SOCIAL WORK WITH GROUPS

SOCIAL WORK WITH GROUPS

by HELEN NORTHEN

COLUMBIA UNIVERSITY PRESS
NEW YORK & LONDON
1969

HELEN NORTHEN is a Professor
in the School of Social Work
at the University of Southern California
in Los Angeles.

Copyright © 1969 Columbia University Press
Library of Congress Catalog Card Number: 69-19462
Printed in the United States of America

Preface

"My love of the group has no need of definition. It is woven of bonds. It is my substance. I am of the group and the group is of me." So wrote Antoine de Saint-Exupery in *Flight to Arras*. I share his sentiment. Fascination with the nature and utility of small groups has been sustained in me for many years. It is clear that the group, in many instances, is an effective instrument for the achievement of social work purposes; in small group interaction lies a potentiality for growth and positive change in individuals and in society.

For groups to be used effectively in social work practice, they must be understood in all their complexity. It is essential for a social worker to perceive the relationship between individual and group; to have a theory that illuminates the nature of the development, structure, and dynamic processes of groups; to discover the meaning of the ways through which both a group and its constituent members develop and change; and to identify the constellation of methods through which a social worker helps a group to achieve its purposes. Such integrated knowledge, combined with the requisite philosophy and skills, should result in services to groups that benefit individuals and the community. To advance the profession of social work, a unified theory of practice is important. I make no claim to have achieved this goal for my book, for the road to the development of sound theory is a long and arduous one; the task requires continued effort on the part of many behavioral scientists and social workers. But I hope that this book will make a modest contribution toward that challenging task.

In the first three chapters a frame of reference is set forth. I have emphasized the generic nature of social work practice and the specific aspects of work with groups, the nature of the group as a unit of social work service, and the role of the social worker. In the remaining chapters the basic theory is related to the social worker's role in a sequence of stages in the development of groups. I have made an effort to describe and clarify concepts, drawing upon a wide range of psychological and social theory; to report relevant research when possible; to set forth generalizations; and to illustrate the content with examples from practice. I have also attempted to demonstrate that there is a logical, orderly approach to understanding and working with groups, from the time of a practitioner's initial planning for a group until service is terminated. The approach is an eclectic one. The selected concepts and principles of practice naturally have been sieved through my own screen of values and perception of the aims and nature of social work service. The generalizations made are *not* to be regarded as absolutes, but as food for thought and, in some instances, as hypotheses for testing.

The book has been written primarily for students in schools of social work and for professional practitioners. The framework of concepts and principles described herein might guide them in their search for understanding of the human group and the practitioner's part in it. The work might stimulate social workers in direct practice, research, administration, or education to test, refine, and extend the ideas set forth or to present alternative theories of practice. If it contributes to the provision of more effective social work services or to the advancement of professional knowledge, it will have fulfilled its purpose.

An author can never repay his indebtedness to the many people who have supported, stimulated, challenged, and enriched him. A teacher always learns as much from his students as they do from him, and I wish my former students to know how grateful I am to them. Especially, it has been my good fortune to teach a doctoral seminar on theoretical bases for social work practice with groups, in which the students have contributed much to my thinking. Particularly helpful were the reactions of a group of advanced students who studied drafts of sections of the manuscript. They are Howard Ancell, Robert Brockman, June Brown, Paul Darnauer, Anne-Marie

Furness, Robert Sidney Justice, Melva Newman, Bertha Simos, Samuel Taylor, and Agnes Trinchero.

Gertrude Wilson and Gladys Ryland, who enhanced my fascination with the group when I was their student many years ago, read an early draft of the manuscript and made valuable suggestions for its improvement. Florence Clemenger read an early draft also and gave me the benefit of her creative thinking and sound judgment. Each of my colleagues in the School of Social Work at the University of Southern California has enriched my understanding of social work, and I am grateful to them for their support and stimulation. I am indebted to many friends in other universities and in professional associations whose experiences and viewpoints have clarified my thinking. Many practitioners have shared generously with me their experiences in work with groups and have contributed valuable records of practice. My sincere thanks go to all these people.

Los Angeles, California   HELEN NORTHEN
August, 1968

Contents

CHAPTER I

The Nature of Social Work Practice

SOCIAL WORK has as its primary concern the individual in his interpersonal relations and in his encounters with his environment. The profession has a rich heritage of activities directed toward reform of conditions that degrade the human personality, provision of services to meet man's basic needs for survival, and improvement of man's capacity for more effective psychosocial functioning. As man's problems in meeting his basic needs, coping with stressful situations, and developing meaningful social relations have become identified and understood, so too has need for knowledge and skill on the part of those persons who are in helping roles. The profession of social work has emerged out of recognition that, if people were to be helped to interact more effectively with each other and within the varied and complex situations of modern life, the nature and quality of the efforts to help could not be left to chance. Good intentions must be buttressed with knowledge and special competence. As Schwartz has pointed out, "Ends without means must, in fact, have recourse to magic . . . there is a mystical, prayerful quality about . . . exhortations to achieve something important without skill and without method, but merely through the sheer power of intent." [1] But the knowledge and technical competence of a professional practitioner must be used for some social ends which are deemed to be essential to the common good of society. Ends and means are inextricably interwoven. In social work, the ends are rooted in values about the good life, knowledge about man and his environment, and competence in the practice of social work.

[1] Schwartz, "Group Work and the Social Scene," in Kahn, ed., *Issues in American Social Work*, p. 129.

Values and Purpose

The ultimate value that guides the social worker's practice is that each individual should have opportunities to realize his potentialities for living in ways that are both personally satisfying and socially desirable. Ashley Montagu has said that, "The deepest personal defeat suffered by human beings is constituted by the difference between what one was capable of becoming and what one has in fact become." [2] With this statement, most social workers would agree.

Underlying this ultimate value of realization of potential are many more specific ones that elaborate on its meaning.[3] A conviction of the inherent worth and the dignity of the individual is a basic tenet of the profession of social work. He who has this conviction will hold dear certain specific values. Each person should be treated with respect—respect both for his likeness and difference in relation to others. He should have opportunities to grow toward the fulfillment of his potential for his own sake and so that he may contribute to the building of a society better able to meet human needs. He should have the right to civil liberties and to equality of opportunity without discrimination because of his race, social class, religion, nationality, or sex. Society should provide those conditions and opportunities that are essential to the fulfillment of man's basic needs requisite not only to survival, but to the development of human potential as well.

A conviction about the democratic spirit and democratic process is another basic tenet of social work. This leads to the views that each person should have freedom to express himself, to maintain his privacy, to participate in making decisions that affect him, and to direct his own life within his accompanying

---

[2] Montagu, *The Cultured Man*, p. 13.

[3] Examples of similar statements of values are: Boehm, "The Nature of Social Work," *Social Work*, III (2), (1958), 10-18; Gordon, "A Critique of the Working Definition," *Social Work*, VII (4), (1962), 3-13; Pumphrey, *The Teaching of Values and Ethics*, pp. 37-54; Hamilton, "Helping People—The Growth of a Profession," in *Social Work as Human Relations*, pp. 3-18; Konopka, *Social Group Work*, pp. 69-77; Wilson and Ryland, *Social Group Work Practice*, pp. 16-22.

responsibility to live constructively with other people. Individuals and groups should assume social responsibility toward the improvement of society, in small or large ways, according to their capacities to do so. The means used in the achievement of goals must be consistent with the ends sought: ends and means are interdependent. These values had their origins in Judaic-Christian beliefs, humanitarianism, and the democratic ethos as embodied in the early political documents of our country. Although not unique to social work, these values provide direction to the practitioner as he fulfills his roles in giving service to individuals, groups, and communities.

The purpose of social work, related directly to its primary values, is improvement in the interaction between man and his environment. To this end, the social worker directs his efforts toward the improvement of psychosocial functioning of individuals and of social institutions and environmental conditions. The social worker has a dual concern for the self-realization of the individual and the betterment of the society of which he is a member. The concept of psychosocial functioning refers to the interaction of people in their social situations. It emphasizes the mutual dependence between the psychological and social components of human behavior. The social worker's concern is not only with what a person can do in the performance of his social roles, but also with what he is and what he can become. His concern is with a person's attitudes toward self and others, his sense of identity and personal adequacy, and the suitability of his values as guides toward the fulfillment of his potentialities. In the individual's interaction with other people, the concern is with adaptation, not blind conformity to the demands of the situation. Adaptation is a "two way process in which the individual reorganizes himself to accommodate to the milieu and at the same time to influence that milieu." [4] In the mature person, his own and society's demands have become fused: he has developed patterns of behavior which are personally satisfying and which permit him to live constructively in his social world.

[4] Cumming and Cumming, *Ego and Milieu*, p. 18.

Within the general purpose of the profession, the focus of
social work practice with small groups may be to help individuals to use the group for coping with and resolving existing
problems in psychosocial functioning, either where effective
functioning has broken down or where, although the level of
functioning is within a normal range, there is a gap between
actuality and potentiality. The focus may be on prevention of
anticipated problems through serving persons with special vul-
nerability to stress, or it may be on the maintenance of a
current level of functioning in situations in which there is
danger of deterioration. Social work service may be directed
also toward the development of more effective patterns of group
functioning, most evident in work with families, and—in some
situations—toward a corporate contribution from the group to
others. With any group, the specific outcomes sought vary with
the desires, needs, capacities, and situations of the individuals
who comprise the group and with the purposes and nature of
the group itself.

The Knowledge Base of Practice

What a social worker does in his practice is for a purpose. It
reflects his values, and is based on knowledge.[5] The nature of
the knowledge essential for all social workers has been set forth
by the Council on Social Work Education, which accredits professional schools of social work.[6] Every social worker needs
considerable knowledge about people and their social situations: the growth, development, and behavior of individuals;
the development, structure, and functioning of groups and
organizations; and the interaction between man and society.
Knowledge about social welfare problems, society's provisions
for services to meet needs, and the formulation of social policy
is similarly relevant to all social workers. But knowledge about

[5] This chapter follows the components of practice as described by Bartlett,
"Toward Clarification and Improvement of Social Work Practice," *Social
Work*, III (2), (1958), 3-9.
[6] Curriculum Policy Statement for the Master's Degree Program in Graduate
Professional Schools of Social Work. New York, Council on Social Work
Education, 1962.

the method by which a professional practitioner enables persons to move toward the achievement of their goals and works toward improvement of social institutions and environmental conditions is crucial. Of special import for work with groups is knowledge of the process by which a practitioner enables groups to form and to develop into viable effective social systems. Other knowledge is essential as it contributes to the competence of the practitioner to render appropriate services to his clientele.

In the provision of direct services to people,[7] social work practice consists of a constellation of activities performed by a practitioner in a planned and systematic way, designed to lead toward the purpose for which services to a particular individual or group is initiated. Its sanction is derived from several sources: the state, the profession of social work, the clients themselves, and, except in private practice, the social agency. The state sanctions practice in a variety of ways. It establishes legislation and appropriates funds for specified services; it provides a legal base for the operation of voluntary agencies through its provisions for their incorporation; it provides special privileges, such as tax exemptions to charitable organizations and it determines whether or not practitioners should be licensed or registered. The profession of social work, through its organizations, sanctions practice by defining standards for and conditions of practice. It has programs that certify competence, accredit professional education, establish codes of ethics, provide channels for complaints against members, and encourage the development of theory and research. The social agency authorizes the particular form of practice. The nature and quality of practice is "profoundly affected and to some extent determined by the purpose, function, and structure of the institution in which it is carried on." [8] The social agency's influence on service may enhance greatly the practitioner's ability to meet the needs of his clientele or it may, alas, impede him from giving appropriate and qualitative service. For the private prac-

[7] Social workers are also engaged in the provision of services to people indirectly, as in the roles of administrator, consultant, or teacher.

[8] Kaiser, "Characteristics of Social Group Work," in *The Social Welfare Forum*, 1957, p. 157.

titioner, the specific conditions under which he provides service are set by his own perceptions of the needs of certain potential clients and by his professional interests and competence. Ultimately, the sanction comes from the people who use the services, for the social worker cannot perform his role unless the participating individuals grant him the status necessary to its fulfillment. The knowledge about sanction is generic to social work with individuals and groups.

The common characteristics of the practice of social work in direct services to people are many and interrelated. They have been stated in different forms by different writers, in either a few abstract generalizations or in specific terms. Some of the essential characteristics of social work practice which apply equally to work with individuals, families, and other small groups, are the following:

1. The social worker's practice is purposeful. The specific purposes toward which the service is directed are determined by the needs of the persons being served within the purpose of the profession. Purposes are defined through a process in which both the worker and the client participate and they change as do the needs of the clientele.

2. The social worker develops a professional relationship as an instrumentality for helping individuals and groups. Acceptance, empathy, self-awareness, and objectivity are components of the social work relationship.

3. The social worker engages in the interrelated processes of social diagnosis, formulation of plans for action, implementation of the plans, and evaluation of outcomes, as these are adapted to particular purposes. The social worker's actions are based upon his understanding of individuals and groups in their varied social situations.

4. The social worker individualizes his work with persons and groups. Individualization occurs when a person's needs and capacities and the unique qualities of his environment are understood and taken into consideration by the practitioner.

5. The social worker clarifies his role and works for con-

gruence between the client's and his own perceptions of role
expectations.

6. The social worker centers his attention simultaneously on
the relationship and on the verbal and nonverbal content of
the interview or group session.

7. The social worker, through the purposeful use of verbal
and nonverbal communication, enables the persons to express
feelings, attitudes, and opinions and to contribute knowledge
which enlightens the content of the transaction.

8. The social worker participates collaboratively with a person or a group in decision-making processes which enable the
client to use the social environment toward improving his life
situation.

9. The social worker facilitates the participation of clients
in all aspects of the service. The rights of people to make and
implement their own decisions are respected within certain
understood limits.

10. The social worker, being aware of the significance of a
time sequence in the provision of service, engages in professional activities that are appropriate to the phase of development of the service which he and his client have reached.

11. The social worker makes use of agency and community
resources, contributes his knowledge toward the development
of new or improved services, collaborates with others who are
serving his clients, and participates in efforts to influence desirable changes in policies and procedures in behalf of his
clientele.

12. The social worker may work with an individual, group,
or a subsystem of a group from whatever his point of contact
with the client, moving from the individual to group or wider
community or from the community to a small group or individual, based on the needs of clients and the availability of appropriate services.

Units of Service

The object of the social service may be an individual, a group, subsystem of a group, or some larger collectivity. The group may be a family or other natural group such as a gang or it may be a group formed specifically for a social work purpose. It may be an intergroup, composed of representatives of other groups or organizations. The specific constellation of persons who receive the service is a client system.[9] A system, according to Allport, is any

. . . recognizable delimited aggregate of dynamic elements that are in some way interconnected and interdependent and that continue to operate together according to certain laws and in such a way as to produce some characteristic total effect.[10]

A person may be viewed as a biopsychosocial system that both influences and is influenced by his physical and social environment. But a person is an element or component of varied social systems such as his family and friendship group, and his educational, work, recreational, and civic associations. A client group is a social system that is a part of the social agency system, and so on. The elements in a social system are conceived both as individuals in interaction and as properties that derive from the interaction, such as positions, roles, patterns of communication, and norms. Although the components of a system may have some functional autonomy, the parts must be organized and integrated if the system is to maintain itself. A system is in continuous interaction with its environment. It is composed of interdependent parts: a change in any one part has repercussions for the other parts and for the entire system. Changes in the system may occur as a consequence of changes within the system or of the impact of environmental forces on the system. Thus, the concept of a system alerts the social worker to the fact that "the individual and the group are inextricably

[9] For references on systems theory, see Chin, "The Utility of Systems Models and Developmental Models for Practitioners," in Bennis, Benne, and Chin, eds., *The Planning of Change*, pp. 201-14; Hearn, *Theory Building in Social Work*.

[10] Allport, *Theories of Perception*, p. 469.

interrelated and the condition of each is bound to affect the other." [11]

There is a tendency for a system to achieve a balance or steady state. The steady state is maintained in part by "the dynamic interplay of its subsystems operating as functional processes." [12] Various forces operating within the system or upon it from outside create stress, tension, or conflict which disturbs the balance or equilibrium. Under stress, the system operates either to maintain or return to its steady state or to move toward some new state. The social worker usually has as his interest not merely the maintenance of equilibrium within the system, but some positive changes in the system or its environment. He therefore seeks to understand the orderly processes of development and change by which a system moves toward some new state. Changes are brought about by the client system itself, with the assistance of the practitioner. The sought-after change is in the direction of growth, defined as "increased ability on the part of the client to face and solve its problems," [13] both those problems that are internal to the system and problems of the relationships of individuals and groups to their environment.

When a social worker enters into a relationship with a client system, he has his own status within the system, and a distinct role to perform in helping the system to move toward the achievement of its purposes. Regardless of the system that is the unit of service at a given time, the worker utilizes knowledge about individuals, groups, and larger social systems. Even in working with persons singly, he needs to understand the transactions of the client within his family, membership groups, and community. In this sense, there is nothing unique in the knowledge about human behavior and social systems required for service to individuals as compared with service to groups. There are generic concepts and principles of practice for use

[11] Somers, "Four Small Group Theories," p. 218.
[12] Hearn, *Theory Building*, p. 46.
[13] Benne, "Deliberate Changing as the Facilitation of Growth," in *The Planning of Change*, p. 230.

with any client system.[14] But there are indeed differences in the way a worker relates to and behaves with a group as contrasted with an individual, derived from the differences in structure, function, and development of varied social systems.

A small group is a particular kind of social system produced by persons in interaction with each other and with other social systems. As Eubank has defined it:

A group is two or more persons in a relationship of psychic interaction, whose relationships with one another may be abstracted and distinguished from their relationships with all others so that they might be thought of as an entity.[15]

Or, in the more recent words of Olmsted, a group is a "plurality of individuals who are in contact with one another, who take one another into account and who are aware of some significant commonality." [16] A group is distinguished from a collection of individuals, according to Hare, if the members are in interaction with one another, share a common purpose and a set of norms which give direction and limits to their activity, and develop a network of interpersonal attractions and a set of roles which serve to differentiate the group from other groups.[17] A small group, normally consisting of two to twenty people, is usually thought of as one in which members are able to engage in direct personal relations with each other at one time. The essential emphasis is pithily stated by Homans, "small enough to let us get all the way around it." [18] The idea is for every member to be able to relate face-to-face with every other member.

The framework for the remainder of this book, then, is one that depicts the social worker's activities in the initiation, development, utilization, and termination of a small group for

---

[14] Generic refers to the body of common concepts, methods, and principles basic to all social work; specific refers to the application of generic aspects to particular situations or segments of practice. See Bartlett, "The Generic-Specific Concept in Social Work Education and Practice," in Kahn, ed., *Issues in American Social Work,* p. 162.

[15] Eubank, *The Concepts of Sociology,* p. 163.

[16] Olmsted, *The Small Group,* p. 23.

[17] Hare, *Handbook of Small Group Research,* p. 10.

[18] Homans, *The Human Group,* p. 3.

the purpose of helping its members with their personal and social functioning.[19] Various forms of verbal and nonverbal communication are directed toward influencing the nature of the structure and processes of the group so that it becomes a potent force upon the growth and development of its members. The dimensions of the small group system that are attended to by the social worker as he participates in the system are: (1) definition and modification of purposes; (2) determination of membership; (3) organizational structure; (4) patterns of relationships as determined by the processes of acceptance, status ranking, differentiation of membership roles, and the evolution of subgroups; (5) values and norms; (6) conflict—its control and management; (7) content of the group; and (8) cohesiveness.

The social worker participates in the group system to influence the ways in which the members work toward facing and solving their problems—those of the individuals, the internal system of the group, and the wider environment. The social worker uses his knowledge and skills to support the group in its current functioning or to change toward some more desired state. One way that systems are influenced is through modifications in the system itself or one or more of its component parts. The worker acts with such intent as: provision of psychological support to an individual, subgroup, or total system; improvement of channels and modes of communication; clarification of attitudes, behavior, and situations; or provision of opportunities for the development of competencies essential to effective functioning. Systems are influenced also through modifications in the environment, brought about by the use of agency and community resources, referrals, the development of new or improved policies or services, or collaboration with others in behalf of individuals or the group system. Often, the

---

[19] Excluded is work with task-oriented groups which are organized for the purpose of accomplishing a particular assignment such as boards and committees, community planning groups, and training courses. For further distinctions between growth-oriented and task-oriented groups, see Wilson, "The Social Worker's Role in Group Situations," in Murphy, *The Social Group Work Method*, 129-68.

worker directs his attention to both the client system and the environment. In working toward these intents, the worker's particular verbal and nonverbal behaviors are based upon his understanding of each individual, the group, and the broader social system. In carrying his responsibility, the worker plans for the formation of new groups and facilitates their developmental processes through several stages of group development.

In summary, the social worker uses his understanding of the small group system in relation to its environment and his professional knowledge and skills to help a group to develop and its members to move toward their desired purposes. This order of content is followed, then, in the succeeding chapters.

CHAPTER II

The Group As a Unit
for Social Work Practice

SOCIAL WORK PRACTICE uses the small group as both the context and means through which its members support and modify their attitudes, interpersonal relationships, and abilities to cope effectively with their environments. The social worker thus recognizes the "potency of social forces that are generated within small groups and seeks to marshall them in the interest of client change." [1] Although groups have power to support and stimulate their members toward the accomplishment of individual and corporate purposes, positive results are not necessarily achieved. Quite the contrary, the group may have very little influence on its members, or it may have a potent influence that is destructive for its members or for society. The development of the group, therefore, must not be left to chance. The social worker requires a body of knowledge about small groups for use in practice. Since the purpose of social work is to improve the relationship between men and their environments, what is needed is a theory of interpersonal and intergroup interaction.

Theoretical Approaches

A well-developed theory, suitable for social work practice, probably does not exist. But until such time as one is developed, a framework of concepts for describing and evaluating a group is useful. The selection of a set of appropriate concepts, however, is not easy. The person who hopes to become knowledgeable about small groups finds a fascinating, diverse, and some-

---

[1] Somers, "The Small Group in Learning and Teaching," in *Learning and Teaching in Public Welfare*, I, 160.

times confusing array of theoretical formulations and research reports for his consideration. The number of books and articles relevant to the study of small groups is burgeoning.[2] Most of the research has been done on short-term groups that were organized for experimental purposes, necessitating caution in generalizing the findings to other types of groups. Terminology is a problem, too, in that different terms are sometimes used to designate quite similar ideas, and the same terms often denote somewhat different concepts. Nevertheless, a framework of basic concepts occurs frequently and has acquired enough common meaning to be communicable to others.

The approaches to the study of small groups which seem to be most widely known have developed since 1930.[3] The theoretical works of such early sociologists as Cooley, Eubank, and Simmel provided impetus for further refinement of concepts and for empirical research. In social work, the early experimental research of Newstetter and his associates, begun in 1926, had great significance for the explication of concepts of particular relevance to work with small groups.[4] Another important related strand was the work of Coyle in which was described a set of sociological concepts for the analysis of social process in organized groups.[5] At approximately the same time, Kaiser and Newstetter were working on methods for recording group process and the leader's role in the group. Several of these records were later published by Coyle, together with criteria for their evaluation.[6] These pioneers, and others, not only influenced social work, but they also influenced some social scientists who

---

[2] In a survey of the literature up to February, 1959, Hare discovered 1,385 references on small groups. From only 5 bibliographical references in the 1890s, Hare estimated that the number has increased to approximately 200 each year. Hare, *Handbook of Small Group Research*, pp. vi-vii.

[3] For reviews of approaches to the study of small groups, see: Lindzey, *Handbook of Social Psychology*, I, 57-259; Olmsted, *The Small Group;* Shepherd, *Small Groups: Some Sociological Perspectives;* Cartwright and Zander, *Group Dynamics: Research and Theory;* Somers, "Four Small Group Theories."

[4] Newstetter, Feldstein, and Newcomb, *Group Adjustment.*

[5] Coyle, *Social Process in Organized Groups.*

[6] Coyle, *Studies in Group Behavior.*

drew heavily on the experiences of group workers in the formulation of their early experimental research.[7]

Perhaps the best-known theoretical approach to the study of small groups is field theory, associated with the pioneering work of Kurt Lewin and his associates.[8] Its basic thesis is that an individual's behavior is a function of the "life space or field," which consists of the person and his environment viewed as one constellation of interdependent factors operating at a given time. The focus is on the gestalt, the totality of factors as they interrelate in a defined situation. Within a group, regarded as a system, there is a continuous process of mutual adaptation of members to each other, labeled as "dynamic interaction." More recent scholars in psychology and sociology who use the field approach tend to emphasize the interrelation between the cohesiveness of a group and such other phenomena as individual motives and the group's goals, standards, leadership, and structure.[9]

Sociometry, another approach, was developed primarily by Jacob Moreno and Helen Jennings.[10] It utilizes field theory, with special emphasis on small groups as networks of affective relations, as identified through the stated choices of persons for others with whom they would like to associate in defined situations. It is interested in the reciprocity of positive choices that bind members of a group together, and with individual differences that account for a member's acceptance or rejection by others. Its major thesis is that the full realization of the individual personality and the effective functioning of social groups depends upon the spontaneity with which given individuals accept others as coparticipants in specified activities.

Psychoanalytic theory has made a contribution to knowledge about groups, with special emphasis on early childhood experiences, emotions, and unconscious processes that are operative

---

[7] Cartwright and Zander, *Group Dynamics*, p. 13.
[8] Lewin, *Field Theory in Social Science*.
[9] Cartwright and Zander, *Group Dynamics*.
[10] Moreno, *Who Shall Survive?*; Jennings, *Leadership and Isolation*.

in group formation and interaction. Unconscious emotional factors partially explain the nature of affective ties of individuals with the leader and among the members, and such processes as scapegoating, contagion, conflict, and cohesiveness. In addition to Freud's own work, some of the principal contributors to this approach to groups are Bion, Redl, Slavson, and Scheidlinger.[11]

Group interaction itself is the focus of the research conducted by Bales and his associates, referred to as Interaction Process Analysis.[12] The group is viewed as a system of individuals in interaction for the purpose of solving some problem. The focus is on patterns and sequences of communicative acts of members. In order to solve problems related to the achievement of the task of the group, members either seek or give information, suggestions, or opinions. Members also deal with the socioemotional problems of management of tension and maintenance of an integrated group. The problem-solving process has certain sequential phases that follow each other in a fairly regular way, each phase being dependent upon the preceding one and each influencing those that follow.

George Homans' work has as its objective the development of a set of concepts drawn from observable facts of group life.[13] The group is analyzed as a social system, utilizing three basic concepts of sentiment, activity, and interaction. These basic concepts are related to such characteristics of the system as the status-ranking process, differentiation of roles, and the norms that regulate the behavior of the members. There is concern with the interdependence between the internal and external systems of the group and between the group and other social systems.

These varied orientations to the small group tend to be supplementary to each other, rather than contradictory. Although

[11] Bion, *Experiences in Groups;* Redl and Wineman, *Controls from Within;* Slavson, *A Textbook in Analytic Group Psychotherapy;* Scheidlinger, *Psychoanalysis and Group Behavior;* Freud, *Group Psychology and the Analysis of the Ego.*

[12] Bales, *Interaction Process Analysis.*

[13] Homans, *The Human Group,* and *Social Behavior.*

there is not full agreement on a conceptual framework, a number of concepts are used over and over again. Selectivity of concepts is related to the underlying theory and to the purpose for which the conceptualization is to be used. For a social worker, a framework of concepts about the structure, process, and development of small groups alerts him to what he should take into account as he seeks to understand what is occurring in a group, thus enhancing his sensitivity to certain important variables in his work that otherwise might be overlooked. The major concepts in the author's scheme are all interrelated; yet they must be categorized and discussed separately for purposes of analysis. What ties them together is the concept of social interaction.

Social Interaction

Social interaction is a term for the dynamic interplay of forces in which contact between persons results in a modification of the attitudes and behavior of the participants. Communication, both verbal and nonverbal, is basic to interaction.[14] There is a structure to communication in that each group carries on its communication through certain agreed-upon chanles, but it is a process, too, of exchanging meanings and making common meanings. Interpersonal communication is a complex social process through which information, feelings, attitudes, and other messages are transmitted, received, and interpreted: it is the very essence of a social system. Communication consists of the verbal, explicit, and intentional transmission of messages between people. It consists also of all the nonverbal processes by which persons influence one another. As a person transmits messages to others, he learns about the feelings, thoughts, hopes, and values of others. As members of a group exchange feelings and thoughts, there is a reciprocal and cyclical influence of members on each other. The sender of a message intends, consciously or not, to influence the receiver in some

[14] References on communication that have been most useful include: Ruesch and Bateson, *Communication: The Social Matrix of Psychiatry;* Ruesch and Kees, *Nonverbal Communication;* Hayakawa, *Language, Meaning, and Maturity;* Satir, *Conjoint Family Therapy.*

way. The receiver needs to perceive and assess the overt and covert meaning and to respond to the message in an appropriate way. People vary in their ability to send clear messages and in their ability to interpret messages accurately.

An open system of communication, based on the right of each individual to be recognized and heard, increases the chances that members will face and solve their own problems and the problems of the group. Within the system, the worker's role is to behave in ways that will facilitate the group's effort. Positive change is facilitated by interaction which is honest, sincere, and meaningful to the participants. It is more likely to occur when an individual is involved in the group and has responsibility for some part of the group's effort to realize its purpose. Thus, each member shares some information and attitudes with others. He does not feel the need to withhold participation due to fear of reprisal, or lack of confidentiality concerning what is shared. The desired pattern of channels of communication is one that is group-centered as contrasted with a leader-centered group in which all communicative acts are channeled through the worker or a particular member of the group. Instead of this, members communicate with each other and with the worker. With genuine involvement in the process, new ideas, experiences, points of view, and emotional responses may become incorporated into the personality of an individual. Although the particular pattern of communication will shift as the group deals with varied situations, the social worker's efforts are directed toward the achievement of a pattern that is predominantly one of integrated interaction.

People come together in a group through some common need or interest. A complicated interplay of social relations among the members and the relations of each member to the group come into play. Members communicate their acceptance or rejection of each other, and they engage in certain activities. As they do so, a configuration of relationships develops, values and norms become established or modified, conflict occurs and is resolved, and a degree of cohesiveness develops sufficient at least for the survival of the group.

Purpose

Every group has a purpose for being.[15] Purpose means any ultimate aim, end, or intention; objective or goal usually refers
to a specific end that is instrumental to the purpose. In the
family, purposes are established by society's expectations concerning such functions as the care and socialization of children,
and the maintenance of certain values, norms, and customs of
the culture. In addition to these general purposes, each family
has its own set of goals. So, too, do other types of groups. The
goals of a group influence the standards by which it will be
evaluated, the patterns of communication that develop, and the
activities of the group. But these other processes also influence
the ways in which motivation toward the achievement of goals
will develop and the goals themselves become strengthened,
modified, or abandoned. In a group, the purpose is a composite of the expressed purposes for the group held by the social
worker and the expressed purposes of the members for the
group. Purpose is a dynamic concept, not a static one. The
desires and needs brought into the group by members become
blended together through social interaction and develop into a
group purpose. The persons who comprise the group have their
own purposes which may or may not be acknowledged. They
have purposes that are overt and conscious, as evidenced by
what they say about why they want to be in the group, but
they also have unavowed purposes of which they may or may
not be aware. Some of these purposes may be rooted in the
person's unconscious needs. Almost always, there is a subtle and
complex combination of individual purposes which may agree
or be in conflict with the stated purpose of the group. Anyone
who would be helpful to a group needs to analyze the similar
and different motives of individuals and the extent to which
there is clarity and consensus about purpose; the extent to
which the aims of individuals are congruent with the general

[15] Group purpose and goals are discussed in Coyle, *Group Work with
American Youth;* Cartwright and Zander, *Group Dynamics,* pp. 345-481; Konopka, *Social Group Work;* Levine, *Fundamentals of Group Treatment.*

purpose; the degree to which the group purpose mobilizes the energies of group members; and the nature and extent to which there is conflict about either objectives or the means toward their achievement. Both the effectiveness of the group and the satisfaction of its members are increased when the members perceive their personal aims as being advanced by the purpose of the group, when individual and group aims are perceived as being in harmony.

Some evidence from research supports the proposition that harmony between the purposes of individuals and the group purpose enhances both the satisfaction of the members and the effectiveness of the group.[16] The perception that one's personal goals are being advanced within the general purpose of the group provides motivation toward the achievement of goals. The social worker therefore needs to help the members to identify and clarify the varied goals of the individuals who comprise the group and to find the common ground within these particular goals. If a group sets its own goals, they will tend to be progressive, so that the members move from one to another under their own motivation.

Affective Ties Among Members

Fundamentally, it is the purpose of the group and the compatibility between persons that determine the nature of the group; in fact, often whether or not a group will develop. This fact points to the necessity for concern with affective forces of attractions and repulsions among members of a group which comprise the emotional bond among the members.[17] Acts of communication in a group convey positive and negative expressions of affect as well as of opinions and information. Both in verbal and nonverbal ways, members of a group communi-

---

[16] Berelson and Steiner, *Human Behavior,* p. 352.

[17] For references on affective ties and interpersonal relations, in addition to those cited in this section, see Coyle, *Group Work with American Youth,* pp. 91-132; Durkin, *The Group in Depth;* Jennings, *Leadership and Isolation;* Konopka, "Resistance and Hostility in Group Members," *The Group,* XVI (1953), 3-10.

cate their feelings of love and affection, hate and dislike, and indifference toward each other. In every human relationship, there are "emotional reactions to one's self, to the other person, and to the specific content of the material expressed." [18] The content of conversation is significant as members of a group tentatively approach each other to learn to what extent they share common orientations toward relationships and interests. But nonverbal communication through actions and gestures is the principal means of expressing and exchanging emotions.[19] Actions may be perceived by the eye and sense of touch, as well as through the ear. Facial expressions, body posture, silence, movements toward or away from another person, and touch are but a few of the ways that persons communicate their perceptions of and feeling toward other people.

The varied responses of a person toward others are means through which he attempts to satisfy his own needs for relationships with others and to avoid threats to himself. According to Schutz, there are three basic interpersonal needs: for inclusion, control, and affection.[20] Persons differ in the extent to which they seek out or desire meaningful relations with others as contrasted with their desire for and use of privacy. Each person, to a certain degree, indicates his desire to have others initiate interaction toward him or to leave him alone. There is his expressed behavior toward others in terms of inclusion or exclusion, and his preference for the behavior of others toward him. People differ, too, in their behavior that controls others and in their preferences for being controlled by others. Although everybody needs to love and to be loved, people vary to some degree between preference for intimate, personal relationships, or for distant and quite impersonal relations with others. Again, each person behaves toward others and prefers that others behave toward him in a certain way with respect to affection.

[18] Phillips, *Essentials of Social Group Work Skill,* p. 93.
[19] Ruesch and Kees, *Nonverbal Communication,* p. 192.
[20] Schutz, "Interpersonal Underworld," in Bennis, Benne, and Chin, eds., *The Planning of Change,* pp. 293-307.

The responses of persons toward others and of others toward them may or may not be reciprocated.[21]

The way in which persons relate to each other is the heart of the group process. "The capacity of individuals to react to one another favorably and unfavorably creates the energy which makes human intercourse possible." [22] The attitudes that persons have for each other are naturally somewhat ambivalent. Human relationships are characterized by various positive ties —love, empathy, cordiality, and positive identification. These are associative in nature and tend to unite people. Relationships are also characterized by various negative ties—hatred, hostility, repulsions, fears, and prejudices. These are dissociative, separating in their effect. When persons come together, through interaction among them, they may accept each other, reject each other, or be indifferent to each other. They may seek to establish intimate, personal relationships, or behave in a distant and impersonal manner. They may prefer that others respond to them with a particular degree of closeness or distance. A positive orientation to others is often reciprocated by the other, but not necessarily. There may or may not be compatibility between the needs of persons for relative intimacy or distance. The extent to which a person finds acceptance in a group depends upon the complex interaction between his own needs and attributes, those of other individuals, and the social climate of the group. Each individual is like all others in many ways; yet he is also a unique human being. Each member of a group has many things in common with other members but also is different in many ways. Similarities and differences in such characteristics as age, sex, religion, race, nationality, and social class are influential in determining the place a person will find in a group. Other important factors are the likeness and difference in the members' goals and aspirations; the nature of their needs and problems; their capacities, achievements, and interests; the opportunities and deprivations of their environments;

[21] This conclusion was drawn from research by Newstetter, *Group Adjustment*, and by Cunningham, *et al.*, *Understanding Group Behavior of Boys and Girls*, p. 203.

[22] Wilson and Ryland, *Social Group Work Practice*, p. 45.

and the groups to which they belong and those to which they aspire.

The combination of affectionate or hostile feelings between members is very subtle at times. It is difficult to know the reasons for liking or not liking others. Positive or negative feelings may be based on distortions in interpersonal perception. A person may have a false perception of another due to ineptness of communication of intent. A child, for example, tries to express friendly interest in another child through a push, but the gesture is misinterpreted as one of hostility. Ignorance of the nuances of language of various subcultural groupings often leads to the use of words that hurt, when no hurt is intended. It is common for a person to stereotype others, that is, to perceive them according to preconceived notions about what they will be like or how they will behave, representing failure to individualize a person and to recognize him as he really is. There is a tendency to stereotype persons who differ from oneself in such characteristics as race, religion, social class, appearance, or generation. Certain distortions in perception of other people are connected with mental illness as part of a constellation of serious problems in the perception of reality.

A person may have a false perception of another, based on transference reactions.[23] Many relationships have within them feelings, attitudes, and patterns of response transferred from other earlier relationships, particularly those with parents. The person misunderstands the present relationship in terms of the past. He tends to relive earlier attitudes with the persons who are in his present situation. He reacts in ways that are not logical or appropriate to the current relationship. A transference reaction may be functional or dysfunctional to the relationship. Emotional attitudes and behavioral patterns evolved in the course of family living and other significant earlier groups are subject to transfer in various degrees to subsequent group

[23] For discussions of transference, see: Menninger, *Theory of Psychoanalytic Technique*, pp. 77-98; Scheidlinger, *Psychoanalysis and Group Behavior*, pp. 80-85.

relationships. In a group, transference reactions may be directed toward the leader, who may represent to the member a parental or other authority figure. Such reactions may also be directed toward other members of the group who have the emotional significance of siblings to the member who distorts the current relationship. Only by observing both the transference characteristics and the reality characteristics of a relationship, and by noting how they contrast, overlap, and interact, is full justice done to the diagnostic process.

As members interact with each other and with a professional practitioner, identifications may be formed.[24] Identification is one form of imitation whereby a person feels like another person. It is a process through which a person adopts some real or imagined attitude, pattern of behavior, or value of another person and through which the desired aspect becomes integrated into the ego. It becomes a part of a person's sense of identity. It is largely an unconscious process, for the person is seldom aware that he is modifying some aspect of himself in accordance with another person. Positive identifications are based on admiration of another person, but there can also be negative identifications, based on fear. In the latter instance, identification is a defense: anxiety may be warded off through identification with the aggressor.[25] As a group develops cohesiveness, identification takes place also with the group as an entity. The values and norms of the group then become incorporated into the egos of the participating members.

A group situation demands that members be able to give to others and to receive from them, and that they be interested in and concerned for each other. In many groups, members do not have the ability to perceive other members as distinct personalities, and to be concerned about them. Mature object relationships, characterized by love of others, are in contrast to the immature, narcissistic relationships of some group members, whose needs are expressed by the phrase, "I want what I want when I want it." In such narcissistic relationships, the orienta-

---

[24] Scheidlinger, *Psychoanalysis and Group Behavior*, pp. 17-25 and 108-33.
[25] Freud, *The Ego and the Mechanisms of Defence*, pp. 117-31.

tion is toward the self rather than toward give and take with others. The behavior toward another person is motivated primarily by the individual's own needs and impulses. Other people are used primarily for purposes of self-gratification. In any group situation, there will be variations in the members' abilities to relate to others in ways that are fairly realistic, that indicate mutuality of concern for and interaction with each other, and that tend toward identification with the positive values and norms of the group. In order for a collection of individuals to become a group, or for an existing group to survive, the positive, unifying forces must predominate over the negative, divisive ones.

A feeling that one is accepted in a group and that he, in turn, accepts other members is a powerful dynamic in the process of change. All people need to feel accepted. Acceptance denotes the quality of being regarded favorably by the group to the extent that continued interaction with others is possible without undue threat. As a person feels accepted, his self-esteem rises. He becomes more open to new ways of feeling and thinking. He feels comfortable enough to reveal some of his feelings, aspirations, and concerns to others. He can dare to look at the unacceptability of some of his behavior, utilizing this knowledge for growth and change. As he feels accepted, a member tends to enhance his identification with the group which, in turn, enhances the group's impact on his attitudes and behavior.

One major reason that the group can become a potent force for development and change is that group practice builds on the powerful fact of interdependency of people one on another. This may be thought of as mutual aid. To be sure, it is mutual aid with a professional worker with his distinctive role in the group. The group provides a give-and-take situation that may reduce feelings of inadequacy or difference, and of dependency on the worker. In any healthy relationship, each participant carries a contributing as well as a taking role. "Shrinkage in self-esteem and resentment occur when people are only the recipients of help—they relate better to people who use and appreciate what they can contribute." [26] This very potential, however, poses problems for many persons who are inadequate in their abilities to enter into the give and take of group participation. The potential value of the group will depend upon whether indeed a member can be helped to find acceptance and to move into interdependence with others. This process results in a feeling of belonging to the group.

As people become acquainted with each other and develop positive or negative ties toward each other, a structure of relationships develops. Statuses and roles become differentiated, and transitory or relatively stable subgroups form.

Status and Role

Status refers to a person's position relative to others in a hierarchy of statuses in a given group.[27] Through a process of evaluation in the group, each individual is given a particular position in the group. The members rank each other, the basis for such ranking depending upon the values and aspirations of the members of the group. A person has a different status in each group to which he belongs or, for that matter, at different times in the same group. He also has generalized status in the community, which may be achieved through such means as education, income, or competence. Or such status may be ascribed to a person on the basis of certain factors other than achievement: color, ethnic origin, social class, age, sex, physical condition, ancestry, or style of life. A person brings this status with him into the group. Depending upon the social welfare setting, a group member may already have a status that labels him as deviant, for example, as an offender, school dropout, or patient. The bases for members' ratings of each other are thus

[26] Overton and Tinker, *Casework Notebook*, p. 162.

[27] The following references on status and role have been useful: Bonner, *Group Dynamics*, pp. 33-65; Coyle, *Group Work with American Youth*, pp. 91-132; Gross, Mason, and McEachern, *Explorations in Role Analysis*; Merton, *Social Theory and Social Structure*, pp. 281-386; Sarbin, "Role Theory," in Lindzey, ed., *Handbook of Social Psychology*, I, 223-58; Stein and Cloward, *Social Perspectives on Behavior*, pp. 171-262; Wilson, "The Social Worker's Role in Group Situations," in Murphy, *The Social Group Work Method*, pp. 129-68.

brought with them into the group from earlier life experiences, their current membership and reference groups, and their cultural values. Values on which members of a group rate each other may be in agreement or in conflict with those of the group leader and the surrounding society. The rating pattern may be predominantly task-centered or it may reflect deep emotional needs. It is often related to a person's likability, the nature and degree of competence or other resources that he has to offer to the group, and his ability to exert force or influence over other members of the group. The ranking process may be unrelated to or even inconsistent with overt purposes of the members, but relevant to their unavowed aims. Finally, the ranking process may be relative to the influence of subcultural values, for example, the bases for prestige in adolescent peer society or within a profession. One's status in a group determines the amount and kind of influence, responsibility, and control he has relative to other members. A reputation, once acquired, tends to be more stable than the actual behavior of a person. Reputations shape expectations and draw out behavior that accords with such expectations; thus prestige is one determinant of behavior. High status is a source of positive self-image and vice versa. The extent to which this is so relates to the importance of the group to the person, and the way in which status in the group is related to status in other groups of significance to the person.

The concept of role is one of those most frequently referred to in the literature on small groups; yet there is no single agreed-upon definition of the term.[28] Many definitions of a role are similar to the one proposed by Hare: a "role is a set of expectations" of a person who occupies a given position in the social system.[29]

The actual behavior of a person occupying a position in a group remains as something to be understood in terms of the expectations which are imposed from without and the tendencies of his personality which express themselves from within.[30]

[28] See Neiman and Hughes, "Problem of the Concept of Role—a Re-survey of the Literature," *Social Forces*, XXX (1951), 141-49.
[29] Hare, *Handbook of Small Group Research*, p. 9.
[30] *Ibid.*, p. 102.

Other social scientists use the term role to mean the actual behavior of the person coordinate with a given status or position.[31] Sarbin says that "roles are defined in terms of the actions performed by the person to validate his occupancy of the position," and as "the organized actions and attributes of a person coordinate with a given status or position." [32] The term position is sometimes used synonymously with status. Gross and his associates suggest position or location as preferable, to distinguish this idea from status which is used frequently, as in the preceding section of this book, to denote the differential ranking among a set of persons or locations. Still other social scientists define role as an "individual's definition of his situation with reference to his and others' social positions." [33]

Although definitions of role vary, most formulations take into account three components of role theory. As Gross puts it: "individuals (1) in social locations (2) behave (3) with reference to expectations." [34] As Stein and Cloward say, whenever the question is asked, "What is the proper way to behave in this situation?" or "What is really expected of me?" there is an implied problem of role definition.[35] Individuals tend to organize their behavior in terms of the structurally defined expectations assigned to each of their multiple social roles. Each position has its organized role relationships which comprise a role set, "that complement of role relationships which persons have by virtue of occupying a particular social status." [36] This idea of role set emphasizes the importance of relationships among and between members of a group, for role relationships are not only between the occupant of the position and each member of the role set but also "between members of the role set itself." [37] Although a role is associated with each of the multiple positions

---

[31] Newcomb, "Role Behaviors in the Study of Individual Personality and of Groups," *Journal of Personality*, XVIII (1950), 273-89; Sarbin, "Role Theory," in Lindzey, *Handbook of Social Psychology*, I, 223-58.

[32] Sarbin, *ibid.*, pp. 224-25.

[33] Gross, Mason, and McEachern, *Explorations in Role Analysis*, p. 13.

[34] *Ibid.*, p. 17.

[35] Stein and Cloward, *Social Perspectives on Behavior*, p. 174.

[36] Merton, *Social Theory and Social Structure*, p. 369.

[37] *Ibid.*, p. 380.

that a person occupies, there may be multiple roles associated with a single status.

When a person enacts or performs a role, he is responding to a set of expectations that others have for his behavior, but he is also acting in accordance with his own expectations and motives. No two persons enact a role identically. When a person meets the expectations, he usually receives positive feedback; when he fails to meet expectations, negative sanctions are likely to be applied. There may or may not be consensus among significant others concerning the expectations for role performance. The expectations for behavior both affect and are affected by the individual in the role, by the social system and its component parts, and by the expectations and demands of the wider social milieu. The roles of an individual are not static, but undergo constant definition and redefinition as the person acts and as other persons respond to his actions.

In a group, a variety of roles becomes differentiated as definitions develop about what is to be done in what way by whom. When a division of labor becomes stabilized over a period of time, expectations for performance of the responsibilities become institutionalized. Thus, the family has conventional roles of husband-father, wife-mother, son, and daughter. These roles are examples of those which are assigned automatically to a person by society on the basis of age, sex, and marital status. In a peer group, there is the basic role of member, associated with the position of being in a particular kind of group. In the member's role set are his relationships with the social worker, other members of the group, and various people in the external system, who have expectations concerning his attributes and behavior. Such diverse expectations need to be articulated sufficiently for effective operation of the status and role structure.[38] Inadequate articulation of expectations suggests that certain social mechanisms be utilized to reduce the amount of conflict concerning expectations. The extent to which this happens determines the effectiveness of the role system. As the group becomes organized, certain members may acquire positions that

[38] *Ibid.*, pp. 380-81.

are related officially to the purpose and structure of the group, for example, officer, committee chairman, or committee member, with their particular expectations. These positions are acquired as a result of certain choices that the person has made or that the group has made for him, usually a combination of both. Authority to influence others in certain ways is inherent in these institutionalized roles. These roles are part of the formal, organized structure of the group.

In addition to conventional or institutional roles, every group develops a set of personal roles. In the family, these are illustrated by such labels as the black sheep, the shy one, the scholar, the clown, and the scapegoat. Within the social work group, too, individual patterns of behavior become evident, some of which may become differentiated into roles as the group develops particular expectations for a member, and the member perceives these behaviors as expected of him.[39] There is disagreement as to whether or not these patterns of behavior become roles in the strict sense of the term. Bales and Slater say that "the degree to which differentiated roles in the fully structural sense appear in these small decision-making groups is perhaps a moot point." [40] Nevertheless, such patterns of behavior are influenced to some extent by the members' own expectations and those of others in the group or society in which they are participants.

Roles that emerge in the group may be constructive for both the individual in the role and the group, or they may be mutually destructive. In order to understand these roles, the social worker needs to ask himself: (1) what is there about the person that accounts for his defining himself in this way in the group; and (2) what is there about the other members and the group situation that accounts for the fact that the group expects one of its members to behave in this way? A complex combination of individual and group influences is at work.

[39] See Benne and Sheats, "Functional Roles of Group Members," *Journal of Social Issues*, IV (1948), 41-49; Coyle, *Group Work with American Youth*, pp. 91-132; Bonner, *Group Dynamics*, pp. 373-407.

[40] Bales and Slater, "Role Differentiation in Small Decision-making Groups," in Parsons and Bales, eds., *Family: Socialization, and Interaction Process*, p. 260.

For social work purposes, an influential group is one in which the member's role is defined as a collaborative one in relation both to other members and to the role of the social worker. The person is not only in a help-using or client role, but in a help-giving to others role. There is a mutual aid system to be built on and used. The word member implies that one belongs to the group and that he participates in interdependence with others. The members are participants in all aspects of the social work process—in the selection of goals, the determination of means, and the diagnostic and evaluative processes. To put it another way, the group operates as a democratic system. This emphasis does not deny the special authority of the worker to influence individuals and the group's structure and processes. It does, however, indicate the way his influence is to be used. Nor does emphasis on mutuality of participation deny the development of leadership functions among the members of the group. It means that members are given freedom of choice within the definition of the group's purpose, their capacities and competencies, and the rights of others. Members are encouraged to do as much for themselves and for each other as they are able. Each is expected to contribute according to his ability, and each is assured that his contribution is valued. The roles of both worker and member are clear to all concerned, and so are the expectations for officially differentiated roles as these are developed in the group.

Subgroups

As members of a group come to discover what they have in common, various subgroups develop which are expressive of common interests, mutuality of feelings of attraction or repulsion, or needs for control and inclusion. These subgroups reflect the personal choices, interests, and interpersonal feelings of the members, not always on a conscious level.[41] Isolates, pairs, and triads combine to form a pattern, often described as the interpersonal structure of the group.

---

[41] For a discussion of subgroups, see Coyle, *Group Work with American Youth,* pp. 91-132.

The smallest subgroup is the pair, or dyad, which is the most intimate and personal of all patterns of relationships. In the pair, harmony brings greater advantages than in any other relationship and discord brings greater disadvantages. The relationship between members of a pair may or may not be healthy according to certain criteria for mental health, as evidenced by the frequency of the sadist-masochist or dominator-dependent relations between members of a pair. The triad, or group of three persons, is another subgroup to be understood. It is famous in fiction as the love triangle for the reason that a third person does affect a pair in that, in a group of three, there is almost always the rivalry of two for the affection or attention of one. A third person may increase the solidarity of the pair but may also bring discord into the relationship. Often a triad evolves into a pair and an isolate or, through the addition of another person, into a double pair. Larger subgroups comprise various combinations of isolates, dyads, and triads. As the group increases in size, there is a tendency for the formation of subgroups to become more prominent.

Subgroups develop out of the interplay of the members' perceptions of likeness and difference, common attributes, and common interests. For some persons, membership in a subgroup may reflect apprehension about meaningful involvement with the group, so that the subgroup becomes a nucleus of security for the fringers in the group. Especially in large groups, subgroups may enhance the cohesiveness of the group, since they may further enable the group to meet members' needs for intimacy, control, and affection beyond what is possible in the total group. A subgroup may temporarily cut itself off from participation in the life of the group. Two or more rival subgroups may emerge, each with its own indigenous leader, resulting in a reduction of the cohesiveness of the group. Or, the conflict between subgroups may provide the means by which issues are recognized and problems are solved. For some isolates in the group, membership in a subgroup may be an indication of movement when such a person is able to relate more frequently with a subgroup which is functioning on a mature level.

In the formation of subgroups, the generalization that "birds of a feather flock together" is supported by evidence from some studies but these findings are confused by evidence from others that "opposites attract." There are some indications, however, that proximity in school, work, or residence; the presence of similar individual atributes such as age, race, intelligence, sex, and ability; common interests and values; and complementarity in certain patterns of needs influence the differential degree of intimacy among members of a group. The more lasting subgroups often stem from strong identifications or mutuality of symptoms. In evaluating the emergence of subgroups, the basic questions concern the way in which they relate to the group as a whole, whether there is cooperation or conflict between the subsystems, and whether they are functional for the particular task of the group at a given time.

Values and Norms

Values are formulations of preferred behavior.[42] They are indications of what is considered to be worthwhile or useless, desirable or undesirable, right or wrong, beautiful or ugly. Values include beliefs and ideologies; appreciative or aesthetic preferences; and moral or ethical principles. As people participate together in a group, a common system of values develops that determines to some extent the norms of behavior for the members of the group. It is probable that these reinforce predominant values in the wider culture.

A norm is a generalization concerning an expected standard of behavior in any matter of consequence to the group. It incorporates a value judgment.[43] It is a rule or standard to

[42] See Pumphrey, *The Teaching of Values and Ethics in Social Work Education*, pp. 32-61.

[43] For discussions of norms and values, see Homans, *The Human Group*, pp. 121-30; Sherif, "The Formation of Social Norms," in Sherif and Sherif, *An Outline of Social Psychology*, pp. 237-79; Thibaut and Kelley, *The Social Psychology of Groups*, pp. 126-48, 237-55; Wilson and Ryland, *Social Group Work Practice*, pp. 37-42.

which the members of a group are expected to adhere. A set of norms defines the range of behavior that will be tolerated within the group. A set of norms introduces a certain amount of regularity and predictability into the group's functioning, since members of a group feel some obligation to adhere to the expectations of the group. A norm implies that certain rewards and punishments will be invoked for conformity to or deviation from the norms of the group. Since these rewards and punishments are often expressed through granting or withholding acceptance and prestige, the nature of the expectations and the manner in which they are enforced play an important part in a group's development. The norms of a group cannot be too far beyond the capacities of the members if they are to be relevant to the functioning of the group. Norms, once developed, tend to become stable. They become susceptible to change, however, when they are deemed inadequate to a particular situation, usually at a time of crisis.

Essentially, the process through which a set of norms is developed is one of identification of the members with what is valued and accepted by the group. Group norms are the product of social interaction based on some consensus about values, yet they are very much the property of individuals, influencing their actions even when they are alone or in other groups. A classic experiment by Sherif illustrates this point.[44] He demonstrated that an individual's specific judgments about the movement of a light in a dark room tended to converge in a direction consistent with the group's range and norm of responses. A conclusion was that after the range and norm in his group have been established, when a person faces the same situation alone, he perceives the situation in terms of the range and norms that he brings from the group. Therefore, the norm formed in interaction with others becomes the individual's own norm. A necessary condition for this internalization of social norms is participation in reciprocal interaction with others.

The development of norms is based on the general psycho-

[44] Sherif, "Group Influences upon the Formation of Norms and Attitudes," in Swanson et al., eds., *Readings in Social Psychology*, pp. 294-362.

logical tendency to experience things in relation to some reference point or standard. Individuals facing an unfamiliar situation tend to form a common basis for reaction to it, rather than for each person to develop a unique mode of reaction. Each person brings his own values and norms with him into the group. Through the process of communication, each person's values are affected by those of others in the group and through the impact of those from the surrounding society. Gradually, those norms are selected which are appropriate to the needs of the group and new ones are developed, as deemed necessary for the pursuit of the group's purposes.

Acceptance of the norms of a group aids in the establishment of procedures and in the coordination and control of the participation of individuals. Control in a social group refers to the social interactional patterns by which the behavior of group members is influenced, restrained, or directed. Norms serve as the principal means of control within a group. They provide pressures toward conformity. As stated by Thibaut and Kelley, "They serve as substitutes for the exercise of personal influence and produce more economically and efficiently certain consequences otherwise dependent upon personal influence processes." [45] Since norms convey expectations and indicate requests that others may not properly make of a person, they protect him from the misuse of power by another. Since norms are usually based on agreement among members, the need for personal power to enforce the norms is reduced and responsibility for enforcement is shared among the members. Norms that are accepted and complied with become intrinsically rewarding, thus reducing the need for external control. Norms thus provide a means for controlling behavior without entailing the costs and uncertainties involved in the unrestrained use of interpersonal power.[46]

The survival of a group is dependent, to some extent, upon the development and acceptance of a set of norms that govern the behavior of its members. Each group applies pressures on

[45] Thibaut and Kelley, *The Social Psychology of Groups,* p. 130.
[46] *Ibid.,* p. 131.

its members to conform to group norms, through various subtle and direct means of reward and punishment. Persons conform to these pressures or they resist them, depending upon many circumstances. There are individual differences in ability to resist pressures from others related to the person's sense of identity, a need to rebel, or strength of conviction. Persons try to meet the requirements of groups to which they most want to belong—hence the degree of attractiveness a group has for a particular person is an important factor. Persons are more apt to conform to values of others who have high prestige in the group. There is a tendency for people to conform on important issues and to differ on minor points. Individuals are more apt to conform to the group's standard if it is supported by a large majority of the members. Fear of psychological punishment or of being rejected by others forces persons to conform to norms which otherwise they would not accept. Finally, the pressures toward conformity vary with a person's perception of the group's attitudes toward nonconformity; that is, if there is a norm that differences are to be recognized and valued, there is a wider range of tolerance for deviance than in groups which do not value differences. It is to be remembered also that when a person conforms to group standards he does not thereby give up his individuality. In a very important sense, a person's attitudes and behavior are always unique to him, but his attitudes and behavior usually are within a range denoted by the norms of the group.

Conflict between the values of a particular group and those of other groups to which a person belongs or to which he aspires is a common phenomenon. In some situations, the norms of different groups may point in quite different, even opposite, directions. Dysfunction may occur when rules overlap, are inconsistent, or too complex; or when there are too few or too many of them. Overconcern with formal decision making about rules and procedures and their enforcement may substitute for working with the real problems facing the group. Norms may either facilitate or hinder the group's movement toward its objectives. Furthermore, the same set of norms may provide support for one person and may reduce the creativity and motivation of another. Thus, the nature of the norms, the manner in which they are enforced, and their impact on each individual and on the group as a whole is an important determinant of the group's development.

To set up rules, customs, and standards to which the members of a group are expected to conform implies that the group or its sponsoring organization regards certain attitudes and patterns of behavior as being of value. The extent to which each individual accepts and adheres to such norms helps to determine and in turn is determined by whether, and to what degree, such attitudes and behavior are regarded by the group as valuable. In effect, then, values and norms together suggest what a group sees as important and what it dismisses as insignificant, what it likes and what it dislikes, what it desires and that to which it objects or is indifferent. The constellation of norms, based on a group's perception of what ought to be, provides weak or strong motivation for its members to use the group for their mutual benefit.

Some shared values of significance to members are indicative of a group that has meaning to its members. Similarity of values occurs as members influence each other, but primarily it occurs through the discovery of those values that are already held in common. Likewise, the norms need to be understood and, to some extent, agreed upon. The norms that develop in a group are crucial determinants, in part, of the group's influence on its members. The desirable norms for a group used for social work purposes may deviate from those considered desirable in other groups to which the members belong or from those of the members' other reference groups.

The social worker helps the group to develop a norm that accepts experimentation and flexibility. In order for change to occur, an individual needs to perceive that the group provides opportunities for him to experiment with new or modified ways of relating and responding to people and to things. A system linked in by traditional and inflexible modes of response is limited in its ability to consider alternatives.[47] An experimental norm permits the introduction of evidence that may suggest alternative responses. It conveys to members the notion that it is safe to try out new things, make mistakes, and ask for and use help from the worker and other members. Such a norm gives permission for a range of idiosyncratic ways of self-expression, so long as these do not impede the achievement of goals and do not hurt others. It invites opportunity to explore, express, and test experiences in a variety of ways of relating to self, others, and materials. Through such experimentation, members learn that others share similar feelings and problems. Such knowledge lessens the sense of being alone with one's problems and enhances ability to face and cope with the reality of various situations. Members learn, too, that differences are acceptable, useful, and valued.

The small group is most effective in bringing about positive growth and change in its members if it combines effective psychological support for efforts to change with adequate stimulation from others to act as a motivation toward change. What is desired is that members learn to interact with each other so that they mutually support each other. The social worker can do things to help the members to accept the norm of mutual support for efforts toward growth. The group can be developed in such a way that it provides effective psychological support for persons in coping with their anxieties about the group experience and in their problem-solving efforts. Even when a person is motivated toward change, some feelings of loss and failure are involved in the anticipation of change. While the group does not remove individual anxiety, it tends to help a person cope with it and render it more manageable and therapeutically useful.[48] In a group, support comes from persons in a peer relationship on a level of equality, in addition to that offered by the professional helper. Support comes partly from a feeling

[47] Benne, "Deliberate Changing in the Facilitation of Growth," in Bennis et al., eds., *The Planning of Change*, p. 231.
[48] Somers, "The Small Group in Learning and Teaching," in *Learning and Teaching*, I, 167.

of commonality, the "we're in the same boat, brother" theme. Knowing that others have similar needs, interests, and problems reduces the sense of stigma that often accompanies being a client.

Support alone is not enough. Stimulation toward different attitudes and behavioral patterns is essential also. A number of studies indicate that the effect of a group upon an individual's motivation is often positive in that a person is more stimulated when in the company of others than when alone.[49] This inter-stimulation facilitates the member's communication with himself and others in terms of perceptions of self-image, adequacy, clarity of beliefs and ideas. It lowers resistance to change. There is a direct experiencing of the self in a variety of interactions with others, which may help to combat the self-confusion and self-diffusion so prevalent in our society. Such positive benefits are not likely to occur, however, unless there is a norm that reinforces the members' sharing of varied feelings, opinions, and points of view.

Groups, including families, tend to promote conformity among members. Insofar as satisfactions derived from group life become essential, the individual tends to conform to the norms of the group in order to gain and retain approval of other members. About this characteristic of group process, Cartwright and Zander have said:

We seem then to face a dilemma: the individual needs social support for his values and social beliefs; he needs to be accepted as a valued member of some group which he values; failure to maintain such group membership produces anxiety and personal disorganization. But, on the other hand, group membership and group participation tend to cost the individual his individuality. If he is to receive support from others, and, in turn, give support to others, he and they must hold in common some values and beliefs. Deviation from these undermines any possibility of group support and acceptance.[50]

[49] Olmsted, *The Small Group*, p. 68.
[50] Cartwright and Zander, "Group Dynamics and the Individual," in Bennis et al., eds., *The Planning of Change*, pp. 268-69.

Yet conformity is not necessarily a negative thing. It is not solely the province of the anxious, the dependent, the maladjusted; unwitting conformity in the face of ambiguity may be so, but conformity to the socially accepted demands of clearly defined situations seems a perfectly healthy response for a child (or for an adult, for that matter).[51]

In social work practice, the task for the worker is to influence the development of norms which further the purpose of the group. One such crucial norm to which it is hoped members will conform is that of acceptance of differences. If members conform to that norm, then the group becomes a means for helping a person to find his own identity through the combination of support and stimulation toward change.

Conflict: Its Control and Management

The sociologist, Cooley, said: "The more one thinks of it, the more he will see that conflict and cooperation are not separable things, but phases of one process which always involves something of both." [52] And Simmel has pointed out that:

Contradiction and conflict not only precede unity but are operative in it at every moment of its existence. . . . There probably exists no social unit in which convergent and divergent currents among its members are not inseparably interwoven.[53]

The word conflict tends to elicit frightened or hostile responses; yet conflict itself is an important ingredient in development and change. It can be destructive in its impact on the self, other members of the group, or society. Yet it also can be a constructive building force in group relations. It is a natural and necessary component of group process, created through the ways people communicate with each other.

Conflict encompasses a wider range of behavior than its usual images of violent struggle and war. The essence of conflict is difference. Three basic elements characterize the conflict situation: there are two or more identifiable focal units or parties

---

[51] Hoffman and Hoffman, *Review of Child Development Research*, p. 312.
[52] Cooley, *Social Process*, p. 39.
[53] Simmel, *Conflict*, pp. 13-14.

to the conflict; the units perceive incompatible differences in needs, goals, problems, values, attitudes, or ideas; and there is interaction between the parties around the differences. Conflict is the behavior as contrasted with certain emotions often connected with it, such as hostility. At the intrapersonal level, conflict refers to contradictory, incompatible, or antagonistic emotions and impulses within a person. At the group level, conflicts arise out of the intrapersonal conflicts of individuals, differences in the members' goals, values, and norms, their motivations for membership, and their interests. At times, conflict has its source in the divergence between the values and norms of the group and those of certain segments of the community of which the group is a part. Differences in goals, values, norms, and interests are caused by differing life experiences and socioeconomic resources within a given culture and in other cultures.

Writers such as Bernstein, Coser, Follett, Simmel, and Wilson and Ryland consider conflict to be an inevitable occurrence which has potentially functional and constructive uses as well as dysfunctional and destructive ones.[54] Conflict has both positive and negative potential at many levels of human interaction.

The person who has learned to manage his internal conflicts may well be what Sanford has called a more fully developed person than one who has never dealt with serious intrapersonal conflict.[55] Such a person's range of coping mechanisms and adaptive behavior may be broader and more flexible and his capacity for empathy may be greatly increased. Conversely, however, intrapersonal conflicts which are too long lasting, too serious, or too basic to the personality structure may lead to severe intrapsychic disintegration and breakdown in functioning.

At the group level, conflict may lead to enhanced understanding and consequent strengthening of relationships among members because differences are aired and not allowed to re-

[54] Bernstein, *Explorations in Group Work;* Coser, *The Functions of Social Conflict;* Follett, *The New State;* Simmel, *Conflict;* Wilson and Ryland, *Social Group Work Practice.*
[55] Sanford, *Self and Society,* p. 33.

main irritatingly below the surface. Conflict provides stimulation and a basis for interaction. Coser points out that it is only through the expression of differences that it is possible for a group to delineate its common values and interests. As areas of disagreement are explored, the areas of agreement become clarified.[56] This clarity, in turn, contributes directly to the cohesiveness of the group. Social conflict may have many consequences that increase rather than decrease the group's ability to engage in successful problem-solving activities. To focus on the useful aspects of conflict is not to deny that much conflict is destructive and may lead to the disintegration of the group. Thus, the way in which members of groups recognize, resolve, and manage conflict is crucial to the very survival of the group.

Conflict may be realistic or unrealistic.[57] Realistic conflict is tied to a rational goal and the conflict concerns the means of achieving the goal. In unrealistic conflict, the conflict becomes the end in itself. This type of conflict springs from the irrational, emotional processes of the parties involved. Frequently, the parties to the conflict are unaware of the emotional processes that have motivated them to enter into the struggle. Most conflicts, transpiring as they do within the complex of the human situation, have both rational and irrational elements. Furthermore, they may be both functional and dysfunctional at the same time.

Efforts to resolve conflict occur throughout the life of any group, but there are differences in the nature and intensity of the conflict at various stages of the group's development. The resolution of major conflicts cannot occur until a group has developed to the point at which the basic consensus within the group is solidly built. Within the decision-making processes lie the methods of control of conflict that are available to every group.[58] Groups often control conflict through the process of *elimination,* that is forcing the withdrawal of the opposing individual or subgroup, sometimes in subtle ways. In *subjuga-*

---

[56] Coser, *The Functions of Social Conflict,* p. 8.
[57] *Ibid.,* p. 49.
[58] Wilson and Ryland, *Social Group Work Practice,* pp. 52-53.

tion, or domination, the strongest members force others to accept their points of view. In one sense, in spite of its use as a democratic procedure, majority rule is an example of subjugation. It does not result in agreement or mutual satisfaction. Through the means of *compromise,* the relatively equal strength of opposing forces leads each of the factions to give up something in order to safeguard the common area of interest or the very life of the group itself. An individual or a subgroup may form an *alliance* with other factions; thus each side maintains its independence, but combines to achieve a common goal. Finally, through *integration,* a group may arrive at a solution that is both satisfying to each member and more productive and creative than any contending suggestion. It is this latter process that, according to Wilson and Ryland, "represents the height of achievement in group life. It has the potentiality of being personally satisfying and socially useful: such action is the basis of democratic government." [59]

In which of these ways a particular group will attempt to resolve a conflict situation will depend upon a number of interrelated individual and group characteristics. Among these are the nature of the conflict: such attributes of the members of the group as emotional maturity, values, knowledge of the subject matter, skills in interpersonal relations; the group's prior experience in working toward the resolution of conflict; and the values and norms that have developed in the group about the way in which differences are dealt with and problems solved.

The concept of conflict is associated with a number of other concepts: uncertainty, crisis, change, and dynamic equilibrium in a cyclical process. Herrick suggests the model on page 44 for viewing conflict, with special reference to group situations.[60]

Some uncertainty exists whenever people convene. There is, for example, uncertainty about goals and means toward their achievement, status and role expectations, acceptance, and norms. Such uncertainty leads quite naturally to conflict. The

[59] *Ibid.,* p. 53.
[60] Herrick, "The Perception of Crisis in a Modified Therapeutic Community," pp. 15-30.

system is under stress. Its members are actively involved in attempting to resolve the conflict through the group's usual means. Apprehension increases if the conflict becomes intensified and if efforts to control it and to resolve it fail. A crisis occurs when the conflict reaches its apex, at which time members become aware that they are incapable of resolving the problems basic to the conflict through their customary problem-solving devices.[61] Emotions reach a peak and group functioning becomes disorganized. A point of maximum disruption and considerable disorganization, accompanied by unusual susceptibility to influence, exists at the stage of crisis. The group's resources are mobilized for the necessary change, since there is

recognition that some change must occur if the group is to continue. The crisis is resolved through more effective means of problem solving. Most groups need a period, following the resolution of a conflict with its accompanying changes in the group, to consolidate the changes. The newly achieved consensus acts as a force toward a steady state. During this period, the members are integrating these changes into themselves and into the group system in such a way that a certain unity and accommodation exists within the parts. A certain unity must develop out of diversity both within the individuals and in the group, if positive change and growth is to result. Within the group unity, there are seeds for further conflict: the existing stability is usually only the temporary balancing of conflicting forces as changes are being worked through.

[61] Crisis is defined as a decisive turning point for better or worse in which normal problem-solving methods no longer work. Lola Selby, "Social Work and Crisis Theory," *Social Work Papers,* X (1963), 3.

In day-to-day practice, a crisis need not occur before appropriate changes are made. Most conflicts can be faced and resolved before they reach a point of crisis. A group in a constant state of crisis usually disintegrates. The successful resolution of conflicts and of the more intense crises strengthens the consensus within the group and enables the members to move toward the accomplishment of their purposes. "We can often measure our progress by watching the nature of our conflicts . . . not how many conflicts you have, for conflict is the essence of life, but what are your conflicts and how do you deal with them." [62] Efforts to deny differences and to suppress conflicts are unsuccessful over the long run: such devices lead to stagnation, dysfunction, or disintegration of the system. Unity in diversity is a value that recognizes differences, uses them to strengthen the group, and makes it possible for conflicts to be resolved through democratic processes.

The social worker's emphasis goes beyond the resolution of single conflict situations to an ability to manage conflict. Since conflict is an inevitable and continuing process in human relationships, one of the worker's goals is to help members to develop more effective means for dealing with the process of conflict as it occurs again and again within the group. The elements which are crucial to integration as a form of conflict resolution are also the factors which contribute to the effective management of conflict. Mutual acceptance, open communication, and respect for differences make it possible for members to become competent to deal with the conflicts which are so characteristic of the human condition.

Group Cohesiveness

Concern with the cohesiveness of a group is based on the results of studies that indicate the influence that the degree of cohesiveness has on a group. Group cohesiveness is defined most simply as "attraction to the group." [63] The concept refers to the forces which bind members of a group to each other and to the group.

[62] Follett, *Dynamic Administration*, p. 35.
[63] Cartwright and Zander, *Group Dynamics*, p. 72.

It has been found that the more cohesive the group, the greater its influence on its members.[64] To the extent that a group is highly attractive to its members, it has the ability to produce changes in attitudes, opinions and behavior. With the increase in influence, the pressures toward conformity also increase. In groups of high cohesiveness, the members may disagree with each other, but they also tend to find solutions to problems and conflicts more quickly. There tends to be greater satisfaction with the group and higher morale, less internal friction, and greater capacity to survive the loss of some of its members. In general, the more cohesive the group, the more satisfying it is to its members.[65]

The attractiveness of a group to its members, then, depends basically upon the extent to which it serves the needs of its members. It will become less attractive to a person if it becomes less suitable as a means of satisfying existing needs, or if it acquires distasteful or unpleasant properties. A person usually leaves a group voluntarily only when the forces driving him away from the group are greater than the sum of the forces attracting him to the group, plus the restraining forces against leaving. Many groups survive only because the members have no strong motivation to leave. Such groups are not cohesive and they exert little influence in the lives of their members.

Cohesiveness can, in a sense, be perceived as the result of the interacting processes within the group. Cohesion results from "the scope and intensity of the members' involvement," according to Merton, which is the bond between the members. The attractiveness of a group to its members is proportional to the motivations of the individuals, their attraction to each other, and the ability of the group to meet their needs. The cohesiveness of a group develops as members strive toward the advancement of their shared purposes. Attraction to the group's purpose and participation in activities devoted to the pursuit of that purpose are essential conditions for the development of a

---

[64] Festinger, Schacter, and Back, "The Operation of Group Standards," in *ibid.*, pp. 241-59.

[65] *Ibid.*, pp. 69-94.

cohesive group. A consensus about the common interests of the members develops. In addition to the interest in the purpose of the group, interpersonal attraction is a crucial factor in the development of cohesiveness. Mutuality of acceptance among members develops out of shared experiences. It must be remembered, however, that in any group there are gradations and continuous shifts, both in the movement toward the achievement of goals and in the process of acceptance and rejection. Gradually, there is an increase in the extent to which members truly involve themselves in the group. Shared values and norms tend to reinforce the forces of attraction to the group. A basic consensus is established whereby the members perceive events, people, and objects from similar, but not identical, perspectives. The recognition of the differences among them creates conflict, the resolution of which provides stimulation toward new and modified common perceptions. The basic process through which cohesiveness develops in a group is effective communication, which frees members to express themselves, encourages comparisons of likeness and difference, and modifies the attitudes of members toward each other and toward the group.

A cohesive group does not just develop. A group's cohesiveness is enhanced if the leader's participation contributes to the group's maintenance and further development. The cohesiveness of a group is demonstrably influenced by its leadership.[66] The social worker, as the technical leader of the group, influences cohesion through the way he uses his professional knowledge, tools, and skills in his work with individuals and the group system.

A cohesive group tends to become a reference group for its members. A reference group is an actual group or a category of people to which a person aspires to relate himself psychologically.[67] It serves as a point of comparison against which a person can evaluate himself and others. A person identifies with

[66] Bonner, *Group Dynamics*, p. 74; Cattell, "New Concepts for Measuring Leadership in Terms of Group Syntality," *Human Relations*, IV (1951), 161-84.
[67] See Sherif and Wilson, *Group Relations at the Crossroads*, pp. 203-31; Merton, *Social Theory and Social Structure*, pp. 225-386.

a reference group and internalizes its values and norms of behavior so that he comes to perceive the group's values as his own. A membership group is not necessarily a reference group, but when a group in which a person is a participant is also a group with which he identifies himself, then his membership group is also a reference group. As Merton has said, "Any of the groups of which one is a member . . . as well as groups of which one is not a member . . . can become points of reference for shaping one's attitudes, evaluations, and behavior." [68] The need then is to develop a reference group through which each member can benefit, and then help him to find his own identity so that he can function effectively when the group is discontinued. The type of group that is developed cannot be left to chance. It should become one in which the relationships and norms are those that promote growth toward more effective psychosocial functioning.

A social worker, then, has a model of a type of group in mind toward which he makes efforts to direct his attention. Briefly, it is a group in which: (1) there is a shared purpose; (2) the role of the members is defined as a collaborative one; (3) relationships are characterized by a preponderance of positive ties and interdependence among the members; (4) communication is characterized by freedom and openness; and (5) the values of the group support healthy growth toward adaptive behavior.

Stages of Group Development

It takes time for a group to develop as an instrument through which positive gains may be achieved for its members. Gradually, from a collection of individuals, a group emerges. As a group develops, there are noticeable differences in the behavior of the members and in the structure and functioning of the group. Although change in the group is a continuous, dynamic process, it seems useful to perceive the group as moving through a number of stages characteristic of its life cycle. The identifica-

[68] *Ibid.*, p. 233.

tion of stages in a group's development provides diagnostic clues for the social worker in his participation in the group. It makes it possible for the practitioner to ascertain where a given group is in it development and then to plan what needs to be done to help it move forward, toward the achievement of its purpose.

A stage is a differentiable period or a discernible degree in the process of development, growth, or change.[69] A phase differs from a stage only in that it is presumed to be recurrent; in the literature these terms tend to be used interchangeably. There seems to be great interest in the process of group development, not only on the part of social workers but also of psychiatrists, psychologists, and social scientists. Two reviews of the literature in 1962 by Hearn,[70] and Sampson,[71] uncovered a total of 117 references on group development, change, or progress. An additional 20 references not noted by either Hearn or Sampson, or written since 1962, were included in Northen's analysis of 45 articles on group development that seemed most pertinent to social work practice.[72]

Although each group is unique in its particular constellation of characteristics, each varies at a given time and changes over time along generic dimensions of purpose, organizational structure, patterns of relationships, values and norms, and management of conflict. Furthermore, each individual changes in significant ways as he becomes a part of a group that is meaningful to him. No author has attempted a full and systematic analysis of changes along each of these dimensions, although the need for such analysis has been indicated. The development of groups is viewed in a multiplicity of ways, depending upon the purpose, size, and duration of the group, the theoretical stance of the observer, and the particular facet of the whole that is selected for emphasis. The number of stages described by various

[69] *Webster's New World Dictionary of the American Language*, p. 1411.
[70] Hearn, "Group Change and Development."
[71] Sampson, "An Inquiry into Knowledge about Stages and Phases of Group Development."
[72] Northen, "An Analysis of Stages of Group Development."

authors ranges from two to eleven. All but two authors deal with at least three stages, and four is the modal number. Only one author dealt with a stage of "origin" that precedes the initial encounter of members with each other, and only a few dealt with a terminal stage. Any division of group life into stages is somewhat arbitrary, for indeed there is a continuous flow of interaction that shifts and changes, with some forward and some backward movement, throughout the life of a group. As one stops the camera, however, to take a still picture, it is evident that a group is different at that moment from what it was earlier. The group has changed.

A model of five stages of group development useful for social work practice will be developed in subsequent chapters. It is thought to be applicable to groups of brief duration, as well as to those that continue over a considerable period of time, and also to groups with varied purposes and forms of organizational structure. A preparatory stage is included which precedes the actual interaction among the persons who are to become a part of the new social system. In the other four stages, four interlocking processes are specified as these remain constant or change over time; namely, the characteristics of the group itself, the predominant patterns of member behavior, the most cogent tasks for the group's attention, and the characteristic patterns of the worker's role.

The reminder needs to be given, however, that no particular group exactly fits the model. Rather the model provides a guide for the practitioner in his diagnostic thinking about the group at a given time. Different groups proceed through the stages at different rates of speed. A group of acting-out delinquent boys or of withdrawn, regressed adult schizophrenic patients will move much more slowly than will a group of fairly adequate adolescents with a need to work out a problem of Jewish identity, or a group of mothers whose primary concern is with their behavior in relation to their adolescent children. A group is composed of individuals, each unique in some way. Individuals progress at different rates, in different ways, and in relation to different problems. A group tends to move irregularly, not uniformly, on all of the relevant dimensions of group structure and process. This does not deny the fact, however, that there is a fundamental core of movement, with variations along both individual and group dimensions, that can be thought of as the development of a group.

CHAPTER III

The Role of the Social Worker: An Overview

THE ROLE of the social worker in reciprocal interaction with the members of a group consists of a sequence of patterns of behavior and attributes expected of him by his profession, the agency which employs him, and the persons he serves. The social worker's is an achieved role, earned through education and experience. Within the group, his actual behaviors are influenced by the expectations of the members of the group and by the nature of the developing group system. His position in the agency and the group gives him certain authority to influence the members toward changes in attitudes and behavior and to influence the structure and processes of the group itself. The manner in which a social worker exerts his authority is crucial. The purpose of the worker's influence is to free the individual to live more effectively. The very essence of his authority is that it is effective only to the degree that an individual permits the worker to influence him. The very fact that man is both influenced by and influences his environment negates any idea that the worker can isolate himself and his clientele from other influences in the environment. One of the advantages of the use of groups in social work is that stimulation toward improvement arises from a network of interpersonal influence in which all members participate. Thus, the practitioner is one important influence but so also is each member of the group.

Relationship

The nature and quality of the social worker's relationship with individuals, subgroups, and the group as a whole has an important effect on each member's use of the group and on the development of the group itself. The use of relationship is of primary importance in motivating members to discover and develop their capacities, to have self-esteem, and to accept and use the contribution of the social worker. Relationship has been described as consisting "primarily of emotional responses which ebb and flow from person to person as human behavior evokes different affective reactions." [1] The social worker in a group situation develops a unique relationship with each member, based on an understanding of the individual. Of equal importance is the ability to facilitate relationships of members to each other. As stated by Helen Phillips, the worker's

relation to each member is important, but if he is to accelerate the group relations and help members to use them, he will need to modify the many diverse, individual strands of his relationship with the members so that they will be in process with each other and so that he will have a connection with the group as a whole.[2]

In one sense, then, the social worker's focus is on the group. Within the group system whatever he does that is directed toward a particular member, affects the group as a whole. Coyle said it this way:

It seems to me that the primary skill is the ability to establish a relationship with a group as a group. This involves the capacity to feel at ease, in fact, to enjoy the social interplay among members and to be able to perceive both individual behavior and its collective manifestations . . . as well as to become a part of the relationships and to affect them.[3]

This focus on the group does not negate the importance of the individual. When the focus is upon interpersonal interaction, neither the individual nor the group is submerged: both are viewed as equally important. Neither can be understood fully except in terms of the other. If he has a connection with the

[1] Trecker, *Social Group Work*, p. 48.
[2] Phillips, *Essentials of Social Group Work Skill*, p. 145.
[3] Coyle, "Some Basic Assumptions about Social Group Work," in Murphy, *The Social Group Work Method*, p. 100.

group as a whole, the worker also simultaneously views the individuals, the network of relationships, and the group. This complexity makes special demands on the worker. The worker seeks to develop and maintain a relationship that is sensitive to the feelings of the members, conveys acceptance of them, is empathic and creative, yet professional in nature. Within these expectations, however, there is ample room for flexibility and innovation in response to others. There is room to respond appropriately to different members in different ways, and to respond to a particular member in different ways at different times.

Feeling accepted by another human being tends to make a person feel that he is of some worth to another and that he is understood by another. Showing genuine interest in a person, giving him recognition as an individual, listening sensitively to what he says, paying attention to what he does, conveying a desire to be helpful, and really caring about the person are some of the evidences of an attitude of acceptance.[4] Acceptance does not require the approval of all behavior: it does, however, convey the hope that the person will be able to move away from self-defeating behavior toward the realization of his potentialities.

In an atmosphere in which a person feels he is of basic worth, he is free to explore his interests and capacities, discover his own identity, and set forth realistic aspirations for himself. The value on which the concept of acceptance is based is the innate worth and dignity of man. As representatives of a profession, and of society, social workers are the bearers of values, but acceptance makes it possible for the members to feel secure and worthy of respect and consideration, even when the worker cannot approve of their behavior. Thus, acceptance does not mean that the worker does not make judgments about the members of the group but rather that, although he evaluates, he does not condemn. His evaluation of members and the group

[4] For discussion of acceptance in social group work practice, see Wilson and Ryland, *Social Group Work Practice*, pp. 85-91. For a similar emphasis in relation to social casework, see Perlman, *Social Casework, A Problem-Solving Process*, pp. 67-69.

is made against the norms that are thought to be conducive to human welfare. Such evaluation is based also upon understanding of the person, the group, and the environment.

Empathy is closely related to acceptance, but it involves specifically the capacity to feel into another in order to understand him better.[5] It is the ability to project oneself into the feeling and thinking of another in order to understand what he experiences. A person's intimate feelings and concerns can be discovered and evaluated only if the social worker and his clientele are involved in the same situation. When the worker can feel with the member, then the member tends to feel free to communicate his feelings and concerns. When the other person senses that the response is an attempt to understand, rather than to judge, it is not necessary for him to cling to defensive distortions of communication. The capacity for empathy demands that the person have warmth of feeling that comes through in communication with others. Empathy is a process that can be either spontaneous or deliberate. Being closely linked to intuition, it is not primarily intellectual. The most distinguishing feature of empathy, compared with other kinds of fellow feelings toward others, lies in the fact that the subject's ego boundaries and coherence of self are maintained. The practitioner not only identifies with the group member insofar as he experiences what the member feels but he also perceives and shares in the member's feelings as though they were his own. He draws on his own relevant life experiences which may aid him in understanding the other. A professional detachment follows which makes possible an objective analysis of what the worker has perceived. Empathic communication is facilitated in a small group when there is identification on the basis of a common purpose or quality sufficient to give the group at least a fair degree of cohesiveness. An anonymous English author is

[5] For good discussions of empathy, see Pernell, "Identifying and Teaching the Skill Components of Social Group Work," in *Educational Developments*, pp. 20-22; Cottrell and Dymond, "The Empathic Responses, A Neglected Field for Research," *Psychiatry*, XXI (1949), 355-59; Scheidlinger, "The Concept of Empathy in Group Psychotherapy," *International Journal of Group Psychotherapy*, XVI (1966), 413-24.

credited with the statement that empathy means "to see with the eyes of another, to hear with the ears of another, and to feel with the heart of another." [6] Empathy is not to be confused with sympathy. In empathy, attention is on the feelings and situation of another person. In sympathy, attention is on the assumed parallel between one's own feelings and situation and the feelings and situation of another.

Several degrees of empathy have been defined operationally, ranging from unawareness of the feelings of a client to a level at which "the message 'I am with you' is unmistakably clear." "Accurate empathy involves both the sensitivity to current feelings and the verbal facility to communicate this understanding in language attuned to the client's current feelings." [7] High empathy has been found to be positively associated with client improvement. The worker communicates his feelings of empathy, or its lack, through the consistency of his verbal and non-verbal acts, listening, observing and feeling into these processes, conveying with honesty his desire to understand, and avoiding such statements as "I know," or "I understand," when indeed he does not and cannot. How much more useful to say, "No, I really don't but I want to understand: will you help me with this?" It is possible to enhance ability to empathize with others through imaginative consideration of the other person in his situation, and through awareness of one's feelings toward other people and situations.

Objectivity, essential to empathy, is the capacity to see things and people as they are, without bias and prejudice. The worker's focus is on the needs of the members. Being aware of his own values and feelings, he is able to refrain from imposing them on others. He is able to evaluate realistically feelings that are expressed toward him. In perceiving other persons, there is a tendency toward a halo effect; that is, to see only positive qualities in persons who are liked and only negative qualities in persons who are disliked. Self-awareness lessens the likelihood

[6] Taken from Katz, *Empathy, Its Nature and Uses,* p. 1.
[7] Truax, "A Scale for Measurement of Accurate Empathy," *Psychiatric Institute Bulletin* (1961), pp. 1-23.

of making faulty judgments about others. Objectivity involves understanding the motives of members in their reactions toward the worker, so that the worker is realistic in his evaluation of feelings and behavior expressed toward him. It involves, as well, understanding one's own reactions to the feelings expressed by members, either covertly or overtly. Self-awareness is not pursued for the satisfaction it brings the worker in his introspective activities, but for use in practice wherein some of his own feelings and reactions may hamper his ability to understand others, or to use himself appropriately in his interaction with individuals, the group, or segments of the social environment. The worker needs sufficient self-acceptance and security to permit disengagement from his own feelings in order to be able to focus on the feelings of others. This necessitates some emotional maturity. Narcissism is incompatible with group leadership. Indeed, if the worker is preoccupied with his own feelings and reactions during a group session, rather than focused on the feelings and reactions of the members, he may not be able to empathize with the members nor act appropriately in response to the interaction.

Members of groups usually develop realistic views about and appreciation of the worker as he is. Some members may, however, perceive the social worker unrealistically, due to erroneous expectations of his role in the group. Or they may transfer reactions from earlier meaningful relationships onto the worker, thus distorting their perceptions of him. Self-awareness is essential for the worker to avoid distortion of his own perceptions of the members through what is termed countertransference. The transference components need to be recognized and, if they are inimical to the progress of an individual or the development of a group, they need to be understood and clarified.

Awareness of one's own values is crucial to understanding and helping others, for a person's values determine many of his choices and actions. In writing on psychotherapy, it has been said:

One cannot live without encountering the problem of values. . . . Nor can one . . . [be] a therapist without bringing certain

convictions about values into one's work. These convictions may
or may not be specifically communicated to the patient, but they
help determine the goal he sets for himself and his patient; and
they are consciously or unconsciously reflected in his questions,
statements, or other reactions.[8]

Herein lies the need for self-awareness: that the social worker
can honestly and openly recognize his own values, separate them
out from those of the members, and act on the basis of knowledge about the distance between his values and those of the
members, rather than deny that values do enter into practice.

Knowledge about the range of values held by persons within
our American culture and its many subcultures may help the
social worker to separate his values from those of others. Understanding and coming to terms with the values of his own important reference groups is necessary for anyone who hopes to
understand the values of others. The worker needs "to realize
that he sees others through the screen of his own personality and
his own life experiences. . . . This is why a social worker must
develop enough awareness of at least the make-up of his own
particular screen." [9] Fortunately, the worker may correct this
screen through careful analysis of his own behavior in relation
to others, and through the use of supervision or consultation.
Such efforts help him to take into account his own bias, even
though he cannot completely eliminate it, thus making it possible to understand better the persons with whom he works.

If a social worker can come to accept, care about, and empathize with the persons with whom he works, he will not need
to worry about using the professional relationship for purposes
inimical to the well-being of his clients. To relate to others
with these qualities is not dependent upon long duration of
the relationship. The worker's attributes can be conveyed in
short-term as well as long-term involvement. The worker can
communicate these intentions to the client only if he truly
possesses the qualities.

[8] Buhler, *Values in Psychotherapy*, p. 1.
[9] Konopka, *Social Group Work*, p. 94.

The Social Worker's Contribution to the Group

How to describe the complex constellation of means by which the social worker uses his personality, knowledge, and professional skills to help a group is a thorny problem. The social worker's contribution to the group has been described in various ways. Wilson and Ryland attempted to conceptualize the behavior and activities of the worker;[10] Saloshin devised a classification scheme of the activities of the worker and the tools used to carry them out;[11] Konopka developed principles of practice that sensitize the practitioner to what he should do;[12] Phillips analyzed four essential components of skill in practice;[13] Vinter and Clemenger, in different ways, described several categories of role behavior; [14] and Schwartz selected tasks, or cate gories of activities, as a concept for use in describing the social worker's contribution.[15] Whatever the scheme, it is generally acknowledged that the worker assumes some degree of leadership in initiating, developing, and terminating a group system. The nature and degree of leadership varies with the capacities of the members to meet the demands of group life and to direct their own activities. When members are unable to cope with a situation themselves, the worker actively uses his authority. On the other hand, when the members are able to participate responsibly in the group, the worker is less active. Authority in the professional relationship is vastly different from the exercise of authoritarian power over others for personal gratification, or for the achievement of one's own ends.[16]

The plan used here to describe the social worker's role be-

[10] Wilson and Ryland, *Social Group Work Practice*, pp. 56-83.

[11] Saloshin, "Development of an Instrument for the Analysis of the Social Group Work Method in Therapeutic Settings."

[12] Konopka, *Social Group Work*.

[13] Phillips, *Essentials of Social Group Work Skill*.

[14] Vinter, "The Essential Components of Social Group Work Practice," in Vinter, ed., *Readings in Group Work Practice;* Clemenger, "Congruence between Members and Workers on Selected Behaviors of the Role of the Social Group Worker."

[15] Schwartz, "The Social Worker in the Group," in *The Social Welfare Forum*, pp. 146-70.

[16] For a discussion of the difference between democratic leadership and domination, see Pigors, *Leadership or Domination*.

haviors is to view his actions as a reflection or instrumentality of his intentions. It builds on Peirce's research.[17] Each major action of the worker is motivated by an intent of some kind. Gordon refers to this notion of intent as "the concrete ends toward which daily social work practice is directed." [18] The worker's intents reflect his values, goals, and understanding of individuals and the group system at a given time. Whatever the worker does takes place within the medium of the worker-group relationship. The categories of intent are based on the theoretical assumption that psychosocial functioning is enhanced when capacities are recognized and used, when obstacles to effective functioning are reduced or eliminated, and when the social milieu supports the efforts of persons, individually and collectively, to strive toward more satisfying and effective functioning. Focus is on ego functions and processes that mediate the individual's efforts to function in his environment.[19]

Essentially, the verbal and nonverbal acts of the social worker are intended to: (1) support an individual, subgroup, group system, or relevant persons in the external system; (2) make more effective the members' modes of communication; (3) improve the accuracy and clarity of members' perceptions of reality; (4) enhance the competence of members to master life experiences relevant to their desires, problems, and situations; and (5) modify the environment so that it can support the members in their efforts toward growth and change, or so that the destructive environmental stresses are reduced. One or more of these intents may predominate in the worker's thinking and doing at a given time in his work with a group. Usually, however, in the course of the group experience, some attention is given to each of these major categories of intent. Together, they form a constellation of means to the achievement of more effective psychosocial functioning.

[17] Peirce. "A Study of the Methodological Components of Social Work with Groups."

[18] Gordon, "A Critique of the Working Definition," *Social Work*, VII (4), (1962), 9-10.

[19] Hartmann, *Ego Psychology and the Problems of Adaptation*.

SUPPORT. If the social worker is to contribute to the improvement of the members' psychosocial functioning, he needs to give sufficient support to the members so that in time the major support to its members will come from the group itself. While the group is still forming, and at times during its later phases of development, the social worker needs to support a member, a subgroup, or the group as a whole. Support means to sustain or keep steady, to give courage, to express faith and confidence, or to give approval to someone. To support suggests a favoring of someone, either by giving active aid or through approval and sanction. Supportive measures sustain the motivation and capacity of a person to seek certain desired experiences or outcomes, and to develop confidence in the group as a means toward growth. What is supported are the strengths and constructive defenses of a person, in order that he may maintain a level of functioning or attain a better one. In social work practice, the aim is to support the ego in its efforts to cope with new or difficult situations.[20]

The relationship between the social worker and the group is itself a means through which the members are supported in their efforts to use the group for their mutual benefit. Indeed, one of the primary responsibilities of the worker is to enhance the supportive potential of the group. The worker sets the tone for mutual support through expressing the expectation that members will become able to do this. To a large extent, however, the members become supportive of each other as they become aware of their common purposes, aspirations, interests, and needs, and as they work out their positive and negative feelings toward each other. They become supportive of each other as they feel security and trust in the worker, as they come to identify with him, and later integrate some of his patterns of supportive behavior.

[20] See: Schmidl, "A Study of Techniques Used in Supportive Treatment," *Social Casework,* XXXII (1951), 413-19; Selby, "Supportive Treatment: The Development of a Concept and a Helping Method," *Social Service Review,* XXX (1956), 413; and Frey, "Support and the Group: Generic Treatment Form," *Social Work,* VII (4), (1962), 35-42.

One specific supportive aim is to enhance the feelings of positive self-esteem and security of the members: this occurs when both inner and outer pressures are reduced. Through support from the group, a member finds courage to express feelings and thoughts that would be suppressed in usual social situations, to express his convictions, to expose some of his vulnerabilities, and to risk trying new experiences. The alleviation of anxiety or guilt when these emotions become intense tends to be felt as support by the members. A moderate level of tension may motivate a person to attain a goal, but when it is extreme, it is disruptive and incapacitating.[21] Support may be used to express confidence that improvement in some area of concern to a member is possible, and that the social worker can be counted upon to do his part to bring it about. Some realistic hope is necessary to develop and sustain motivation to enter a group, remain in it, and make optimal use of the opportunities it provides. A person's sense of confidence may be increased through the provision of social experiences in which he can be successful and can perceive the achievement as success.

Realistic reassurance tends to reduce feelings of insecurity and anxiety. Persons often come into a new group, especially if they have been referred to it because of a problem perceived by a relative or a person in a position of authority, with feelings of guilt, stigma, and abnormality. Realistic reassurance of normality is usually supportive. When realistic reassurance cannot be given, it is more supportive to acknowledge the difficulty and to suggest that ways can be found to improve the situation. Denial of the reality is seldom felt as support. Persons feel secure when they know what is expected of them. When members are clear about what is expected of them, their energies can become mobilized around the accomplishment of their purposes, rather than being tied up with uncertainty about their own rights and responsibilities in the situation. A person develops a sense of security in his role in the group if he is provided with encouragement to remain in the group, to continue to participate in its varied conversations and social experi-

[21] Berelson and Steiner, *Human Behavior*, p. 264.

ences, and to try out new modes of functioning. Support may be given, to reinforce strengths or efforts to explore areas of difficulties, through the use of approval and encouragement. When some members of groups are offered small, concrete evidences of the social worker's interest in them, they feel supported. It is often desirable to support members of a group through modification of some aspects of their environments. Working with relatives may result in their provision of support to the member's use of the group. These persons may, in turn, need support from the social worker in order to do their part in supporting the member.

Support may be given through the verbalization or through nonverbal demonstration of the worker's interest. To be supportive to one or more members of the group, the social worker's behavior needs to be based on sound judgment about the individual needs and the group climate at a given time, since the worker's acts intended to be supportive are apt to feel like support to the members only if they are rooted in reality, rather than in the worker's need to be pleasant and to deny feelings and troubles. Even when a practitioner's intent is sound and his acts appropriate, they may not be perceived as supportive by the persons to whom they are directed. The support may not be accepted because the person distorts reality, or because he is unable to accept evidences of concern and acceptance from another. The feedback that a particular member gets from a group may support acceptance of the worker's messages to the member or may tend to contradict them. Such results are evidences of the importance of the worker's accurate assessment of the group as well as of the particular person about whom he may have a special concern at a particular moment in the life of the group. To the extent that a worker is sensitive to the feelings and needs of each member of the group, and their relations with each other, his use of supportive techniques will probably be effective. Certainly, the social worker's efforts to sustain the motivation and enhance the capacity of the members of the group toward achievement of their purposes is an important ingredient in serving people well.

COMMUNICATION. "In a sense, all communication involves giving a little of the self into interaction and getting something of the other in return. If the input is all on one side, the process breaks down." [22] This quotation emphasizes the interdependence of the members of the group for meeting each other's needs and accomplishing the group purpose. The social worker hopes that the group will provide opportunities for each member to participate according to his ability and that the quality of communication will enhance the group's positive influence on each of its members. He hopes, too, that each member will improve his own ability to communicate effectively, not only within the group but with the various people whom he encounters in his daily living.

There are guidelines to aid the social worker in his assessment of the adequacy of the communication within the group. Adequate communication is direct and open, and conveys the intended meaning with clarity. If communication is adequate, there is consistency between the intents and the words or actions used, and consistency between affect and cognition; there is a balance between listening to or observing others and contributing to others; and there is acknowledgment of personal responsibility for the intent and content of the communication. Such communication assumes a high degree of emotional maturity, and expectations therefore need to be in line with the developmental phase of members and their particular vulnerabilities.

Ability to communicate with other people is basic to effective psychosocial functioning. Unless a person understands the intent of messages sent to him, he cannot respond in a way that meets the expectations of the other. Likewise, unless a person can convey his intents to others in such a way that they can be perceived with accuracy, he cannot make his desires known. When a person cannot understand others, he tends to become anxious. The result is often confusion, misunderstanding, and distrust. Many difficulties in interpersonal relations and role performance derive from inability to make clear one's desires,

[22] Cumming and Cumming, *Ego and Milieu*, p. 192.

knowledge, feelings, and ideas. Difficulties derive from misin-
terpretations of what others are intending to communicate. If
members do not participate actively in the communicative network within a group, they miss an opportunity to give to others
and to receive validation of their feelings and thoughts from
others. It is not implied that each member must "tell all," but
rather that each is entitled to what privacy he feels he needs
at a given time. The development of a sense of identity is dependent to some extent upon validations from others. Without
feedback from others, there is a lack of knowledge about the
extent of congruence between one's own perceptions of self and
the world and the perceptions of other people.

In a group, the network of communication is more complex
than in a one-to-one relationship. Each member, with his own
values and styles of communication, needs to be understood
and to be responded to in appropriate ways. Within the interacting processes of the group, correction of distortions in perception of intent and content of communication may be delayed.
Some messages may get lost in the welter of competing messages
so that responses are missing. Lack of commonage of experience
may make communication difficult.

There is a close interrelationship between facility in verbalization and exposure to and use of experiences in the physical
and social environment. Stimulation from dealing with a variety
of nonhuman objects, within supportive social relationships,
seems essential to the development of adequate verbal skills.
In the course of normal development, the basic speech skills are
acquired during the preschool years. The progression is from
experiencing many objects to learning the verbal symbols for
these things and experiences. Dearth of language skills may
often be reflected in poor performance at school or work. In
working with members of groups who have suffered early
deprivation in this respect, development of skills in verbal
communication may be dependent upon the provision of experiences with objects and people to make up for these lacks.

Some cultures place much more value on verbalization than
do others, so that members from different cultural backgrounds

may have different perceptions about the relative importance of verbal and nonverbal forms of communication. Middle-class families tend to have the resources that facilitate the development of language, which gives their children an advantage in school and other situations in which a premium is placed on the use of verbal skills. There is, on the other hand, evidence that persons identified with lower and working classes share some characteristics that impede their ability to participate in the verbal world of the dominant middle class.[23] One such characteristic is the first person perspective, in which reality is described through the person's own perspectives and in relation to himself only. Modes of conceptualization tend to be oriented to the concrete. Both depth and breadth of verbal communication are therefore somewhat curtailed. Furthermore, such persons are further impaired by the inadequate grammatical structure of their communication.

Culturally derived attitudes toward authority influence the nature of participation in groups. For example, in many Japanese families, ultimate authority is vested in males. The nonacceptance of the authority of women, combined with conventional courtesy toward them, might be reflected in an overly polite manner and avoidance of expression of feelings in the group. In some cultures, as in some segments of the Mexican and American Indian cultures, persons are taught not to share personal problems with outsiders. Social distance, due to such cultural differences, can be reduced through discussion of feelings about various forms of self-expression.

At the other extreme, some middle-class clients of European origin have a pseudosophistication with verbalization that masks misunderstanding of reality and that makes the expression of feelings extremely difficult. Words are used as a defense against understanding, or as an avoidance of taking responsi-

[23] See Deutsch, "The Role of Social Class in Language Development and Cognition," *American Journal of Orthopsychiatry*, XXXV (1965), 78-88; Siller, "Socioeconomic Status and Conceptual Thinking," *Journal of Abnormal and Social Psychology*, LV (1957), 365-67; and Bernstein, "Language and Social Class," *British Journal of Sociology*, XL (1960), 27.

bility for behavior. Overintellectualization can be a common defense against involvement.

Knowledge about people's differences in comfort and facility with verbalization has several implications for the social worker. The worker considers verbal accessibility and styles of verbalization in setting realistic expectations for the members' participation in the group's discussions or action-oriented experiences. His expectations take into account the members' own expectations for each other. When a member feels incapable of meeting the worker's or the group's expectations concerning verbal communication, feelings of inadequacy are bound to be accentuated. The outcome may be reticence to participate, withdrawal from the group, or assumption of a role of dominator or monopolizer. The worker is concerned with whatever hinders a member from learning to communicate effectively.

In most group situations, the social worker directs some effort toward helping the members to communicate more effectively with other people. The ways he does this depend upon the particular problems that the members of groups are having in communication, the values and norms of the members related to communication, and the motivation and capacities of the members to work on this particular aspect of functioning.

With small children, the worker may teach them the elements of verbal communication: how to label the sights, sounds, colors, and objects they encounter. He may teach them how to ask questions or make a request of an adult or another child. Often children need to talk about those things with which they have direct experience in the group, so that social experiences and conversations go hand in hand. With older children and adults who have difficulty in the use of verbal communication, the worker may need to provide indirect modes for practicing communication through such experiences as role playing, sociodrama, use of microphones, puppets, word games, or charades. He moves them, however, into direct verbalization as soon as they are ready to benefit from it.

There often is a need to help persons to check out the intent of a message with the message as perceived by others, through such means as questioning others as to what they understand, and requesting restatement of the message that was sent.[24] The worker may seek feedback from the members as to whether or not his own intent was perceived accurately by the members, and correct himself when necessary. He may mirror back to the members what was felt, seen, or heard. When a person has expressed an emotion or an idea, a reaction is expected which contributes to the extension, clarification, or alteration of the original message. When a person is aware of the results produced by his own actions, his subsequent actions are influenced by this knowledge. Some members of groups need to be asked to listen to others, to indicate when a message is not clear, and to offer correction of messages, when requested. The worker may need to point out to members when their messages are not clear, when they are confused, incoherent, or incongruent, or when others have misinterpreted an intended message. There is a need to call attention to double-bind messages and ask that they be clarified. A double-bind message is one in which the latent message contradicts the manifest or cognitive message, or in which one set of words contradicts another. Words may convey one attitude or request, and tone of voice a different one. In double-binds, there often is no right response, so that the person is caught in a dilemma and may become anxious, inactive, or withdrawn.

The specific acts of the social worker in opening up and clarifying verbal communication are varied and many. He may make comments and ask questions that invite certain members to speak. He may need to limit a member who attempts to monopolize the conversation. He may request further amplification of a feeling or thought. He may connect up what one member says with what has gone before it in order to help members to follow the sequence of communication. He may ask for the reactions from others to the comments of one member. He may notice points of difference or stress, and help bring these into the open where they may be examined and explored,

[24] Satir, *Conjoint Family Therapy*, pp. 63-90.

through sharing his observations of these tensions with the members and eliciting broad and varied reactions to his observation. He may restate an idea to verify his and the group's understanding, which tends to make it the possession of the group, as well as to make its understanding clear. Whenever this happens, the commonage of experience of the group is broadened which, in turn, facilitates communication among the members. Above all, perhaps, the practitioner's own skills in communication are important. If he is direct, clear, and honest, there will be consistency between his verbal and nonverbal acts of communication. In these respects, he needs to be a model for the members to emulate. The concern is with communication both as a tool in working toward other goals, and with ineffective communication as a problem in itself. The level of communication sought is, therefore, of a practical applied nature, as contrasted with abstract thinking.

ENHANCEMENT OF PERCEPTION OF REALITY. Flexibility in adapting to the needs and interests of others in the pursuit of one's own realistic goals requires the ability to perceive the relevant factors in a social situation realistically and to act in accordance with this understanding. Improvement in functioning is enhanced when realities are faced and appropriate coping methods are developed. Almost everyone has some difficulty in perceiving himself accurately in relation to other people and to his environment. A person may have a distorted perception of the environment as it really exists. Distortion may stem from bias, isolation, lack of knowledge or experience, a frame of reference not shared by others, strong emotion, or unconscious transference reactions.

In a sense, a small group is a microcosm of society, providing for its members an opportunity for reality testing, that is, for testing their perceptions against those of the worker and their peers. The group situation may be likened to a wall of mirrors through which is reflected to an individual various views of different aspects of himself. He comes to see himself in and through the group, gradually discovering his own identity.

Positive evaluation from one's peers is a source of reassurance and satisfaction; negative evaluation is painful, but often a valid source of learning about oneself. When perceptions of reality are affirmed or challenged by peers, there may be a more powerful impact than when this is done only by a professional helper.

One of the major intentions of the social worker is to help the members of a group to recognize and identify the various aspects of a social situation, then extend or elaborate on their understanding, and move ahead to clarify the problems and the situations. These are procedures used to enhance a person's perception of himself in his varied social situations. There are two major aspects that need clarification by the members of a group: (1) the social situation, including the outer environment, the agency, and the group; and (2) the attitudes and behavior of the members in various social situations.

An essential step in working toward either modification of one's attitudes and behavior, or toward modification of some aspect of the environment itself, is accurate perception of the situation. People often do not have adequate understanding of situations in the community that influence their attitudes and behavior. They may lack knowledge about the organization of the community in terms of its institutions and resources for the provision of opportunities and special services. They may have a distorted or one-sided picture of varied situations and people in the community. They may lack knowledge of or be unable to accept the legal requirements for certain privileges, such as use of public buildings, becoming a licensed driver, remaining on probation or parole, or having chaperons for a public event.

Members often need help with the recognition or elaboration of their knowledge about the agency as it influences the service given, or they may need to clarify their perceptions of the group itself. The members may simply need information about these matters or they may have misperceptions about some aspect of the agency or the group that requires working toward its clarification. Attitudes and responses to the social worker may be brought into the group's discussion as may attitudes and responses to each other. Clarification of such matters tends to remove obstacles to a sound relationship between worker and the group, and among the members. It makes it possible for members to turn their attention to working on other problems of concern to them. Clarification of the nature of the group and agency is predominant during the early stage of the group's development, as will be seen in Chapter V.

A major task of the social worker is to contribute ideas, facts, and value concepts which are not available to the members and which may prove useful to them as they attempt to become oriented to and cope with their situations. As Schwartz has put it:

. . . the worker's grasp of social reality is one of the important attributes that fit him to his function. While his life experiences cannot be transferred intact to other human beings, the products of these experiences can be immensely valuable to those who are moving through their own struggles and stages of mastery.[25]

The worker asks members to share experiences, opinions, information, and feelings about the external situation, and to assist the members to distinguish between subjective perceptions and external reality. It is to be noted, however, that reality itself is not usually clear and definite. He requests that the group share knowledge and experiences and then evaluate them, in which process the worker contributes what data the group needs to continue its discussion or activity in an effective way. The worker presents his views not as absolutes, but as opinions for the group's consideration. Another means to achieve this intent is to clarify the situation through firsthand experience with what is unknown or misunderstood: for example, through trips around the agency, encounters with the police, or visits to community resources.

One aspect of reality with which members of groups almost always need help is the reality of their own feelings about themselves, other people, and situations. Persons need to express

[25] Schwartz, "The Social Worker in the Group," in *The Social Welfare Forum*, p. 164.

feelings in order to identify and accept them. The expression and recognition of them seem to be necessary prerequisites to strengthening or changing them. Ventilation of feelings is helpful because emotion often blocks intellect. Feelings tend to distort perceptions and consume energy that might otherwise be available for the achievement of desired ends. Feelings also reinforce cognition and enrich experience. So long as feelings remain indistinct and unrecognized, there is little to take hold of to influence change in attitudes. Coser reports that Kurt Lewin, the famous social psychologist, liked to quote the following ditty:

> I was angry with my friend:
> I told my wrath, my wrath did end.
> I was angry with my foe:
> I told it not, my wrath did grow.[26]

Although oversimplified and somewhat misleading, this poem does illustrate vividly the point that direct expression of feelings is potentially helpful. Some ventilation is generally thought to be essential to the recognition and control of harmful feelings. To disclose the varied feelings that one has, and still find acceptance in a group, constitutes a revelation of self and the foundation for intimacy.

The worker can, by attitudes and words, indicate his acceptance of both positive and negative feelings, and of the one who has them. It is natural, to some extent, for social workers to like and support harmony within the group and to avoid unpleasantness. Yet, to be able to permit the expression of negative feelings, particularly interpersonal hostility, is a crucial component of professional skill. By allowing some ventilation, the worker can show that such feelings are not devastating. By stopping the flow of excessively hurtful feelings, he can lend assurance that he will not let the members hurt themselves or each other. Some people seem to get gratification from pouring out feelings without any evidence of movement toward using such ventilation as a step toward changes in themselves or their

---

[26] Coser, *The Functions of Social Conflict*, p. 271.

situation. In such instances, the worker needs to limit the ventilation and to focus on problem-solving activities. Some persons have great difficulty in expressing feelings directly. When this occurs, certain action-oriented experiences may be used through which members can express their feelings indirectly. Examples of suitable media are play, dramatics, or crafts that provide for free expression, such as clay or paints. Gradually, the worker can help such members to verbalize their feelings, through comments that sanction the right to have them and that indicate interest, concern, and empathy.

Ventilation of feelings is not enough. Troubled people need to come to recognize the content of the feeling. Emotions are recognized more clearly and acknowledged as being influential when they are named, when cognitive components become integrated with affective components. A simple, "You look sad today," or "You were angry when you said that," may help a person to acknowledge the feeling. A simple reflection of what has been said, or an exploratory comment, is often effective in aiding members to express and identify feelings. The worker, in order to encourage members to share feelings, observes the reactions of the group to the messages communicated to him or by others. He relates comments made by one member to similar or different reactions of others. He selects and uses certain materials and activities to facilitate expression of feelings, and he uses nonverbal gestures as well as words.

Recognition, elaboration, and clarification of behavior comprise a set of interrelated intents of the social worker in enabling more realistic perceptions of oneself and his situation. Destructive ego patterns may be modified if a person can examine and reevaluate the nature of significant experiences or situations, and the consequences of his particular pattern of functioning. There are varied ways through which changes in behavior occur. Understanding of the feelings behind the behavior is an initial aid in understanding and modifying the behavior. Growth in the ego's capacity is encouraged by facing and coping with the reality of one's behavior. In working toward adaptive change, it is thought that some understanding of one's behavior is an essential prerequisite to change in that behavior.

Establishing as nearly as possible what is the nature of the pattern of behavior, and the situation in which it occurs, is most usefully done by the members themselves, but the worker adds to the group members' contributions. Gentle confrontations by the worker may be necessary to help a member to acknowledge his behavior. This does not mean assaultive directness; rather it means challenge with "an arm around the shoulder." [27] Direct confrontation is a form of statement that faces or confronts a person with the reality of a feeling, behavior, or situation. It faces the person with the fact that there is some inconsistency between his own statements and those of other sources, or with the consequences of his behavior. It may be in the form of confrontation with positive attitudes or performance, as well as negative behavior.

Confrontation needs to be based on sound diagnostic thinking concerning both individuals and group. It is not the worker alone who uses confrontation. The members may confront each other, often quite bluntly, requiring that the social worker evaluate the impact of such statements on particular individuals and on the group, following up in whatever way seems necessary. The worker may ask the group itself to evaluate the consequences of such confrontations on the progress of individuals and the movement of the group. In order to find patterns of behavior, the worker may comment on omissions and contradictions in the descriptions of the members. A comment that seeks to understand what happened tends to be more effective than questioning why it happened. It tends to focus on the chain of events which makes clear the nature of the behavioral pattern to the members.

The practitioner shares with the members responsibility for working toward clarification of a person's behavior or the group's progress when lack of understanding seems to block progress toward improvement in behavior. In respect to behavior, clarification simply means to make understandable, or

[27] Overton and Tinker, *Casework Notebook*, p. 68.

to come to perceive clearly the motive, meaning, or functioning of the behavior.

In the process of clarification, the worker needs to remind himself that such defenses of the ego as denial, displacement, or projection, are self-protective devices that need to be respected and often supported.[28] In some instances, they may be opened up to examination gently, in nonthreatening ways. The members of the group often are most effective in recognizing defenses in each other, as they reflect on each other's behavior. Exploratory comments by the worker, such as "I wonder what that means?" or "Have you ever noticed that?" can open up group discussion that leads to clarification of behavior, in ways that the group can deal with successfully. Sometimes, members can utilize simple explanations by the worker of the way a defense works or, for example, of how the superego can be too harsh in its demands. The worker may comment also on the possible existence of connections, implications, and meanings that tend to elude the group. Such contributions help the members to objectify and understand the connections between bits of behavior, emotion, and experience. Putting connections into words helps toward their integration.

Insight, if defined as the understanding of unconscious, repressed material that is made conscious through techniques of free association and interpretation, is usually not a part of social

---

[28] For references on the structure of the personality and the defenses, see Alexander and Ross, eds., *Dynamic Psychiatry;* Brenner, *An Elementary Textbook of Psychoanalysis;* Freud, *The Ego and the Mechanisms of Defence;* Stamm, "Ego Psychology in the Emerging Theoretical Base of Casework," in Kahn, ed., *Issues in American Social Work,* pp. 80-109.

Defenses frequently referred to are: *displacement,* by which a feeling is redirected onto something other than the original person or object; *projection,* by which responsibility and blame for one's behavior is placed on someone or something other than oneself; *denial,* through which a person affirms that he does not possess certain thoughts and feelings, even though his behavior shows that he does, or through which he affirms that some aspect of his environment is different from what it is in reality; *regression,* in which the person reverts to a pattern of behavior that was appropriate at an earlier phase of development; *avoidance, or restriction of the ego,* in which the person turns away from experiences, rather than trying them out or participating in them; and *sublimation,* by which unacceptable desires are directed into acceptable outlets that bring satisfaction to the self.

work practice. In social work, interpretation of the meaning of behavior is done at the conscious or preconscious level of the personality. Recall of the past is facilitated or encouraged only when such recall helps the members to understand the present. This statement does not deny the importance of earlier events for shaping the future, but does recognize that recollection is not necessarily therapeutic. When a person needs to hold to the past, he can be helped to reevaluate it in light of its implications for present circumstances. The group is encouraged to find its own meanings. When the worker adds his contributions to the group's own efforts, he participates according to his judgment that the group is ready for this; that the members are almost ready to acknowledge the meanings themselves; and that there is a strong worker-group relationship to sustain the group in its work.

The social worker formulates and tests diagnostic impressions of individual behavior and group process, and may share these with the group. He indicates these impressions in an exploratory way; seldom does he make a direct verbal diagnostic statement. In this view, social diagnosis is a dynamic, continuing, and collaborative process. It is a component of the process of change itself, as contrasted with diagnosis as a step preliminary to treatment. Diagnosis is often thought of as an inactive listening, observing, and analytical behavior on the part of the worker. The worker does listen, observe, and analyze. But he does more than this; he responds to the members' own diagnostic and evaluative statements. He tests some of his diagnostic impressions with the group when he judges that such action seems desirable in order to know what he should do next in his work with the group. Feedback is essential to the perception of stability or change in the members of the group. Recognition of progress, or of obstacles to progress, serves as a positive force in enhancing motivation toward further change. The social worker, therefore, shares his perceptions of blocks to progress, accredits specific evidences of progress, and seeks reactions of members to these comments.

Achievement of Competence in Action

Clarification of a person's attitudes and behavior in relation to his social situation may be beneficial only if it helps him to master problematic situations. The social worker uses his influence toward the actual achievement of competence on the part of the members of the group. Competence is the ability of a person to interact effectively with his environment. A realistic perception of oneself, the other persons, and situations is a prerequisite to effective interaction with the environment.[29]

It is a natural development in work with groups to move from understanding situations and behavior to doing something about the situation or behavior. The ego is strengthened as a person develops effective means of communication and has more clear perceptions of himself in relation to other people and varied situations. But it is strengthened also as these skills are translated into competence in the performance of varied social roles in a way that is personally satisfying and that meets the demands of the situation. If a person is confronted with situations and tasks which can be mastered, the resulting feeling of success may strengthen the ego and make possible further success. A damaged self-image may be bolstered. It is especially important that there be an opportunity to master those situations or tasks in which a person has previously found himself wanting or lacking.[30] It may be that "social competence leads to increased ego strength and that this stronger ego is in turn inherently better able to cope with conflict and anxiety."[31] This, in turn, may lead to increased social competence.

Members of groups often need to enhance their competence to make and implement decisions. In one sense, all purposeful discussion within the group aims at some decision or choice.

[29] See Inkeles, "Social Structure and the Socialization of Competence," *Harvard Educational Review*, XXXVI (1966), 270; Rae-Grant, Gladwin, and Bower, "Mental Health, Social Competence, and the War on Poverty"; White, "Motivation Reconsidered: The Concept of Competence," *Psychological Review*, LXVI (1959), 297-333.

[30] Redl and Wineman, *Controls from Within*, p. 141.

[31] Rae-Grant, Gladwin, and Bower, "Mental Health, Social Competence, and the War on Poverty."

The decision may be effected within the personality of an individual member, influencing his feelings or behavior. It may affect the group itself through the form of corporate agreement or action. The decision may be a very minor one, or one of major concern either to the individuals concerned or to the life of the group itself. All of the steps in the decision-making process come into play: identification of the problem, procurement of proposals for solution, analysis of the proposals, and the actual choice or decision. Based on clarification of the problem and the situation, a choice is made and, if put into practice successfully, the executive function of the ego is enhanced.

The social worker's task is to engage the group in discussion of how to apply what has been decided in the group to other situations that are of concern to the members. The topics may cover the range of problematic situations of the members, such as appropriate use of and responses to medical care, cooperation with the school in behalf of a child who is having trouble there, improvement of child rearing practices, problems in heterosexual relations, alternatives to membership in delinquent gangs, and dealing with prejudice and discrimination. The worker initiates or participates purposefully in the discussion; he provides information needed by the group and follows up on its usefulness to the members; he provides support to the members as they try out their choices in the community. He may prescribe, through making suggestions or recommendations, new patterns of behavior or new perspectives on what might be done about a situation. He may engage the members in participation in social experiences that focus on alternative solutions to problems and making choices from among them. He may teach or demonstrate ways of doing things that implement decisions. For example, a decision to budget income may need to be followed by learning about and practicing budgeting. A decision to have a conference with a school principal may need to be rehearsed in the group prior to the actual experience. A decision to seek specialized service in another community institution may require concrete help from the worker to connect the person with the desired service. These are but some of the ways that a worker helps members of a group to become competent in acting on their choices.

When there has been relative deprivation of opportunities for successful achievement, these need to be provided, either within the content of the group or in addition to the group experience, through referral to other resources. One criterion to be used in making this decision would be the extent to which other opportunities are available that would be appropriate to the readiness and capacities of the members who need the experience. The social worker then makes the referral and follows through with the members' use of the service. Another criterion would be sufficient common need among the members to use the group itself for learning. If the experience is provided within the group, the worker may take direct leadership in teaching or guiding the members in the use of the activity, or he may bring a resource person into the group. The decision to use a particular form of experience with a group depends upon the members' interests, the worker's diagnosis of the members and the group, and his knowledge of a variety of forms of activities and their potential contributions to the process of treatment.

Action-oriented experience is a phrase that is meant to convey all the myriad of activities, other than discussion, that comprise the content of the group experience.[32] Program is the word that is frequently used to designate this pattern of activities; yet program is also defined as everything that enters into the group experience. Varied activities may be used to accomplish different objectives in relation to the improvement of the psychosocial functioning of members. Activities are experienced within the network of relationships in the group. Both verbal and nonverbal communication are integral components of most social experiences. Almost all activity has verbal aspects: a social worker may pick up on informal conversations that occur in the midst of activities. Group discussion is used to make decisions about activities, to plan for them, or to talk over problems

[32] For major contributions to understanding the use of activities in social work with groups, see Wilson and Ryland, *Social Group Work Practice;* Redl and Wineman, *Controls from Within;* and Middleman, *The Nonverbal Method in Working with Groups.*

that are encountered in doing the activity. The use of activities is based on knowledge that improvement in social functioning comes from experiencing together, usually combined with talking about the experiences.

A variety of experiences contributes to strengthening the ego's capacity to cope with the give and take of social relationships and expectations for performance. The group can be used as an "arena for trying out and living out new experiences. . . ." [33] Through selected experiences, members come to discover the consequences of their behavior and means for coping more effectively with difficult tasks. They may demonstrate to each other their actual competence, and be faced with questions about areas of competence. The culture of the group is crucial in the selection and use of experiences. There needs to be a norm that accredits trying and learning and one that helps members to face a realistic appraisal of their efforts, without blame or negative criticism for failures.

In order to function adaptively, a person's behavior needs to meet the realistic demands of the environment. People need to learn to meet these demands and to be protected from the destructive tendencies of themselves and each other. It is the rightful authority of a community to establish and maintain its own standards, and there is a positive, unavoidable need for limitations on individual freedom. Within the prescribed limits, there is ample room for the individual to make choices. The social worker, therefore, needs to balance his use of permissiveness with the use of limits on behavior that is harmful to self, others, relationships, or materials.[34] The forms that limits can take are manifold: rules governing behavior in certain situations, direct physical or verbal interference, temporary exclusion from the group, use of play situations for channeling aggressive

[33] Maier, ed., *Group Work as Part of Residential Treatment*, p. 28.

[34] References of value concerning the use of limits include: Falsberg, "Setting Limits with the Juvenile Delinquent," *Social Casework*, XXXVIII (1957); Hacker and Gelered, "Freedom and Authority in Adolescence," *American Journal of Orthopsychiatry*, XV (1945); Milner, "Freedom and Authority in Social Work," in *Social Work Papers*, VIII (1961); Redl and Wineman, *Controls from Within;* Wilson and Ryland, *Social Group Work Practice*, pp. 91-96; and Wittenburg, *The Art of Group Discipline.*

behavior and alleviating conflict, confrontation, and recognition of feelings underlying the need for unacceptable behavior.

External controls are not an end in themselves but serve as a means to the goal of self-control. The rationale for setting limits is that they stabilize the immediate situation, are a crutch for the ego with respect to controlling impulses, relieve external and internal pressures, meet the need for security, and prevent the undesirable consequences of socially unacceptable behavior. Effective limits are realistic and reasonable, specific, nonpunitive, treatment oriented, consistent, and placed on the person's behavior, not his feelings.

The fact that competence can be achieved by people only to the extent that there are opportunities available to develop and use it should not be lost sight of by the social worker. When desirable opportunities are not available, the worker has a responsibility to report the needs to responsible organizations in the community and to work toward the development of more adequate services.

Use of Environmental Resources

The environment, "as experienced by the individual is a set of interacting forces impinging upon him simultaneously from many different directions and interacting with an equally complex set of forces within his own personality." [35] The reduction of environmental stress and the provision of more adequate opportunities for fulfilling the potentials of his clients is one of the social worker's responsibilities. Sometimes the first priority for social work treatment is to meet the basic need for survival, from both a physical and social stance. Some persons come into group situations with great uncertainty about whether or not it will be possible for them to eat, be sheltered, clothed, nurtured, or employed with any continuity and dependability. Such concerns may well be brought into the content of the group experience where the commonality of problems may suggest means for alleviating them, or such concerns may be dealt with through the use of resources. The worker may need to work

[35] Hollis, *Casework: A Psychosocial Therapy*, pp. 14-15.

directly with other agencies in the community to secure the necessary resources for one or more of his members. Some clients may be so overcome with grief or anxiety that they cannot be expected to participate in a group situation until they have been given immediate help with their particular critical needs on a one-to-one basis. Or some such persons may benefit from concurrent individual and group service.

Since a social work group is a small social system that must be viewed as connecting with other social systems, it is influenced by and in turn influences these other systems. Social work has at least an indirect responsibility to the people with whom the client is interacting, and sometimes a direct one. When the client can gain enough confidence and skill to handle a situation himself, of course, he does, for one principle is that the social worker supports the client's ego functioning by strengthening his ability to handle his own affairs. There are times, however, when the client cannot or when the person in the environment will respond better to the worker than to the client, because of the former's status and professional knowledge. So the social worker may need to intervene in behalf of the person.

Members of groups belong to families, each with its own particular physical and social environment. A social worker needs to understand the particular culture of the families from which his members come, the similarities and differences among them, and the ways in which they conform to or deviate from the predominant culture of the community. Work with relatives of members is an important component of the worker's role. If the worker recognizes the strengths in the family, he will relate to each member differentially, based on his understanding of the patterns of roles within the family. He will relate to the father in families where he is the center of authority. He may work with relatives to help them to understand the nature of the problems of his client. He may offer service to the family as a unit. Conferences may be aimed toward securing the support of the family for the service planned for the member who is in his group. When a child is the group member, the minimal involvement of the parents is that of granting permission for the child to be served for a particular purpose. Relatives may be helped to consider how they can alter some of their behavior toward him. The focus should be on strengthening the relationship of the client to his family and of his family to other social institutions. The social worker serves as both a helper to his clients and as an interpreter to other agencies and the community.

Members of groups may need to be referred to other social or health agencies for help with needs not within the function of the agency that serves the group. Knowledge of social, health, and educational agencies in the community is necessary for effective referrals; knowledge of their functions, auspices, concepts of service, and interrelationships. Referrals to employment services, work training programs, health and medical care, or religious organizations should be part of treatment if clients are to be helped to function nearer or at their full capacities. The worker may need to mediate between the client and the desired service so that the client does not get lost between slots of agency functions and policies. It may mean explaining to the agency the client's goals, problems, capacities, and special needs. It may mean giving considerable assistance to the client, to help him understand the intake procedures and to make concrete plans for the first encounter. Successful referral involves clarification of the specific problems, motivation to initiate an application, and follow through procedures.

Lack of resources and conditions in the community often make it difficult for clients to function effectively. Some persons need to be taught to use available resources. The lack of use of resources is sometimes striking: a group of mothers never thought of using a park within walking distance; an adolescent with an infected finger did not think of going to a nearby clinic; a mother had not thought of applying for a special nutrition program for her children. Such failures to use resources may stem from lack of knowledge about the resources and how to use them, or from fear and distrust.

The worker may help groups to take direct action in behalf of their members when this is appropriate to the purpose of the group and is within the function of the agency. Although the focus is on action that will directly benefit the members themselves, hopefully social change of a broader nature may also be the outcome of such efforts. Practitioners have also a responsibility to note facts about conditions that need to be changed and to report these facts to appropriate persons within the agency, the professional organization, or community planning and action bodies.

In order to serve his groups most effectively, the worker needs to work collaboratively with other social workers and with members of other professions such as education, psychiatry, medicine, and recreation. Conferences with other personnel, such as teachers or nurses, are usually focused on members who are having difficulty. The content may be an exchange of information, joint planning for integrated service to the person, attempts to modify the behavior of others toward the client, or reports on the client's progress with the hope that this will start a chain reaction in the client's favor. When there is a team of personnel responsible for a given client, early planning about the division of responsibility among each person can assure good service. It can, incidentally, alleviate later misunderstanding. Each participant needs to understand the goals and values of each of the other persons who has some part in the constellation of services being provided his client. Each needs to understand the functions and policies of the agencies concerned. Each needs to respect the specific contributions of the others as well as being willing to share some tasks with others. In any team work, there needs to be a mutuality rooted in respect for the differing contributions of each member of the team. This, as Grace Coyle has said, "is the crux of the relationship. No mechanical division of function can provide the basis for it. True mutuality is a matter of attitude, not layout." [36] It is a matter of each party being deeply concerned about rendering the best possible network of services to those who need them most.

Through the use of his relationship with the group, and

[36] Coyle, *Group Experience and Democratic Values*, p. 47.

content designed to fulfill particular purposes, the social worker fulfills his role. His behaviors are intended to provide support for the members of the group, develop skills in communication, enhance the accuracy of perceptions of self in relation to varied situations, develop competence, and influence the environment. Knowledge of the means for carrying out intents comprises the basic methodological knowledge of the practitioner. The selection of procedures, however, is always specific to a situation. Sound social diagnosis of individuals, the group system, and the external system is essential. Where the group is in its development is one of the basic guides for determining the ways in which a social worker uses particular tools and procedures to help the group to achieve its purposes. In the succeeding chapters, attention is thus directed to the social worker's role in the developmental processes of groups.

CHAPTER IV

Planning and Intake Processes

MANY complex forces determine the meaning and value a group will have for its members. In order that people be served effectively, sound preparation for the initiation and subsequent development of a group is essential. In the literature on group development, almost no attention has been given to a preparatory stage as a necessary prerequisite to the formation of a group. Nor has attention been given to the impact of particular policies and procedures upon the individuals concerned and the later development of the group. Only two authors specifically set forth a phase of origin in which the focus is mainly on the social worker's actions in the determination of group purpose and composition, the establishment of a contract with individual members about the service to be provided, and the determination of such elements of structure as time, place, and frequency of meetings.[1] Writings on intake processes, criteria for group composition, and the impact of organizational structure on group life, however, are pertinent to understanding this stage.

Prior to the formation of a social work group, a complicated set of circumstances determines whether or not a group will be developed and served by a social worker. Group service begins with the identification of need for services which can be implemented within and through a small group. Persons seek out and apply for a service because they perceive it as being necessary or beneficial to them in some way. Other persons are referred, perhaps, by a relative or institution in the community

---

[1] Levine, *Fundamentals of Group Treatment,* pp. 4-40; Sarri and Galinsky, "A Conceptual Framework for Teaching Group Development in Social Group Work," in *A Conceptual Framework for the Teaching of the Social Group Work Method in the Classroom.*

that has become alerted to their needs. The persons to be
served may be living in an open community or in an institutional setting. The group may start from a collection of individuals or service may be given to an already formed group
such as a family, a friendship group, or a gang. Although some
work with groups is done by private practitioners, service usually is given in a social agency or social service department of
an institution. Whatever the form of the organization, the
agency needs to have policies governing the general purpose
for the use of groups, the selection of membership, types of
groups to be served, and the necessary facilities and resources to
support effective practice. The nature of the policies and facilities, and the manner in which the initial planning for a new
group service is done, have significant impacts upon an individual's use of the group and upon the development of the
group itself. During this phase, the major task for the prospective member is to make a tentative decision about membership
in a group. The major tasks for the social worker are to plan
for the formation of a new group or the acceptance of an
existing group for social work service and to engage prospective
members in a decision-making process.

Purposes of Groups

It has been said that

the group is a system of relationships which, in its own unique
way, represents a special case of the general relationship between
individuals and their society; in other words, it is one of the
special forms through which members interact with social values,
social objectives and social resources.[2]

Belonging to and participating actively in a small group is a
basic constructive experience in life for all people. In addition
to the family, society provides varied opportunities for people
to have such experiences. But the need for social work is evident when there is lack of suitable resources, or when persons
need professional help in order to maintain a current level of

---

[2] Schwartz, "The Social Worker in the Group," in *The Social Welfare Forum,*
p. 158.

functioning or to move toward more effective psychological functioning. Thus, groups have specific purposes that relate to this general one.[3] The purposes need also to meet human need and to be in harmony with the functions of the sponsoring agency. Clarity of purpose is essential: it provides the basic guide for both the worker and the clientele. It provides a framework for the social worker's diagnostic and treatment activities. It becomes a primary determinant of the group's motivation and focus. The initial purpose for a group stems from the recognition of certain recurrent needs of people who are within the jurisdiction of the agency—needs which can be met through a group. When common needs of applicants or clientele are identified, and used as a basis for the organization of a group, it is likely that the goals of each member will be related to the general purposes of the group. Groups may be appropriate modalities for serving clientele in the various fields of practice.[4]

Groups are organized in public and private agencies that provide services aimed at the enhancement of the social functioning of the family. In work with public assistance clients, groups may be organized to orient applicants to their rights and responsibilities as clients, and to prepare them to use resources that can contribute to more adequate family life. For groups of unwed mothers, the purpose may be to help them to use community

[3] There is considerable emphasis on the importance of clarity of purpose in the literature, regardless of the theoretical orientation of the authors. See, for example, Coyle, *Group Work with American Youth;* Konopka, *Social Group Work;* Levine, *Fundamentals of Group Treatment;* Phillips, *Essentials of Social Group Work Skill;* Vinter, *Readings in Group Work Practice;* Wilson and Ryland, *Social Group Work Practice;* Trecker, *Social Group Work.*

[4] For references on purposes of groups in varied fields of practice, see Child Welfare League of America, *Group Methods and Services in Child Welfare;* Coyle, *Group Work with American Youth;* Fenton and Wiltse, eds., *Group Methods in the Public Welfare Program;* Frey, ed., *Use of Groups in the Health Field;* Glasser, "Group Methods in Child Welfare: Review and Preview," *Child Welfare,* XLII 1963), 213-19; Konopka, *Group Work in the Institution;* Konopka, *Therapeutic Group Work with Children;* Kraft and Chilman, *Helping Low-income Families through Parent Education;* Maier, ed., *Group Work as Part of Residential Treatment;* Northen, "Interrelated Functions of the Social Group Worker," *Social Work,* II (1), (1957), 63-69; Spergel, *Street Gang Work;* Trecker, ed., *Group Work in the Psychiatric Setting; Use of Groups in the Psychiatric Setting;* Wilson and Ryland, *Social Group Work Practice,* Part IV.

resources, achieve better understanding of their situations, and make realistic plans for themselves and their children. Groups for potentially employable adults may be focused on the enhancement of motivation, realistic assessment of the feasibility of employment, and preparation for employment, when indicated. Groups of parents from varied socioeconomic backgrounds may be designed to help them to improve their family relationships and cope with problems that impede a more adequate family life. Parent education groups may help parents to discover the strengths within themselves, develop more effective social relationships, and use the resources of their communities to change the situations in which they live and rear their children. Other similar groups add to these goals those of identifying unmet community needs, making decisions, and planning strategies for action relevant to the conditions that influence family functioning. Groups of couples may be organized for the purpose of working through conflicts in marital or parent-child relationships. The family itself may be the unit of service for the achievement of such objectives as decision making around issues and problems that affect the family as a whole, or the resolution of interpersonal conflicts within the family group.

In the field of child welfare services, parents of children in placement may use group services to resolve some of their own problems in role functioning within the family and the community, and to relate these to the need for a placement service for their children. Foster parents, as well as houseparents in children's institutions, often need help to understand the needs and behavior of the children in their care, and to learn effective means of carrying their particular roles. Parents in a protective service program used a group to face up to the complaints that they had neglected or abused their children, and to understand and find solutions to their problems. For many children in foster care, the onset of adolescence requires special help as the youth come into conflict in their relationship with foster parents and other adults in positions of authority. Objectives of groups may be to help such adolescents to overcome the dif-

ficulties they are having with their foster parents and other
authorities. In children's institutions, the living group itself
may be served in order to help the residents with the interpersonal conflicts that are inevitably a part of group life. Other
groups may be formed to help the children to cope with the
feelings and behavior associated with separation from family
and neighborhood life.

A polyglot constellation of community based social agencies
provide group services to some segment of the community,
based on age, sex, educational status, religious affiliation, or
residence in a neighborhood. A settlement may develop a
variety of family oriented services in which the group is used
as the modality of treatment. It may develop a group whose
purpose is to study, plan for, and implement improvements in
environmental conditions that are inimical to healthy individual and family functioning. A Jewish Community Center may
have a group for aged members, to help them to improve their
social relationships and to find satisfying and useful roles in
the community. Or, it may work with children in order to
enhance their sense of Jewish identity or to resolve specific
conflicts between their identification with the Jewish culture
and with other significant reference groups. A number of agencies including Camp Fire Girls, Young Men's Christian Associations, Young Women's Christian Associations, the Boy and
Girl Scouts, Salvation Army, and settlements, may cooperate
with schools to provide groups for children who are having
academic and social difficulties in school to help them to improve their roles as pupils, and to make better use of educational opportunities. Similar experiences are provided to groups
of children or parents by school social workers. Many groups
are organized to provide help in making effective use of opportunities in the community. Some groups focus on helping
persons to overcome problems that are rooted in economic or
cultural deprivation, or cultural conflict. One example is the
increased emphasis being placed on programs for preschool children whose homes provide inadequate stimulation and relationships for learning which lead to lack of success in school.

The group approach may be a treatment of choice in many cases of chronic disability arising from mental illness. A sizable proportion of the population of most psychiatric hospitals consists of chronic, regressed schizophrenic patients. They show the behavioral responses peculiar to prolonged institutionalization and characterized by withdrawal, seclusive behavior, muteness, or incoherent speech. They become socially and emotionally isolated. Their inability to talk about their problems makes participation in a typical one-to-one relationship difficult. The purpose of a group service may be to help such patients to relate to others more effectively, develop more accurate perceptions of selves in relation to others, and behave more appropriately toward others.

The discharged mental patient has similar needs. He is "often clinically improved but socially disabled." [5] The purpose of group work for such patients may be to help them to maintain and enhance their social relationships and to become more socially able. The mental patient, as he is discharged from the hospital, faces many fears and realistic problems in finding a place to live, reestablishing himself in his family, and returning to or securing employment. He is fearful about his ability to stand the test of living in the community. In addition, he carries a new burden, for he has been branded with a stigma of mental illness. He needs, therefore, a group situation in which he can find acceptance and cope with his problems.

Medical hospitals exist to treat patients for some illness or to overcome a physical handicap. Within this general purpose, many patients or their relatives need help with the psychosocial problems that impede recovery. The focus of a particular group may be on helping parents of hospitalized children to understand how some of their behavior has a negative influence on the child's recovery, and to become more cooperative in their relationships with hospital personnel. Or groups may be used to help children cope with the anxieties connected with their illness or with treatment procedures. They may be focused on

[5] Lerner, "The Therapeutic Social Club: Social Rehabilitation for Mental Patients," *International Journal of Social Psychiatry*, VI (1960).

helping long-term patients to learn to live with handicaps or to make decisions about their futures when they return to the community.

Agencies in the field of corrections view their purpose as one of helping clients to learn new attitudes and patterns of behavior that are in harmony with society's norms of law-abiding behavior. The purposes for groups in correctional agencies are usually viewed as related to a process of resocialization which attempts to correct inadequate earlier socialization so that the offender can function as an acceptable member of a community.[6] Groups may focus on the initial adaptation of new residents to a correctional institution, or on their preparation for return to family and community living. In work with gangs in the community, the purpose is usually to effect more satisfying and socially acceptable behavior. Specific goals for work with a gang may be on several levels: to decrease group disturbance, violence, and delinquency; to provide some satisfactions and some new relationships with the community and some new perceptions of the world and the individuals' roles in it; and to help members with individual problems in relation to school, employment, health, or legal situations. There are, therefore, a combination of concerns for the group and the individual, for community protection, and for group assistance and guidance.[7] One or more of these goals is usually cited for the use of groups with adolescents or adults who are on probation.

The preceding descriptions of purpose in varied social agencies are not meant to be exhaustive, but rather to serve as illustrations of the similarities and differences in purposes for groups that are used in social work. Note that, although agency auspice is an important determinant of the focus of the service, there is a considerable amount of overlapping. Agencies which on the surface seem quite different may offer services with very similar goals and to persons with similar needs. Many of the

[6] Studt, "Correctional Services," in Lurie, ed., *Encyclopedia of Social Work*, pp. 219-25.

[7] Austin, "What About Reaching-out—An Account of the Boston Youth Project," *The Round Table*, XIX (1955), 2-3.

policies and procedures that govern the specific way a service is given vary, however. Note also that it is difficult to describe purpose without also describing the clientele for whom the service is intended.

Membership Determination and Group Composition

Basically, a social worker serves several types of groups. Within groups developed for some social work purpose in direct service to people, one type consists of groups for which the social worker, alone or as a member of a professional team, takes primary responsibility for the initial selection of membership. This type is differentiated from those groups which had a life span prior to the social worker's entrance. For lack of more precise words, the first are referred to as formed groups and the latter as natural or autonomous groups. The formed group may have varied structures such as a social club, a play group, an activity group, or a discussion group. The natural group may be a family, a neighborhood friendship group, or a gang. Another important differentiation is whether a group is served within an institution or in the open community. In any institutional setting, such as hospitals, residential treatment centers, correctional institutions, and homes for dependent children or aged persons, the members of social groups usually have multiple relationships with each other outside of the social work group; indeed, they may live together in a ward, cottage, or dormitory. In the open community setting, clients often see each other only in the social work group. This is most true in such agencies as clinics, family service associations, and such child welfare agencies as those dealing with adoptions and foster care. Some neighborhood-based agencies such as settlements, schools, or decentralized youth-service centers, often have members with some additional associations within the agency or the community. Another important consideration is the extent to which membership in a group is voluntary or compulsory: voluntary in that the person or an existing group has sought out or at least accepted the offer of help; involuntary in that he may be required to attend a group by parents, court, or other concerned segment of the community. These factors are important in making plans for the composition of a group.

Regardless of whether a group is formed or natural, neighborhood based or isolated from other aspects of life, the social worker and his agency exert some control over the membership of a group. This control is usually minimal in natural groups, neighborhood groups, and voluntary membership groups. It is most evident in formed groups, those within institutions, and those in which membership is prescribed or compulsory. Even in serving a natural gang, however, the social worker has a responsibility to make a preliminary social diagnosis of the individuals, and an evaluation of the group's structure and patterns of interaction in order to determine whether or not he will regard the entire gang as his client system or select some core group or segment of the gang for his attention. Likewise, in instances in which the family is the primary unit of service, the worker has some part in the definition of family for this particular purpose.

The particular constellation of persons who interact with each other is an important determinant of whether or not a group will be satisfying to its members and successful in its hoped for outcomes. "The very fact of group mixture in itself," according to Redl, "may sometimes play a great part in what happens in a group, even when the best conditions and the most skillful professional leadership are taken for granted." [8] If persons are placed in unsuitable groups, they may become a serious disturbance to the group, be harmed by the experience, or drop out of the group. If the composition of a group is faulty, it is less likely to become a viable and cohesive social system.

Knowledge of the factors that influence the participation of members is used by the social worker to determine which ones seem most crucial to the purpose and the anticipated focus of the group. There is no such thing as a perfectly composed group, but it is important that the worker know with what he is dealing in this respect. The basic questions to be raised are:

[8] Redl, "The Art of Group Composition,' in Schulze, ed., *Creative Group Living*, pp. 76-96.

will an individual benefit from the group? Will he be able to participate in such a way that his presence and his behavior will not interfere seriously with the realization of the purpose of the group for others?

Although there are many opinions about criteria for group composition, there has been little systematic study of who should be together in groups.[9] Perhaps the most generally accepted principle is what Redl calls "the law of optimum distance": groups should be homogeneous in enough ways to insure their stability and heterogeneous in enough ways to insure their vitality.[10] This principle is based on the premise that the major dynamics in a group are mutuality of support and mutuality of stimulation among the members. Some balance is necessary so that no single member represents an extreme difference from other members, for this usually makes integration into the group unlikely. Clients who represent extremes on any one factor of significance in human relations are usually not placed together. It is inappropriate to refer to groups as either homogeneous or heterogeneous; rather there will be certain common characteristics, making for homogeneity, and certain differences that make for heterogeneity. This principle does not offer a simple formula; rather it requires sound diagnostic thinking about individuals and the group.

The most important consideration in group composition is its purpose. The specific goals and needs of prospective members should be those that can be met through the purpose of the group. Within the purpose, it is essential that there be some common need or problematic situation that can provide some focus for the content of group life. The content is related to common concerns, capacities, and shared significant experiences. The combination of some commonality of goals and

---

[9] For references on group composition, see Ryland, "Social Group Work in Medical Settings," in *Group Work and Community Organization*, pp. 80-90; Sloan, "Factors in Forming Treatment Groups," in *Use of Groups in the Psychiatric Setting*, pp. 73-93; Wax, "Criteria for Grouping Hospitalized Mental Patients," *ibid.*, pp. 91-100; Wilson and Ryland, *Social Group Work Practice*, pp. 101-52.

[10] Redl, "The Art of Group Composition," in Schulze, ed., *Creative Group Living*, pp. 76-96.

shared experiences provides for a community of interest that
can outweigh certain other differences among people. Persons
may need a group experience in the initial phase of becoming
oriented to an institution, be it a mental hospital, correctional
facility, or residential treatment center. The feelings connected
with being institutionalized and the usual problems in adjustment to the demands of the new situation provide for shared
experiences of sufficient significance to make less important
other factors in group composition. Although adults who have
problems in parent-child relationships have much in common,
such differences as age of children and marital status of parents
may need to be used as a basis for organizing groups. These
two examples illustrate the point that certain variables among
members reflect the nature of life experiences and feelings of
likeness and difference that influence the development of a
group bond. What is desirable is not similarity, but compatibility and complementarity.

Members of groups who share the experience of being in a
similar stage of psychosocial development tend to share certain
life tasks to be mastered and common interests. Within the
several stages in the life cycle, differences in age influence
group participation, but are more important in childhood than
adulthood. Sex, however, is at least as important as is age. There
are sex-linked values and norms of behavior in our culture
that are important to the development of identity and successful
role performance. Yet, there are also values and norms for
heterosexual relationships. Grouping by age and sex is often
useful in providing support for learning varied social roles.
Yet, at other times, and with different purposes in view, people
need to learn new patterns of heterosexual relationships directly with members of the other sex.

There is a tendency for small groups in our society to be
based on similarity in cultural values and practices associated
with social class, race, religion, and nationality. Differences in
such characteristics tend to separate people from one another in
work, play, education, place of residence, and style of life.
These factors may be relevant to the purpose of the group par-

ticularly, for example, when groups are formed to work toward improved interracial relationships, or to help members of a minority group to accept their own cultural background as a basis for integrating this facet into their basic sense of identity. These factors may not be relevant to the purpose of the group but, since cultural differences do influence attitudes, patterns of behavior, and interests, they cannot be ignored. They must be recognized and plans made for utilizing differences as positive dynamics toward growth and change rather than impediments to such movement.

The social worker is concerned not only with the nature of the problems and capacities of persons, but with modes of coping with problems. How individuals express themselves, deal with tension and conflict, and defend themselves from threat and hurt influence the nature and content of group interaction. Diversity of ways of coping with problems facilitates the exchange of feelings and ideas among members, providing there is a potential for a strong bond in relation to purpose and focus of the group. An individual's tendency to withdraw from relationships or to reach out aggressively to other people is especially important. Usually, extremely shy, withdrawn persons are not placed in groups with aggressive, acting-out ones, because of what is referred to as "shock effect." Members who are too far from the behavioral level of others in the group may find themselves in intolerable inner conflict, stirred up by faulty placement.[11] An individual's ability to communicate through the use of verbal symbols is another important factor. If a group is to use predominately verbal means of communication, the ability to express oneself verbally is essential. A nonverbal person often finds his problem intensified in a group of very active, talkative members. There is need, however, in groups of relatively nonverbal members, for some who can stimulate conversation at a level others can achieve.

When people live together and their problems are those of communication, relationships, and cooperative living, it is usually desirable to work with the unit as a whole. Examples

[11] *Ibid.*, p. 86.

would be a cottage group in a residential setting, a small group foster home, or a family. It is necessary to add the caution that sometimes persons need to get away from the living group to be able to look at it more objectively, and to consider and practice new patterns of behavior which can later be tested out within the group itself.

Closely related to purpose of group and needs of individuals are the agency policies and conditions that necessarily influence the particular persons to be selected for a group. Administrative considerations play an important role in determining who can become a member. These include such matters as the schedule of hours that an agency is open; the geographical distance from which clients come; money available for transportation, baby sitting services, and other expenses connected with using a service. Patterns of staff assignments may determine who will be served. If, by policy, a worker serves all members of a family, a particular member of that family who needs a group may not be placed in one unless the particular worker is able to organize a group at that time. The number of available potential members at a given time influences the number of criteria that can be taken into account in forming new groups: thus size of agency itself is an influence here. Often, such practical considerations make possible the use of only a limited number of other criteria in determining membership in groups. If the variety of other factors are considered in planning for a new group, however, whether or not they can be implemented, the social worker begins his work with knowledge of factors of homogeneity and heterogeneity for use in his work with the group.

In planning a new group, the optimum size should be in relation to the nature of the interaction desired.[12] The smaller the group, the more it demands that each member become fully involved in it, the greater is both the potential and de-

---

[12] For research on size of group, see Bales and Borgatta, "Size of Group as a Factor in the Interaction Profile," in Hare et al., eds., *Small Groups; Studies in Social Interaction,* pp. 495-512; Thomas and Fink, "Effects of Group Size," in *ibid.,* pp. 525-35; Berelson and Steiner, *Human Behavior,* pp. 358-59; Vinter, *Readings in Group Work Practice,* pp. 76-77.

mand for intimacy of relationships, the least anonymous are the actions and feelings of participants, the higher are the rates of membership participation, and the greater is the influence on each member. There is more time available for each person to test his attitudes and ideas with others. The smaller the group, the stronger are the group pressures on each individual; so also is the ease of access of a member to the worker and the access of the worker to each member. The smaller the group, the greater is its flexibility in modifying goals to meet changing needs of members. With some groups, particularly of children and adolescents, if a group is larger than ten or twelve members, the worker cannot be readily available to each member and the group's controls tend to become ineffective. It must be noted, however, that too small a group may disintegrate with absences, or as members leave.

As the size of the group increases, each member has a larger number of relationships to maintain. Formality in leadership emerges beyond the number of approximately eight, and so do subgroups within the larger group. As groups increase in size, there is a tendency for more communication to be directed toward the worker rather than toward the other members. Communication tends to be directed to the group rather than to specific individuals. Beyond a size of eight to ten, there is greater anonymity and greater difficulty in achieving consensus in decision making. A larger group tends to have greater tolerance for direction from a leader and the more active members tend to dominate the interaction.

There are differences between persons as to the range of relationships they can encompass, based on prior experiences and factors of personality. It has been found that "increasing maturity of the personality associated with age permits effective participation in larger groups." [13] But, note that people may be retarded in their social development. Age does influence size, to some extent. Young children become overstimulated and confused in a group that seems large; they need to work out

[13] Bales et al., "Structure and Dynamics of Small Groups: A Review of Four Variables," in Gittler, ed., *Review of Sociology: Analysis of a Decade,* p. 394.

their problems in relationships with a few as they move toward efforts in cooperation. Latency age children usually need small groups to provide security as they work toward mastery of situations, but there are some cultural differences in this respect. Children from large, economically deprived families often are not ready for the intimacy of a very small group. These are examples of the need to determine size of group in terms of its purpose and the capacities of its members. There is no substitute for sound judgment in planning.

Initial Organizational Structure

Structure has an impact on the quality of group life. It consists of the relatively stable instruments which determine the distribution of authority and responsibility, the governing procedures, and the manner in which coordination of activity is effected.[14] It gives order and direction to group life. Structure may be formal and official, or it may be informal and unofficial. Where there is a formal structure, there is also an informal one within it, which may have as much influence on the members as does the formal structure. In social work, the organizational structure of a group ought to facilitate the achievement of its purpose.

Social work groups seem to be organized with two basic types of structure, although there are variations within these types. In one type, often designated as the informal group, the only officially designated roles are those of member and worker. Other informal membership roles emerge out of the interaction within the group itself, as each member comes to influence others and others respond to this informal influence. Such groups are thought to provide for a maximum of group-centered communication and spontaneity of individual participation. They favor informal decision-making processes and the possibility that each member will have equal access to the worker and to every other member. A group of this type may further

[14] See Coyle, *Social Process in Organized Groups;* Vinter, "The Essential Components of Social Group Work Practice," in *Readings in Group Work Practice.*

be designated as a play group, activity group, discussion group, or discussion-activity group, based on the nature of the primary content of group life. It may be a natural group or a formed group.

The social club or self-governing group is the second major type of structure.[15] Relations become organized into well-defined positions and roles are acquired through election by members, or appointment by a member in a position of higher authority. This form of structure requires that members engage in making corporate decisions and work out conflicts in values and norms as they do so. It provides for opportunities to learn to carry responsible roles, use officers appropriately, and experiment with parliamentary procedures. It has the potential for providing a high degree of autonomy for the members. In such groups, the network of communication is formalized, making it necessary for a member to use the official channel for speaking and to obey rules pertaining to the conduct of the group's business. Such procedures tend to limit both the spontaneity and spread of participation among members, and dilute the relationships between the worker and each member of the group. Such groups frequently are in the nature of social clubs in youth-serving agencies and in self-government or ward groups in hospitals and other institutions.

The initial structure is usually set during the time that organization of a new group is being considered. But the worker may not have a choice in the determination of the structure, since a natural group already has a system of structural arrangements which the worker needs to understand and respect. Later, whatever the initial structure, it will be changed as the worker and members interact during the course of the group's life.

Some anticipation of the duration of the group is a part of planning. It is anticipated that some groups will continue over a period of many months. Some groups are planned as brief services, ranging from a single session to approximately eight

---

[15] Tropp, "Group Intent and Group Structure; Essential Criteria for Group Work Practice," *Journal of Jewish Communal Service*, XLI (1965), 229-50.

sessions. Others range in duration between these two extremes. The duration of the service, of course, should be related to the purpose of the group and the particular needs and capacities of the members.

Groups of relatively long duration, several months or more, have predominated in social work practice until recently. Such groups have been directed toward the improvement of a constellation of identified problems in psychosocial functioning of the members, or toward maximum development of potential for effective functioning. If a major purpose is to develop maximum or restore effective functioning in social relationships and social competence, when there are serious obstacles to the achievement of these goals, then short-term treatment is usually inadequate. It takes time for many people to develop meaningful relationships with a social worker and each other and to use such relationships for their own and others' benefit, to work through the problems, and to stabilize positive gains before the group terminates.[16]

In short-term groups, all of the phases of development are condensed. Cohesiveness in terms of mutual attraction of members to each other does not often take place. The cohesiveness that does develop is dependent upon attraction of members to the stated purpose of the group, clearly focused content, and relatively strong motivation to use the group. Short-term groups seem to be appropriate for several important social work purposes. They have been used to prepare the participants for a new role, such as becoming a foster or adoptive parent, a recipient of public assistance, a resident of an institution, or a foster child. They have been used for family life education in which the focus is to present a limited amount of content, within an atmosphere that makes possible some expression of

[16] One family service agency found that in family life education groups having four to six sessions the groups were disbanding just at the point that the members were becoming a group and able to participate quite fully and appropriately. The changed plan is for groups to meet from eight to fifteen times with sessions lasting for $1\frac{1}{2}$ to 2 hours. Meyer and Power, "The Family Caseworker's Contribution to Parent Education Through the Medium of the Discussion Group," *American Journal of Orthopsychiatry*, XXIII (1953), pp. 621-28.

feelings and ideas, and some modification of attitudes and behavior. They have been used to help persons to cope with personal or family crises, as when a child is suspended from school or runs away, when a member of a family is arrested, or when there is a new conflict in family relationships or in the family's relationships with significant reference groups. With children served by child guidance clinics, diagnostic group sessions are used to clarify the specific manner in which problems of children are manifested in social situations. A by-product often is helping a child to accept other treatment. As more use is made of short-term services to groups, both the benefits and limitations need to be studied; more experience and research is necessary to evaluate this trend in practice.

Frequency and length of meetings are factors to be considered in planning for a new group. The length of each meeting should be determined by its purposes, the size of the group, and the interests and time span of the members. Very ill patients or aggressive children may at first be able to tolerate less than a half hour and gradually become able to participate for longer periods of time. Work with adolescents seems to be more effective if the meetings last for at least one and a half hours. If the group is large, more time is required for participation of each member. The frequency of meetings is also affected by the aforementioned factors. Unfortunately, decisions about length, time, and frequency of meetings are too often made on the basis of tradition, rather than the needs of the members.

A group session is influenced by the physical and social environment in which it takes place. The physical environment may either facilitate or impede the group in its development. The adequacy and atmosphere of the room in which the group meets has an important impact on the development of relationships and group cohesiveness. In a room in an agency where groups of adults meet, the room is bright, light, furniture is informally arranged around a table, and an urn of coffee is provided from which members may help themselves. A contrast is a room with a very long board-type table, stiff chairs, and one in which no smoking or eating is permitted. To foster participation in discussion and intimacy of relationships, the ideal is a room that is quiet and large enough only for an informal circle of chairs within such distance that each member can readily be seen and heard by others. The circle itself is a symbol of closeness. The space in the center provides some distance, and the space between the chairs can indicate varied degrees of closeness and remoteness. In an open circle, however, no hiding is possible. A table tends to support members and often reduces self-consciousness. In situations in which groups meet in schools, churches, playground buildings, or other host facilities, there are always necessary rules and regulations to which all must conform. Basically, the worker needs to think through the impact of the physical setting on the members, do what he can to plan for an adequate setting, and then make the best use of what is available. Within even very poor physical facilities, it is possible for the social worker to create and maintain a physical atmosphere that is consistent, supportive, and trustworthy.

In planning for a group service, a decision needs to be made as to whether or not to permit additional members to join after the group has started; that is, to have an open group or to close it to new members after an initial period of time. The decision to have an open or closed group is often made during the period of preparation. In some instances, the plan is that the decision will be made later by the group itself. The plan for a given group needs to be made with recognition that each new person who comes into a group changes it, alters the interpersonal relations in which the original members are involved, and provides a new stimulus and situation to which the members need to adapt. The loss of a member from a group likewise requires an alteration in the network of relationships.

Obviously, any group which will regularly lose members must have a means for replacing them if the group is to continue. Examples are predischarge groups or groups of patients in short-term hospitalization. An open group may be suitable for certain purposes. In predischarge groups, for example, a flow of patients may serve to emphasize the out-of-hospital pace and community orientation of the group. Other groups are more appropriately closed, for example, groups in which interrelationships among members are of primary importance, or groups of regressed patients for whom time is necessary to develop trust in and ability to relate to others. In open-ended groups, there is frequent orientation of new members, and reorientation of the group to its purpose and to the focus of the content. Progress toward the achievement of purposes that require consistent attention is usually slowed down. In open groups, replacement of lost members may be done at regular or irregular intervals, again dependent upon professional judgment.

Application and Intake

APPLICATION PROCEDURES. In planning for formed groups, the decision by the applicant to elect group service or of the worker to recommend it, is related to the many factors of purpose, need, and group composition previously explored and to the constellation of services provided by the agency. The many different procedures used by agencies to reach people who need the service, to accept requests for service, and to admit persons into particular groups make generalization difficult. Many different procedures are used, but the basic purposes are similar: to help an individual to begin to know about the availability and nature of the service, determine his eligibility for service, ascertain if his purposes are sufficiently similar to those of others to be met through a group, and prepare him for entry into a particular group.

One procedure for recruitment that is used in such diverse agencies as settlements, youth-serving agencies, family service associations, and community mental health clinics is to publicize the fact that groups are being organized for a given purpose. A community center, for example, makes known the fact that it is starting a group for parents of preschool children focused on child development and preparation for school entry, or that it is starting a club for senior high school students who are interested in vocational exploration. A community-oriented

child guidance clinic provides announcements for junior high
school students, through the cooperation of the schools, indicating that group treatment is available to them and their parents
for help with crises. When persons respond to such recruitment,
there is usually a screening or a registration process prior to the
first session in the group. A short interview, prior to attendance
in the group, takes place to provide information about the
nature of the service, to screen out those applicants who seem
not suitable for the service, and to orient applicants to the
nature of the help that is being sought and that which is being
offered. Even though the initial interview is brief and informal,
the intake worker is sensitive to the mixed feelings of positive
motivation and apprehension of the applicant, and helps the
applicant to understand what he is seeking in relation to what
can be offered. Essentially, in these types of application and intake, the process is largely one of self-selection of clientele who
meet the objective criteria established by the agency for group
composition, eligibility requirements, and for children, parental
permission for participation in the group. There is the greatest
amount of informality in the procedures used in these instances.

There is some evidence that these relatively informal and
brief application and intake procedures are particularly effective
in reaching people from the lower social classes and for reaching adolescents and young adults. Such informality tends to
reduce social distance between staff and clientele. It has been
proposed that in settlement houses which typically are located
in low income areas, "where social distance is great, there is
little likelihood that efforts to influence members will be effective, where social distance is minimal, the possibilities for influencing members in constructive directions are maximized." [17]
It is suggested that the more formalized the agency, the more
likely it will selectively attract persons who have middle-class
orientations. Gouldner found that there was a tendency for
lower-class clientele to perceive bureaucratic procedures as red

[17] Cloward, "Agency Structure as a Variable in Services to Groups," in
Group Work and Community Organization.

tape.[18] The disadvantage of such initial approaches is that the practitioner begins his work with a minimal of prior knowledge about his prospective members.

In some agencies, application and intake procedures are formal and continue through a period of study, diagnosis, and planning for treatment prior to the assignment of a person to a group. Sometimes a group experience, particularly for young children, may be a part of the preliminary process, used for purposes of diagnosis and treatment planning. Or a conference with an entire family, often in its home, is a part of the intake process in instances where faulty functioning of the family as a group is thought to be central to the problem of an individual or the family unit. The most prolonged intake procedures usually occur in outpatient mental health clinics. A staff member, usually a social worker, is assigned responsibility for interviewing the applicant to determine his eligibility and to make a psychosocial study of the applicant's problem and situation. Often, the applicant is seen also by other team members, such as psychologists or psychiatrists. It is in a meeting of the professional team, then, that a decision is made about whether or not the agency will accept the case and, if so, the type of treatment to be offered. The needs of applicants are assessed in relation to the constellation of individual and group services which comprise the function of the agency. The applicant may be assigned for service immediately or he may be placed on a waiting list to receive service at some future time.

The social worker's relationship with a prospective group member may, but usually does not, begin at the point of the person's application for service. It more often begins once the decision has been made to invite him to a particular group for which the worker has responsibility. Whatever has been learned about the person in the intake process needs to be conveyed to the social worker who now has responsibility for the case. This latter worker often then has one or more interviews with the

[18] Gouldner, "Red Tape as a Social Problem," in Merton, *et al.*, *Reader in Bureaucracy*, pp. 410-18.

prospective member. Such interviews enable the worker to
establish an initial relationship with a person. They provide an
opportunity for exploring the person's reactions to placement
in a group. The prospective member, likewise, has an opportunity to become acquainted with the worker. Preliminary
interviews tend to diminish the anxiety and confusion which are
characteristic of first sessions. Often persons are asked to use
a group when group situations are very difficult for them.
Through one or more preliminary interviews, a relationship
may be initiated between the worker and the member which
can serve as a bridge for member-to-member relationships
within the group.[19]

REACHING OUT APPROACHES. There has been increasing interest
over the years in reaching out to prospective clients who themselves do not seek service. In these instances, there is no typical
application process by the recipients of service, but rather a
seeking out of persons thought to be in need and an active
offering of service to them. Such an approach is used in schools,
where the initial concern is usually expressed by a teacher or
administrator who then refers the child to a social worker for
individual or group service. The child or his parents may or
may not respond positively, but an agent of the community has
decided that help must be attempted. This is typical also in
the prescription of group services for patients in hospitals.
Cases in probation, work with delinquent gangs, and protective
services in child welfare are other examples of this approach.

In reaching out to persons who do not seek service, the
specific procedures will vary with the agency's function, the
proposed purpose of the group, the agency's geographical jurisdiction, the potential sources of referral, and the reputation of
the agency with those thought to need its help. Public school
personnel, probation officers, police, and courts often refer
people to social agencies. Once an agency has established a
reputation for being helpful to previously hard-to-reach clients,

[19] Levine, "Principles for Developing an Ego-supportive Group Treatment
Service," *Social Service Review*, XXXIX (1965), 422-32.

the volume of referrals tends to increase and the problem then becomes one of limiting intake.

When the social worker has a list of potential members or of potential existing groups, he learns about them through the person making the referral. Many children or adolescents are too suspicious of adults or too nonverbal to participate in formal intake interviews prior to the beginning of group experience. Information from referral sources helps the staff to assess the need for service, and the suitability of the agency's service for the referred clientele.

Agencies have used several approaches to facilitate acceptance of service. A written invitation has been effective. So, too, have introductions of the worker to the individual or group by the person making the referral. Home or street corner visits or telephone calls have been used also by some workers. The particular procedure to be used in reaching members is a matter of professional judgment based on knowledge of the particular people and their situations. Sometimes, when a person or group is wary of the service, the offer of help must be made over and over again. An honest presentation of the service to be offered and the conditions under which it will be given seems to be effective in motivating the prospective members toward a decision to at least try out the service.

In a reaching out approach, the agency must be very clear about the reasons for choosing to serve one group rather than another, based on needs of members and purpose and knowledge of the community. An example is that of a small delinquent gang, referred by a policeman. It was a subsystem of a larger group that split as a result of a conflict around a boys' gang. In investigating the situation, the worker learned that the most delinquent subgroup called itself the Spiders and the members aligned themselves with a boys' gang, the Scorpions. The patterns of delinquent behavior including fighting, truancy, and suspected thievery. The girls were ages fifteen to seventeen in grades nine to eleven in two different schools. Most of the girls were in a school for students with serious problems in social adjustment. They were of Mexican-American background. Since this seemed to be the subgroup with the most serious problems, it was selected for service. The worker secured the girls' names from various sources, met with them in pairs or triads, and later as a group. Within three weeks, nine of the girls said they'd be willing to "try a sponsor."

Social agencies may offer service to existing groups or a group may apply for service. In such instances, one major task that faces the worker is to determine the purpose for which affiliation with an agency is sought, and whether the group's purpose can be achieved within the agency's function or modified to the extent that service is possible. Another task is to determine the membership of the group and its membership policies as these exist. From here it is necessary to secure enough information about each member to make a tentative judgment about the workability of the present composition and size of the group for a social work purpose. If not suitable, are there ways the membership can be redefined for this purpose? Some of the decisions about membership may occur quite naturally as there is exploration of the purpose for which the group is seeking affiliation with the agency. Such exploration may be with the group as a whole or with persons who speak for the group.

The process of determining the suitability of a group for service may be clarified through an example. A minister telephoned an intake worker in a community center to say that there was a group of troublesome eleven-year-old boys who needed someone to work with them. The social work supervisor went to the church for a conference with the minister and later with the boys. The boys expressed a desire to have a football coach. The supervisor talked with them about this request, explaining that the center did not provide this service. He said that there was a playground just two blocks away and he'd be glad to see if the boys could learn to play football there. The boys resisted this idea, and finally said they weren't welcome at the playground—they'd been thrown out. There followed tales of the unfairness of the recreational staff about this, but it also became clear that these boys could not participate

in organized sports without starting fights and disorganizing
the activity. The supervisor said that he understood from the
minister that it was not easy for him to welcome them here
either, that apparently they were having some of the same
troubles here as at the playground. At first there were denials,
but then one boy said that, "Well, we'd be good if we could
have a coach." The supervisor said he could not do that: what
he could do would be to work with the playground director
and the boys to reopen the question of their use of the playground, or he could provide a social worker who could meet
with them as a group and who could perhaps help them to get
along better with each other and within the church. They
could do things together—even play with a football—and then
talk about how the activity went and what they could do to
make it better next time. Then when the boys could get along
all right and play well together, he would help them to find a
way to become a team. It took two more conferences before
the boys accepted this notion of service. This example illustrates
the need for clarity of purpose, based on the social worker's
skill in looking beyond a verbalized request to the underlying
need.

In application and intake processes, the social worker uses
all of his interviewing skills. He sets a climate conducive to the
task. He makes the applicant as comfortable as possible. He
shares his perception of the purpose of service with the applicants. He assures the person of his and the agency's desire to
be helpful. He engages the applicant's participation in the
decision-making process about the use of the agency's services.
He observes and accepts the feelings of the applicant; he initiates and develops a time-limited working relationship. He
secures enough information about the person or the group situation to decide tentatively whether or not the request falls within
the agency's purposes. He orients the applicant to next steps in
his use of the worker and the agency's services, and clarifies
how the applicant will be introduced to the group situation, if
this seems suitable. If a group is the unit, he clarifies how the

social worker will proceed with the group. The intake process serves as a bridge to the next stage, namely work with a group in its beginning as a unit of social work service.

Social Diagnosis

During all of his work thus far, the social worker has been securing and analyzing facts and using them in order to understand the applicant in relation to the proposed group service. In other words, he has been engaging in the process of social diagnosis. Some persons have criticized the use of the term diagnosis in social work, for to them it smacks of medicine. Although the term may indeed be a medical one, it does have a broader meaning, "a careful investigation of the facts to determine the nature of a thing," and "the decision or opinion resulting from such examination or investigation." It is in this sense that the word is used here, with the adjective social preceding the noun, to indicate that the thing being understood is not medical but social in nature; a person in his situation, a small group, a community, a social milieu. In social work an appropriate diagnostic scheme must rest upon a concept of interaction between persons and their environment as its foundation.

The purpose of social diagnosis is to understand and to arrive at an opinion. Social workers vary in preferences for use of the term diagnosis or assessment to refer to this process. Diagnosis is preferred to assessment by this author, since the common dictionary meaning of assess is "to set an estimated value on: usually of property for taxation." The purpose of assessment is, therefore, an evaluative one rather than one of understanding the nature of something which is central to the concept of diagnosis.

Social diagnosis is an ongoing process as well as a first step in practice. From fact finding in order to understand the client system, the social worker formulates an opinion about the nature of the system, including its characteristics, problems, and potentials. This leads quite logically and naturally to planning for what should be done to enable a client system to improve its functioning or to influence changes in the wider social system that has an impact on the client system. Based on such a decision, the practitioner uses himself to influence the system in some way. This is social treatment. After a worker acts, he evaluates the impact of the treatment on the system which itself involves further fact finding and opinion forming, and so the cycle of understand, plan, treat, and evaluate goes on in a dynamic way.

It is neither necessary nor possible to have all of the facts about a person in order to make a preliminary judgment about the suitability of a particular group for him. The social worker begins with what facts are relevant to the decision to accept a person for service and for his placement in a particular group. He then continues to add to his storehouse of knowledge as he judges what additional information will be helpful to him in serving individuals and the group as a whole.

A concern with the goals of the applicant should be paramount, as a social worker first encounters a person or a group as applicants for service. A person's positive motivations in seeking help or his aspirations are at least as important as are his problems or, in the words of Mary Richmond, "our examinations of the yesterdays and the todays should be with special reference to the client's tomorrows." [20] If the worker starts with the applicant's interest in having something be better in himself or his situation, his subsequent acts are apt to be goal-directed. The applicant may be clear about what he hopes for or have only vague feelings of discontent with the current situation. He may be articulate or need much help in expressing himself. Accompanying the positive motivations toward the opportunity available, resistance toward change may be evident. Fear of the unknown and of his own capacities to meet expectations may interfere with his ability to identify some goals related to agency purpose.

To observe and test for capacities, positive attitudes, areas of successful accomplishment, and supports in the environment are

[20] Richmond, "Some Next Steps in Social Treatment," in *The Long View*, p. 487.

equally as important as is knowledge of the nature of a person's troubles. For it is such strengths that can be used and built on as the applicant becomes a member of a group. Knowledge of normal growth, development, and behavior relevant to particular subcultures and situations, as well as deviations from norms, is used by workers to make possible a valid social diagnosis of the person and his social situation.

A problem encompasses any question, matter, or situation that is perplexing or difficult. Problems in human relations are usually identified by stress or some discomfort with the present situation. It is to be noted that in social work a problem is usually occasioned by a combination of inner and outer forces. The problems with which social workers are concerned are in the psychosocial realm. There tends to be some discrepancy between actual and potential performance. A problem therefore does not necessarily denote pathology or dysfunction. Problems are often evidenced by maladaptive attitudes toward oneself, differences among people, authority, or society's values and norms. The range of relationships with other people may be very narrow or their quality troublesome to the person or to others. Certain patterns of behavior may be maladaptive, hampering the person's use of his full potential in the achievement of his varied social roles.

To come to know the applicant's perception of his goals and the problems that are barriers to goal achievement also requires knowledge about his views of the severity of the difficulties and their onset and duration. Primary concern with the person's current situation and immediate future does not deny the importance of selective understanding of his past. If the worker is to contribute to positive growth and change in the members of a group, he has to be able to establish a relationship between change in the future and from the past. He cannot purposefully and effectively enable change if he does not know what has contributed to the situation that needs modification. As the worker seeks to understand the applicant, he tries to assess the constellation of factors that might be contributing to the person's stress, almost always some combination of inner and outer aspects. Environmental pressures are often troublesome to applicants, including deprivations and lack of opportunities in the past or in the current situation. There may be physical or intellectual disabilities. Inadequate or faulty development of the ego or superego are relevant personality factors. There may be conflict between values and norms within the person and between him and his various reference groups.

During the intake process, social diagnosis leads to a decision about an applicant's eligibility for service according to the requirements of the particular agency. It is used to determine a particular group placement or other service for an individual. It is used to determine the purpose, composition, and structure of a new group, or the basis for the provision of social work service to an existing group. The crucial aspect of initial social diagnosis in group work is the individual's potential contribution to as well as benefit from others who will share the adventure of group living with him.

CHAPTER V

The Orientation Stage

BEFORE a viable group develops as a means through which its members grow and change, a complex process of group formation begins at the time of preparation for a new group and continues until a group emerges. For "collective behavior is something more than and different from the sum of the individuals who produce it." [1] As members interact, a new entity is created: a group is born. This "groupness" occurs as a result of a process of orientation and a subsequent one of testing out and achieving commonality of perception of purpose, relationships, and structure. The primary task of the social worker during the early phases is to help a group to form—a group that will be beneficial to its members.

Characteristics of the Group

Regardless of the theoretical differences of writers reflected in the literature of social work, psychotherapy, and the social sciences, there is common recognition that there is a point of initial formation when the members of a group come into face-to-face association. In the literature on group development, the most frequently used title for this stage is orientation, to reflect the needs of the members for familiarization and adaptation to a situation or environment in reference to space, time, objects, and persons.[2] Other titles given to this stage reflect a similar focus.[3] They include: definitions of goals, roles, and norms;

---

[1] Coyle, *Group Work with American Youth*, p. 45.

[2] *Webster's New World Dictionary of the American Language*, p. 1411.

[3] The basic data for generalizations about the literature on group development throughout the remainder of this book are Hearn, "Group Change and Development"; Northen, "An Analysis of Stages of Group Development"; Sampson, "An Inquiry into Knowledge about Stages and Phases of Group Development."

definition of direction; locating commonness; initial situation; establishing initial contact; establishing the situation; pre-affiliation; and basal stage. There is considerable consensus that the stage is characterized by initial anxiety on the part of members toward the unknown situation. Members enter into the new situation with feelings and behavior characterized by uncertainty, anxiety, and tension and by self-conscious and noncommittal behavior. The relationship of the members with the leader is seen as a central problem. As members become acquainted with each other and oriented to the situation, there begins to emerge a pattern of interpersonal relations, values and norms, and processes of communication. Relationships of members with each other evolve out of the efforts to adapt to the expectations for the role of members in the particular group.

When a collection of persons comes together for the first time, a group does not yet exist. Likewise, when an existing group meets with a social worker for the first time, a group for social work purposes has not evolved. There is lack of congruence among members and with the worker about the purpose. The aggregate tends to be a collection of individuals with the center of attention on selves rather than on others. Membership is not stabilized; there is often lack of knowledge about who is to be included in the group. In a formed group, the structure of the group is the one established initially by the social worker. In a natural group, with its own structure, there is lack of clarity about how this will be modified to include the worker and the requirements of the agency which sanctions the group. In either instance, there is a lack of clarity about the interacting roles of client-member and worker. Except in natural groups, subgroup structure has not developed. Members of formed groups have not developed relationships with each other nor with the worker. In the case of natural groups, not only is there not an established relationship with the worker, but relationships with each other will become modified in unknown ways as the members engage in a new enterprise.

The members bring their own norms of behavior into the

group situation, based on their values. The worker has his own norms as a person, as a representative of an agency, and as a member of the social work profession. There is lack of knowledge about each other's values and norms, with lack of mutuality around this aspect of group process. Established patterns of verbal communication have not yet emerged so that discussion is apt to be scattered, diffuse, and lacking in continuity. Similarly, attention to any activity may be short-lived. There is lack of clarity about and acceptance of the boundaries to the group's self-determination as related to the authority of the social worker. Cohesiveness is indeed weak, for there is not a common basis for members' attraction to the group.

If a social work group is to form, the major task for the members is to become oriented to the situation. Initial working relations with each other and with the social worker are established around the task of orientation. In the process of intake, there was some orientation to the group experience; yet such preparation is not enough. The principal orientation remains to be done in the group. The task for the social worker is to become oriented to the developing group and to take leadership in the establishment of relationships and the process of orientation.

Initiation and Early Development of Relationships

At the point of entry into a new group, there is copresence among the members, but psychological bonds are not present unless members have known each other previously. Coming together psychologically is accomplished through psychological interplay and social exchange among the members. Someone makes an overture and, according to Goffman, the "adaptive line of action attempted by one will be insightfully facilitated by the other or insightfully countered, or both. . . ." [4] Thus a pattern of affective ties and communication emerges. It cannot be known in advance what the configuration will be, for this depends upon the interaction among many individual, group, and environmental factors.

[4] Goffman, *Behavior in Public Places*, p. 16.

When a person enters a new group, he scans the situation for signals that indicate to what extent he is welcome. He may be especially sensitive to those signals that indicate aloofness, in difference, or mild hostility as these are communicated to him through tone of voice, facial expressions, or gestures. Such messages are often more potent than are verbalized ones. They may communicate warnings to be wary, retreat, wait and see, or approach and reach out to others. The entering person may perceive the signals fairly accurately or he may distort and misinterpret them. People have highly selective awareness of others, predominantly unconscious, so that they see and hear only certain things. Such distortions interfere with the person's effective entry into the group. In his efforts to cope with the new situation, a member may have positive feelings of interest, hope, trust, pleasure, comfort, curiosity, friendliness, or satisfaction. Negative feelings may run a gamut of insecurity, anxiety, distrust, rejection, doubt, confusion, discomfort, disinterest, self-consciousness, resentment, or disappointment. Combinations of positive and negative feelings seem to be quite universal. They seem to be as prevalent in members of groups in youth service agencies, in which membership is thought of as desirable and voluntary, as in members of groups in hospitals or correctional institutions.[5]

Initial motivation is influenced by the personal and social characteristics of members, the adequacy of members' psychosocial functioning, the social agency and its place in the community, and cultural factors that influence attitudes toward and use of institutional resources. These, in turn, are often related to the initial application or referral, whether initiated by the group member or someone else in his behalf and the extent to which membership in the group is voluntary. But even voluntary attendance does not imply eagerness and motivation to become a part of a group. Most people come to a new experience both wanting it and fearing it. As Osborn has said vividly:

[5] Gore, "Analysis of Members' Expressions of Feelings in First Meetings of Groups," pp. 13-35.

Just as we must remind ourselves that there are many shades of grey between black and white, so we must recognize that all voluntary affiliations are not equally fervid. Joining is more like a five to three vote than the miniature landslide we might prefer.[6]

Whatever the initial motivation, it is modified as a person has experiences in the group. The fact that most people want the goals of improved personal adequacy and social functioning for themselves is an ally to the social worker in his efforts to support the initial motivation of members. Another ally is the powerful fact that all people have potential for growth and development. Yet most people also have some resistance to involving themselves in a group experience. Change means discomfort or disequilibrium, for it means giving up the comfort of the familiar present for an unknown future. There may be fear, too, of inability to succeed or an underlying feeling of hopelessness about oneself and his situation. What the social worker strives for is to motivate the members to select one or more specific goals toward which they may work. The worker's own value system, in part, determines his skill in this important area. A belief in the potential for change in each human being tends to be communicated nonverbally to the group. If this feeling is picked up by one or more members of the group, such members may in turn influence others toward hoping for something better for themselves.

Within some of the common reactions to becoming involved in a group, there are striking differences in initial motivation. Sometimes, there is eager anticipation of belonging to a group. In a children's hospital, for example, a group was initiated for five- and six-year-old girls and boys. Its purpose was to help the children to understand the varied treatment procedures and develop relationships with other children that might sustain them through the difficult period of hospitalization. When the social worker entered the ward to invite the children to come to the group, she found poignant desire combined with appre-

[6] Osborn, "Some Factors of Resistance Which Affect Group Participation," in Sullivan, ed., *Readings in Group Work*, pp. 1-14.

hension about exclusion. One little boy in a wheelchair asked, "Do you want *me?*" in a tone of voice that expressed both wonder and fear. A girl tugged at the worker's skirt and in a high-pitched voice asked, "Me, too—me, too?" The oldest boy asked, "Is there room for one more—is there room for me?" How different is this initial behavior from the hostile reactions to service of adolescent boys who were referred by a judge with the admonition to: "Be in this man's group or go to Juvenile Hall," hardly a positive motivation toward the service. Such differences in motivation are reflected in the members' feelings about and reactions to the social worker.

The social worker uses his understanding of the meaning of the new experience to the members of the group in order to develop an initial working relationship that will sustain the members through the period of initial uncertainty and anxiety, and that will serve as a catalyst for promoting the development of relationships among members. He needs to deal with the members' varied abilities to trust him and each other and their related dependency-independency conflicts, feelings of psychological and social distance, and reactions toward his authority.

In each new situation, an individual faces, to some extent, renewal of the basic conflict of his sense of trust versus distrust and the need for synthesis of these polarities.[7] The extent to which he has achieved a basic sense of trust influences the amount and duration of uncertainty and anxiety that is typical of encounters with new situations. Each new experience offers some occasion for mistrust until the unknown becomes familiar. Until members can come to trust the people involved and the situation, they cannot participate in an interdependent relationship with others. The social worker develops trust by conveying, through his own attitudes and behavior, the qualities of acceptance, empathy, and objectivity that are components of the professional relationship. He helps members to relate to him and each other through the many small courtesies that indicate interest in one's comfort and that acquaint members with each

[7] Erikson, *Childhood and Society*, pp. 219-34.

other. Simple acknowledgments that the experience is a new one, that it is natural to feel uncertain, and that he has confidence that the group experience will be a valuable one for the members are specific means for developing an atmosphere of mutual trust. With the necessary amount of support and direction from the worker, members of groups who have a healthy sense of trust will move rather quickly into fuller exploration of the potentials and demands in the group experience. In groups composed of such individuals, an initial working relationship with the worker and each other develops quickly. An example is a group of parents who voluntarily joined a parent education group to learn how to understand better and communicate more effectively with their teen-age children. With a minimum of anxiety and basically positive motivations toward the service, the period of orientation was achieved within the first session.

Many persons lack a basic sense of trust in others and in their own ability to cope with situations. For some, the symptoms will be withdrawal and fearful responses to efforts to engage their participation. With regressed schizophrenic patients, for example, work usually involves a prolonged period in which the social worker nurtures and develops the capacity for trust. He may do this through providing opportunity for the members to be dependent upon him and engaging them in a variety of simple activities that are clearly within their capacities and that focus on individual or parallel participation, but also make possible cooperative work. He may encourage, but with a minimum of pressure, discussion of everyday events and common experiences and provide some gratification in the form of food or concrete achievements. Within a protective and permissive environment, he gradually encourages the members to express their feelings, ideals, and goals. It may take a period of several weeks before a relationship of trust in the worker and each other is established. This process is somewhat similar to that used with very shy and fearful young children.

Personal characteristics and qualities of the social worker

influence the development of the worker-group relationship. It is desirable that the member like the worker as a person and respect his abilities. Initially, some members of groups assume that the worker has professional competence on which they can depend. Clientele from middle-class backgrounds tend to establish relationships with a practitioner on the basis of their perception of his knowledge and skills primarily, but also need to feel his acceptance. Other people, such as children and adults from lower socioeconomic backgrounds, tend to respond initially in terms of the worker's personal qualities. Such persons need to feel that they know and like the worker as a person as a basis for using him for help with their problems. Spergel emphasizes that in street gang work, it is essential that the worker "achieve a specific person identity in his role rather than an abstract identity with an agency." [8] The members may inquire about the worker's background, experiences, and values in an effort to find out what he is like, what motivates him to work with them, and often out of a desire to get closer to him psychologically. There is some evidence that mental patients tended to remain in groups when the practitioner interacted freely with them, and that they dropped out when he was an enigma to them. Further, there is evidence that there was a higher improvement rate if the practitioner showed active personal participation with them than when he showed a less personal and less understanding attitude.[9] An informal atmosphere is usually conducive to the development of trust in the worker as well as to the development of relationships among members. If appropriate to his knowledge about the members' preferences and purpose of the group, an informal action-oriented experience, no matter if as simple as sharing coffee, touring the facilities, or making name tags, may facilitate the development of relationships. With some groups, such devices are unnecessary.

Members often come to a group situation with some fear of

[8] Spergel, *Street Gang Work*, p. 73.
[9] Frank, *Persuasion and Healing*, p. 132.

the worker's power over them. One common fear is that the worker will violate the individual's right to privacy by revealing to others what he knows about him, and that this will be used to the detriment of the individual. Hence, dealing with these fears is essential if membership in the group is to be sustained. A direct statement that this group is one in which the worker respects the right of the members to express what they feel and think without fear that he will talk about them outside the group, unless he tells them about it first, usually suffices for a first meeting. His sensitivity to the reactions of the members is a clue as to whether or not he needs to pursue this theme further. Confidentiality, though, is not limited to the worker, for members acquire information about each other. The worker serves as a model for the members in this respect, and in addition he expresses the hope that they will not share information about each other outside the group.

The client has a right to expect that, when it is desirable, the agency will use information constructively in his behalf. Pertinent information may be shared with appropriate persons in order that the best possible service may be given to the individual. The agency is responsible to the client, and also to the community which supports it and makes its services possible. This dual responsibility may create problems in applying the principle of confidentiality to specific situations. Mutual trust will be developed between the worker and the group as varied situations occur that are of concern to the members, and as the worker deals with these in the person's best interests without violating the community's interest.[10]

The social worker hopefully feels some eagerness and zest in regard to his involvement with the group. If he does, he can convey to the group his willingness to involve himself openly and spontaneously, within his responsibility to them as a helping person. Inasmuch as the core of work with groups is the alleviation of obstacles that prevent gratifying relationships and

[10] For a good statement on confidentiality see National Social Welfare Assembly, *Confidentiality in Social Services.*

productive interaction, it is essential that the worker be able to interact freely in this, a relationship with other human beings.

Orientation to the Purpose of the Group

Orientation to the worker, other members, and the plans for the use of the group is necessary to reduce some of the uncertainty and anxiety, and to enhance the potential value of the group for its members.

The purpose of the group needs to become explicit if the group is to be of optimum benefit to its members. The members of the group are most receptive to change when their goals and aspirations are similar and are meshed with the social worker's purpose. When members of groups are not clear about the motives of the social worker, they tend to become confused and distrustful. To say, "I'm here to help," without indicating for what purpose, implies that the worker is omnipotent and the members are dependent upon him.[11] In her research, Hartford found that workers frequently failed to make explicit the purposes, or they intervened inappropriately in the process of goal formulation. In such instances, there was a tendency for the group not to form.[12] This finding supports the principle that it is the social worker's responsibility to help the group to become aware of its reason for being in terms of both his purpose and the members' goals for themselves. Yet workers often find it difficult to express clearly, simply, and explicitly their perceptions of the social work focus of the group. Or, they find it difficult to use action-oriented devices to help groups of nonverbal members to play out the purpose. They often avoid encouraging the members to react to the stated purpose with varied degrees of positive and negative expressions and to relate the general purpose to their own goals. Even though the initial purpose of the group as perceived by the

[11] An unpublished paper by Overton, "Establishing the Relationship," has helped to clarify the use of purpose with involuntary clients.
[12] Hartford, "The Social Group Worker and Group Formation."

agency has been explained to members during an intake process, it still is important that the group hears it and has an opportunity to react to the worker's explanation.

To present the purpose in positive terms of what members can expect to achieve through the group, as contrasted with a focus on the problems of members, connects the purpose to the positive motivations of members. To express hope that members will become able to "get along better with others," "be able to understand and bring up your children better," or "find out how you might be able to complete high school" does not deny the need for help, but does tend to enhance motivation toward change. It is important that the members express, as best they are able, what they hope will happen and what they hope can be achieved in the group. From a therapeutic standpoint, the process of goal formulation is to bring to the awareness of all participants the direction toward which they are moving. In the orientation phase, this is done in accordance with the worker's judgment of what the members can take hold of at a given time.

There is skill in stating a purpose with both sufficient breadth and explicitness that, within the generalization, the group members can begin to formulate their own purposes. The difficulty is greater in those instances in which the recipients of service do not apply voluntarily but are referred or for whom a group is prescribed. With some prospective members, the worker and the members may be far apart in their perceptions of mutually agreed-upon goals. For example, inmates in a correctional institution want nothing but to get out. The worker sees a need for changes in their behavior. He, too, wants them released as soon as possible, but only after they have made sufficient progress in modifying their attitudes and behavior to be able to live in the open community. The worker can thus begin by defining the conditions under which release can take place.

A professional relationship is developed through activity that is related to the purpose, not through subterfuge, as when a worker offers a recreational activity without clarification of his purpose and role. This subterfuge leads to confusion about the role of the worker and to further difficulty in achieving congruence of social work purpose. Rather, a clear and simple presentation of who the worker is, how he sees the purpose of the group, and why the group or an individual was referred to the agency is effective. The worker makes it clear that he is interested in the members' views about their aspirations, goals, problems, and possible solutions. Even young, disturbed children accept an explanation of the reason for the group and can express their feelings about membership and their concepts about help. When the children become aware of their need for help, they are able to share many problems and feelings in the group. There is less evasion and tension is reduced. Listening and reacting verbally to the explanation by the worker may often be supplemented with play, through which the children dramatize their views of the situation. Activities lead to discussion, and talk leads into activity. When members are able to find the words that belong to their feelings and ideas, verbalization may be the most useful activity.[13] The worker seeks to find the common threads of purpose that seem to underlie differences in goals. It is his task to seek combatibility between his view of what the group needs and the composite of members' motives.

Structure and Membership of the Group

The social worker provides direction for the initial organizational structure of the group. Although the degree of his activity may vary somewhat according to the group, it is usually more apparent during the stage of orientation than at any other point in the group's development. It is the worker's responsibility to orient the group to the agency's rationale for the particular form of organization, and for the decisions concerning time, place, frequency, and content of meetings. The members' reactions to these plans are sought and modifications

[13] Ganter, "The Group Worker in the Child Guidance Center," in Trecker, ed., *Group Work in the Psychiatric Setting*, p. 31.

may be made, based on the members' judgments about the
suitability of the proposed structure. The members need to
know the source of authority for establishing and changing
procedures, including the part they have in this process.

Uncertainty and anxiety about the basis of membership in a
group is usually present in formed groups. In natural groups
the concern tends to be one of ambivalence about the inclusion
of a social worker in the group. Questions from members as to
the reasons why they were referred to or selected for the group
need to be responded to with brevity and honesty. Later, there
can be clarification of the members' questions and concerns
about this. Even in groups in which the individuals have sought
a place, the provision of information about the major criteria
for group composition may enable members to feel some sense
of commonality, a necessary first step toward identification with
the group. Similarly, sharing with them information about
anticipated changes in membership helps to provide a sense of
security. Members need to know if there are expectations that
they be prompt and attend regularly. They need to know under
what circumstances others will be added or they will be
dropped.

Norms

Persons often come to social work situations ignorant of what
particular role behaviors will be expected of them. They bring
their own norms with them into the group but, if this is a first
experience with a social worker, they have no experiential base
for knowing what to expect of the worker and what is expected of them. An illustration is of a group composed of
eleven- and twelve-year-old boys who were making a poor adjustment in school and had been referred to a group for help
with their problems related to school. The worker sensed the
members' discomfort about the silence that followed his suggestion that the members talk about what they might discuss
or do in the group. He then repeated an earlier explanation
that the purpose of the group was to help them get along better

in school, and added that he knew it could be very hard to do well in school. One member then told a story about a new boy in school who was "teased by the kids and given a rough time by the teacher." A silence followed which the worker interrupted, saying that he knew it would be hard for the new boy in school; that they were in a somewhat similar situation, coming to a new group and not knowing what to expect from the worker and maybe from each other, too. "Yeah, that's exactly it," was the boy's response. A worker's sensitivity and appropriate response to such indirect forms of communication facilitates the members' orientation to the group.

There may be wide disparity between the expectations that the worker has for the members and those of the members themselves, or there may be wide disparities among the members of the group. If they are to make appropriate use of the group, the members need to know what rights and responsibilities they have in relation to each other and to the worker, and what the base rules are that govern their relationships with each other. An unequal power distribution is inherent in the differences between roles of worker and member. The members' perceptions, however, may exaggerate the extent or the facets of the worker's power. Clarification of expectations helps members to understand and assume the rights and responsibilities that are theirs. The worker likewise needs to be sure that his expectations are relevant to the capacities and the sociocultural milieu of his clients.

The worker strives to develop mutuality of expectations between himself and the group. There is some evidence that similarities of expectations tend to create both stability and progress in therapeutic social systems. Mutuality concerning several types of expectations has been found to be crucial in this regard: patterns of participation concerning the spread of verbal communication—who shall speak and how much; the relevance of communication—what shall be said; rules about when to communicate; expectations concerning the conversations and social experiences that comprise the content of the group; and expectations regarding progress and length of service. When asymmetry of expectations occurs, strain in communication is likely to follow.[14] One manifestation of this strain is apt to be withdrawal from the group. Periodic strain is bound to occur and is essential to progress. But when it is too severe in initial meetings, it is more likely to be disruptive to what is still a tenuous connection between the worker and the members. To resolve the problem of what a person may expect and what may be expected of him appears to be an indispensable requisite for maintaining the therapeutic system. Without some resolution of the problem of discrepancy in expectations, continuation becomes doubtful.

That social class differences are one of the more important influences of clients' expectations about help has been suggested by a number of studies.[15] Clients from middle-class orientations tend to expect that value will be placed on introspective and reflective discussion and on verbal sophistication; that the helper's role will be a relatively inactive one; that other family members may be involved in treatment; and that the treatment will be prolonged. Clients from less advantaged socioeconomic backgrounds, on the other hand, tend to expect that the practitioner will be direct, supportive, and active; that "cure" will occur more rapidly; and that the practitioner will do something in an immediate, tangible way to relieve discomfort. They are confused by the demand for verbalization as contrasted with action. Too often it has been assumed that the reluctance of these clients to question the expectations and their passive compliance with the worker's definition of role are due to lack

[14] Lennard and Bernstein, *The Anatomy of Psychotherapy*, pp. 154-61. Other references useful to understanding mutuality of expectations are: Spiegel, "The Social Roles of Doctor and Patient in Psychoanalysis and Psychotherapy," *Psychiatry*, XVII (1954), 369-76; Schaeffer and Meyers, "Psychotherapy and Social Stratification," in Cohen, ed., *Advances in Psychiatry*, pp. 71-91.

[15] Maas, "Group Influences on Client-Worker Interaction," *Social Work*, IX (2), (1964). Maas, *et al.*, "Socio-cultural Factors in Psychiatric Clinic Services for Children," *Smith College Studies*, XXV (1955), 1-90. Aronson and Overall, "Treatment Expectations of Patients in Two Social Classes," *Social Work*, XI (1), (1966), 35-41. Wiltse, "The Hopeless Family," *Social Work*, III (4), (1958), 22.

of motivation. Rather, such behavior may be a sign of confusion and uncertainty. Hence, the worker needs to give time and attention to setting reciprocal responsibilities and forms of communication.

The Social Worker's Role in Group Interaction

As members come into the first meeting, the social worker's responsibility is to support each member's entry into the group. Attending to the members' comfort, introducing himself and members to each other, and suggesting ways for members to initiate interpersonal exchange are simple everyday courtesies, but important ones. It is usually suitable for the social worker to review briefly what he understands the members have already been told about the reason for the new group or the group's referral for service. He tells them briefly what the nature of his participation will be. He presents the essential facts simply and succinctly in an informal manner. He notices the non-verbal responses to these statements and invites verbal reactions, giving each member an opportunity to comment and ask questions. What happens next depends upon the type of group, the individuals who comprise it, and the specific responses of the members to the introductory comments. Whatever his next act and regardless of whether the content is talk or activity, however, he attempts to set up a pattern of participation that gives recognition to each member's efforts and facilitates communication among the members, according to the readiness of particular members. He may request, either through words or nonverbal signals, that the members respond to each other's suggestions and reactions, but he does not usually pressure them to do so. He may make comments that connect up the contribution of one member to that of another. In such ways, he makes clear that one aspect of his role is to help the members to interact with each other.

In his participation in the group, the social worker selects and uses specific techniques within all of the major categories of support, communication, clarification, development of social competence, and use of resources, as described in Chapter III. Within the general categories, some techniques are most appropriate during the early stage and some are less appropriate. Although there are common elements in all groups, the worker's particular focus and activity is different with every group. Two examples from practice may serve to clarify the similarities and differences in the worker's participation in group interaction during first meetings.

Ten seven- and eight-year-old girls came into a first meeting, excited about the invitation to be in a Blue Bird group, whose special purpose was to enhance the members' ability to succeed in school. The girls had been referred to the group because they were behaving in unacceptable ways in school, their academic work was unsatisfactory, and they were economically and socially deprived. Initially, the children were exceedingly quiet and conformed rigidly to their perceptions of good "pupil" behavior. The worker introduced herself. She explained in simple words what the group was for. She said that their teachers had said that they wanted to be in the group so they could learn to do better in school, that their parents had given permission for them to attend, and that they would play and talk together in the group. She asked how that seemed to them. The children were silent until one girl raised her hand and asked, "Do we all get to come, teacher; is it for sure?" The worker reassured the girls about this, told them that she was not a teacher but a social worker, and reviewed her name for them. She then suggested that they get acquainted by playing a simple game. All enjoyed this, so another game was introduced to help the girls to learn each other's and the worker's name. The girls had difficulty in following directions, so the worker simplified both her directions and the game itself. Some members enjoyed this and succeeded in it, but others gave up quickly when they could not remember a name. A few girls became restless and roamed around the room investigating the equipment and supplies, but came back into the core of the group when it was time for refreshments. In closing this short meeting, the girls were told about the schedule of twice-weekly meetings, but it was apparent that they had no idea when Thursday would be. The worker said that they need not worry about the day for she would make plans with their teachers to remind them of the next meeting. In such a group, it will take many sessions for the members to achieve orientation to the worker, each other, and the group.

A second example is of a group of six mothers of preschool children; this was organized in a child guidance clinic for the purpose of helping the mothers to become more effective in dealing with their young children. Through an intake process, the women had become well acquainted with the clinic's purpose and procedures, and had had several interviews with clinic personnel concerning the plan for treatment of their children and the nature of their expected participation in the plan. Basic orientation to the group had been done through interviews. Furthermore, the women had all at least seen each other before as they waited for their children who were together in group therapy. These facts did not mean that orientation in the group was unnecessary, however. In the first meeting, the social worker was able rather quickly to review the purpose and plan for the group with the mothers, and to engage them in some discussion of the group. The discussion then focused on the reasons perceived by each mother for referral to the group and on identifying common concerns. Although each member differed in her pattern of participation, there was a general tendency to direct statements to the worker rather than to each other, to take turns in reporting on the symptoms of their children that brought them to the clinic in a contained manner with little expression of affect, to look to the worker for approval of their comments, and to express their goals in terms of knowledge about children rather than modification of their own attitudes and behavior. There was little spontaneous interaction among the members. From here on, the major tasks in orientation for the worker were to elicit the expression of feelings about the situations that brought them to the clinic, to search for the common ground underlying seemingly different goals and problems, to establish a network of communication among the members themselves rather than the perpetuation of individual to worker communication, and to discover some preliminary focus for their work together.

During this phase, the worker needs to be a supportive person. He does not withhold information or support when the group needs it. He provides whatever information is relevant to the situation. Turning questions back to a group when the members simply do not have the necessary information is not helpful. Knowing when to give information directly to members, and when to help them to use resources to find out the facts for themselves, is an essential skill.

One of his most crucial skills is to identify, understand, and respond sensitively to the feelings of members. As he observes the members and listens to them, he becomes able to recognize their feelings. He does this through observation of nonverbal cues such as facial expression, body posture, and gestures, as well as through the verbalized content. He understands the members' uncertainty and ambivalence and the meaning of some of their defensive maneuvers. As feelings are expressed, he meets them with a feeling response rather than an intellectual one. Certain types of activity facilitate the expression of feelings; others inhibit such expression. Some forms of communication seem to be more effective than others. One effective technique is to show genuine interest in individuals or the group, through giving special attention or recognition. Through recognition, the worker communicates that he is taking in the uniqueness of a person and is paying attention to him. Another type of comment conveys acceptance of a member's feelings, particularly those which express doubt, hostility, or distrust. Whether or not the members can yet trust the worker's responses, they come to feel his acceptance and understanding.

The free but protected atmosphere of the group may be a new experience for many members. Particularly during a first session, the worker avoids asking questions concerning the members' reasons for feeling or behaving in certain ways. Asking why tends to elicit defensive responses, rather than releasing feelings and setting a problem-solving process at work. Such questions may be perceived as reprimands or be confusing to members who do not know what kind of answer is expected. A restatement of the feelings expressed by members can be effective, if accurately perceived by the worker. He puts into words some feelings which he senses members are trying to express, or restates them in a way that they are named and hence recognized. Often, the simplest responses are the most effective. In order to bring a feeling of one member into the commonage of group experience, the worker may test with the group whether or not the acknowledged feeling is shared by others. To be able to respond to the underlying meaning of the members' requests, challenges, or comments is an important skill. Within a climate that supports the expression of feelings, the worker tries not to stir up feelings that cannot be dealt with during the course of the session. He may note mentally sensitive areas but hold them for discussion until the person or the group is ready to focus on them. If a worker really desires to be helpful to the members and is sensitive to their feelings, his responses are apt to be appropriate.

Contagion of feelings from member to member and group as a whole seems to occur very infrequently in initial meetings of groups.[16] Rather, the feelings tend to be idiosyncratic to individual needs and reactions to the new situation. Usually there is not yet mutual identification or much capacity for empathy. The worker, therefore, takes responsibility for assessing the flow of feelings and for noting the common elements within the myriad of individual responses.

In making his contribution to the group interaction, the social worker needs to follow the manifest content of the conversation at the same time that he seeks understanding of the latent content. The manifest content consists of the literal and

[16] Gore, "Analysis of Members' Expressions of Feelings in First Meetings of Groups," pp. 56-59.

obvious meanings of the verbal communication; the latent
content is that which is below the threshold of superficial observation or that is the essential motivation for the contribution.[17] It may be just below the level of awareness, subject to
ready recall, or it may be at the unconscious level. The latent
content may extend and add meaning to the manifest content
or it may contradict it. If the former, the process of communication is enhanced; if the latter, mutual understanding is
hampered.

To make sense out of the often apparently unrelated contributions of the members, the worker searches for the underlying common threads of feelings and meaning and responds to
these. He tries to discover how a succession of comments and
questions by members are linked together around an underlying
concern which is common to a number of members. For example, one common concern of members in first meetings may
be whether or not they will be accepted by the worker and
other members. This concern is seldom expressed at the
manifest level, but the sensitive worker makes the generalization from his observation of both verbal and nonverbal cues
that are provided in subtle ways during the meeting.

The social worker needs to follow the interaction process
itself. The process is transactional in nature by the mutual
effect and reciprocal influence of people on each other as they
participate in the conversation. The practitioner's concern is
with the nature and spread of feelings, opinions, and ideas;
who interacts with whom; who initiates behaviors and who
follows the initiator. He is interested in discovering the factors
that create a beginning sense of mutuality among the members
and, on the other hand, with the sources of tension and conflict
in the group.

In relation to his interest in opening up communication
among members, the worker seeks out the blocks to communication in the group which may be due to interpersonal hostili-

[17] For a valuable discussion of these distinctions, see Merton, *Social Theory
and Social Structure*, pp. 61-66.

ties or to differences in culture, knowledge, or values. He assesses each member's ability to listen, to observe, and to respond to the communication of others with or without distortion of the messages. Young children need to learn to communicate with the social worker, often in new ways. Many children are expected to listen to and obey adults and to respond only to specific questions asked them. Often they are not expected to enter into discussions with adults present—to give as well as take in reciprocal verbal communication. The worker needs to develop interest in the children's viewpoints and to be able to enter into the world of childhood so that he and they can talk with each other. To talk with children, in language suitable to the children's level of understanding without talking down to them is a precious attribute in a worker. Children are not as nonverbal as is often assumed. The clue, to a large extent, is in the adult who is able to listen, to enter into the child's world, to talk simply and concretely, with the appropriate amount of seriousness or playfulness that is indicated by the child's moods. Adults, too, have their troubles in listening and talking. Observations of the capacities for communication of the members are used by the worker in making a professional judgment about when to enter the conversation, or intervene in an activity for a particular reason, and when to support silently the interacting processes within the group.

In the early period of group life, it is desirable to focus on shared experiences as a basis for the development of motivation. Initially, discussion or activity should provide for some immediate sense of learning something that is valued or that brings gratification. Early discussion, though scattered, tends to promote a feeling of belonging and reduces the members' anxious feelings. At any one time, there are diverse topics available for consideration by the group, from which a selection is made, either by formal decision or through the influence of a central theme that underlies informal free-flowing discussion. Although there is a model for phases in the process of decision making that is useful for purposes of analysis, in reality each group deviates from the model, influenced by its objectives and the interests and capacities of its members at a given time. Informal chats may be interspersed with more formal discussion. A topic may be introduced at one time, set aside by the group either consciously or not, and then picked up again at some later time when there is greater interest in or readiness to pursue it. If a group experience is to be helpful to the members, some order must underlie the diverse strands of communicative messages within the group. The social worker finds this order and helps the group toward some focus.

Certain action-oriented experiences may be used to further the specific goal of helping members to become oriented to the group. Through carefully selected experiences, members may become better acquainted with the worker and each other; verbal communication can be opened up to express feelings and concerns; and some immediate sense of gratification can be gained.

The diagnostic value of certain action-oriented content has long been recognized. When members are engaged in working alone or together on some task, the social worker can observe directly the capacities and problems of the members. He can observe their behavior as they interact with others in varied situations. Perceiving their performance in varied situations helps the members as well as the worker to recognize the members' responses to situations, the things that give satisfaction as contrasted with those that frustrate, the conditions under which individuals approach new relationships and materials and those in which they avoid them, the situations in which they are able to engage in cooperative activity and those in which they cannot share, and the tendencies toward hostile aggression or withdrawal from people or activities. Many activities free people to express and thereby reveal their attitudes, feelings, and desires more fully than they are able to do in words.

Action is a crucial means through which people communicate with each other. Action-oriented content is useful to facilitate communication with clients of all ages, but it is essential for young children and people, whatever their age, who have low tolerance for or lack of ability to communicate verbally in effective ways. Some activities tend to lower defensive barriers to verbalization so they are often used to facilitate discussion. Smoking, sharing food, working with clay, or the use of audio-visual aids are common experiences for achieving this purpose. Engaging in some activity permits a person to enter into conversation as he is ready to do so, without the sense of pressure that is often present when discussion is the only activity. This is not meant to imply that some anxiety, discomfort, or pressures toward verbal participation are not useful motivations. Rather, it is meant to emphasize the value of aiding discussion under circumstances in which the members could not participate otherwise or in which the quality and content of communication is enhanced through such devices. Frequently, the discussion stimulated by an experience is of at least as much value as the activity itself.

Speech is but one means of communication, but it is a basic tool for all human beings. Nonverbal communication usually must be understood in verbal terms before it can be integrated and used by a person. Verbal skills are essential to success in education, and to the successful fulfillment of almost any social role.

It is important to meet the clients' requests for concrete services even before a full understanding of the needs of each member is developed. With some individuals, material and physical deprivation may be primary, or the need may be for the resolution of some immediate crisis. Even when there exists other problems of an interpersonal nature with which the person would like help, the request for concrete assistance is much easier to communicate. The concrete request often serves as a feeler to test out the worker's interest and intent. It is possible in certain instances that the worker maximizes the chances of sustaining a relationship if he responds to and attempts to meet an individual's or the group's request for some specific service. In a group of young adults in a maternity home, after the worker reviewed the institution's purpose for inviting them to the group, the members requested permission to set up a club and elect officers. This was done in a perfunctory way, for the interest of most members was in ventilating their own complaints about the institution. The worker accepted the outpouring of complaints and, before the meeting closed, asked if there was any agreement about a complaint that seriously concerned all of them and about which something might be done by them. The president suggested that the worker talk with the director of the home in their behalf concerning one complaint. The worker accepted this task, but mentioned that together they could work on some of the other concerns that had been expressed during the meeting. This willingness to intervene in their behalf enhanced the members' perception of the worker as someone interested in and willing to help them. In working with children and with lower-class families, particularly, "a concrete service often has more meaning than an early attempt to deal with feelings and attitudes. We build trust in the distrustful by first dealing with specific and urgent needs." [18] Fantl similarly points out that, in the beginning phase, service to hard-to-reach families should be focused on situational problems.[19]

While it is not always possible or desirable that the worker directly provide the concrete services being asked for, because they fall outside the agency's function, he can usually be instrumental in helping the person or group to locate and use the service that is requested. When the worker suspects that further service beyond this immediate problem may be needed, serving as an intermediary to help the client find relief for the pressing environmental problem may be an excellent basis upon which to build a continuing relationship.

It is not easy to get started with a new group. The social worker cannot really know the members well enough for

[18] Overton and Tinker, *Casework Notebook*, p. 49.
[19] Fantl, "Integrating Psychological, Social, and Cultural Factors in Assertive Casework," *Social Work*, IV (4) (1958), 30-37.

accurate diagnosis of their goals, expectations, problems and capacities. The worker, as well as the members, feels some anxiety with a new group. He is uncertain of the responses of the members to him. If he is not comfortable, he may over-direct or underdirect the group. He may present introductory material in such a didactic manner that members tend toward passive agreement. He may become anxious over silence and enter into the discussion prematurely. He may tend to answer questions or make comments when turning them back to the group would be beneficial. A worker who is too passive usually makes a group restless and insecure. In such cases, the members often leave a meeting feeling let down, that nothing has been accomplished. A worker must give direction and simultaneously allow for freedom of expression and self-direction.

Motivation to Continue in the Group

Prior to the group's closing during first meetings, the social worker often gives some brief summary of what has happened in the group thus far. He makes sure that the members under-stand the arrangements for meetings in terms of time and place, and explores any concerns or problems about such matters. He engages them in a decision to try out the group a little longer. He elicits from members, or suggests himself, some immediate goals to be worked on in the next session. He creates a bridge to the next meeting. Hopefully, during the meeting, he has provided a fair test of what it will be like to be in the group through the provision of some immediate satisfactions in doing something together, identifying interests and concerns, and making some satisfying decisions of a personal or corporate nature.

The social worker hopes that the experience that each member has had in the first meeting will be such that he will want to continue. Far too often, persons drop out before they have had sufficient experience to make a wise decision for themselves. A number of studies in social casework have reported that difficulties in communication and lack of understanding between the worker and the client are factors related to unplanned discontinuance after the first interview.[20] In a study of adult clients' reactions to initial interviews, it was learned that a client's willingness to commit himself to a relationship with a helping person was related to two goals: the achievement of some progress in the solution of a problem, and a degree of social satisfaction from the relationship with the helping person.[21] In another study, the willingness of adolescents to see a helping person again was positively associated with a perception of the practitioner's desire to help and his ability to understand.[22] It is likely that these same conditions would hold for work with groups, with the added complication of the nature of the members' interactions with each other. Factors in the social environment also influence continuation. When there are readily available alternative resources for service or when there are relevant other persons who do not support the person's quest for professional help, the client is less likely to tolerate any dissatisfaction with the service and hence is more likely to discontinue.[23]

The conclusion is that it is likely that a member of a group will continue beyond the first meeting if he feels that the worker has recognized him, is interested in him, and was able to be helpful; that he felt recognized by other members and had something in common with them; that something happened in the first meeting that was useful to him, in the way of a relationship, an attitude of hopefulness, a concrete experience,

[20] Kogan, "The Short Term Case in a Family Agency, Part I: The Study Plan," *Social Casework*, XXXVIII (1957), 231-38; "Part II: Results of Study," *ibid*. 296-302; and "Part III: Further Results and Conclusions," *ibid*., 366-74; Ripple, "Factors Associated with Continuance in Casework Service," *Social Work*, II (2)· (1957), 87-94; Shyne, "What Research Tells Us about Short-term Cases in Family Agencies," *Social Casework*, XXXVIII (1957), 223-31; and Stark, "Barriers to Client-Worker Communication at Intake," *Social Casework*, XL (1959), 177-83.

[21] Polansky and Kounin, "Clients' Reactions to Initial Interviews: A Field Study," *Human Relations*, IX (1956), 237-64.

[22] Worby, "The Adolescents' Expectations of How a Potentially Helpful Person Will Act," *Smith College Studies*, XXVI (1955), 19-59.

[23] Mayer and Rosenblatt, "The Client's Social Context: Its Effect on Continuance in Treatment," *Social Casework*, XLV (1964), 511-18.

or an idea; and finally, that he has some sense of knowing what to expect next time, that he knows in a very general way what the group is for and what he might hope to get from it. If other significant persons in his milieu support his decision to join the group, his own positive attitudes toward it will be reinforced. He will be ready to engage himself in an active process of exploring and testing out the potential in the group for meeting his needs.

CHAPTER VI

Exploring and Testing the Group

INVOLVEMENT of members in a group does not occur during a brief period of orientation. Following the initial phase in which the members' behavior tends to be passive and conventional, there follows a period characterized by the development of patterns of social interaction. A large majority of writers state that the interaction is characterized by exploring and testing out the situation and by unrest, conflict, and tension. Phrases used for titles of this stage include: relationship negotiation and conflict; ideological conflict and polarization around issues; conflict and tension; testing and struggle for power and control; competition for leadership; leadership and power struggle; increasing tension; hostility, projection, and ambivalence; frustration and conflict; and counter-dependence fight. These phrases give some of the flavor of this crucial stage of group life. But other phrases are used to reflect the other facet of the interaction, that is the formation of a cohesive group. These include exploration of the interpersonal potential in the group, working toward emotional integration, creating exchange, or a period of organization. Through their exploration and testing, there is an increase in the members' perceptions of and response to the group as a whole. As conflicts are resolved, the satisfaction of the members is enhanced and the members are freed to work together on other problems which further the group's transition into the next stage.

In social work groups, the members interact with each other to test out the varied aspects of the group experience in order to determine their status in the group and the value of the group to them. Through communication, the members examine themselves in relation to the group. Each one seeks to understand the varied perceptions that the social worker and the members have of the group; its purpose, structure, norms, and developing relationships. As the members explore each other in relation to the group, their awareness of similarities and differences among them becomes acute, resulting in considerable ambiguity and conflict. Through dynamic decision-making processes, the members modify their original perceptions of the group and develop their own group with which they identify and which becomes an important reference group for them. The major tasks of the worker are to develop understanding of the group as a social system, support the members in their exploration of the group, clarify the various facets of the situation as necessary, engage the members in decision-making processes concerning the group and their use of it, regulate conflict and tension, and strengthen the positive ties among the members.

Guidelines for Diagnostic Evaluation

Crucial to the worker's success in helping members to use this stage of group life toward the achievement of individual and group purposes is his diagnostic acumen. During the planning stage, attention was given to the process of diagnosis and to certain knowledge about individuals requisite to determining group composition, eligibility for service, and placement of a person in a particular group. During the orientation phase, the worker derived additional understanding of the members as he talked with them and observed their behavior in a variety of situations. It is his responsibility to review and organize the facts about each individual and the group's structure and process, ascertain the meaning of the facts, and evaluate the members' problems and potentials as these relate to the group. The task of fact finding and diagnostic evaluation is somewhat different for each group, depending upon the particular purposes of the group, its composition, and its structure. Nevertheless, certain guidelines provide the workers with a frame of reference for viewing the individual in relation to the group and to the external situation.

A basic asumption underlying this diagnostic framework is

that human behavior is the product of the interaction between the individual and his environment. Every individual has an interdependent relationship with others; he is a part of a number of interlocking social systems, and certain dimensions of his behavior can be understood only in terms of the structure and function of these networks of interaction and his status and role in them.[1] The worker's diagnosis is, therefore, related both to individuals and the significant social systems of which they are a part. At both individual and group levels, the worker is concerned with the nature of stresses from internal and external forces, and the capacity and motivation of the system to withstand strain, cope with change, and find new or modified ways of functioning.

Knowledge of the psychosocial development of individuals throughout the life cycle alerts the social worker to what he should observe and check out if he would serve his members well.[2] Assessment of a person's position on a continuum of functioning, ranging from very effective to very ineffective functioning, cues the worker in to both problems and capacities of the person. Such assessment is made against standards of physical, cognitive, emotional, and social functioning deemed to be normal for persons within various stages of the life cycle. Each stage of development has its characteristic opportunities and tasks to be mastered.[3] But these norms need to be differentiated according to such important influences on psychosocial functioning as sex, urban or rural community, school grade or occupation, race, nationality, religion, and economic status. It is necessary to recognize that all phases are overlapping, that each person has his own rate of growth and development, that there are many variations within a normal pattern of functioning, and that the norms themselves are in a process of change. It is necessary to determine variations of effectiveness of functioning in different social systems—whether ineffective functioning in one system is affecting ability to function elsewhere,

[1] Hearn, *Theory Building in Social Work,* p. 36.
[2] For a somewhat different outline for diagnosis, see Vinter, *Readings in Group Work Practice,* pp. 58-66.
[3] Erikson, *Childhood and Society.*

and if successful functioning in one system can be used as a bridge to more effective functioning elsewhere.

Certain facets of personal and social functioning are particularly pertinent to service through groups. The worker assesses a member's attitudes toward himself, as expressed in a sense of self-esteem and realistic identity. He ascertains the member's attitudes toward the social worker, members of the group, and significant people outside the group, both peers and persons in positions of authority. He seeks to learn the member's attitudes toward different values and norms. Another important category is the range and quality of each member's relationships with others; his acceptance by and of other members of the group, his status and role within the group, the subgroups to which he belongs, his social sensitivity and empathy with others, and his patterns of relationships within his family and other groups in the community. In assessing capacities and problems, the social competencies of individuals are considered: the adequacy of verbal and nonverbal communication of feelings and ideas, evidences of positive and negative contributions to the content of the group experience, adequacy of performance of roles outside the group, balance between freedom of expression and self-control, the appropriateness of ego defenses, and adequacy of perception of reality.

The motivation of a member to participate in the group and to work toward improvement of functioning outside of the group is a clue to the use he will make of the group. Of importance are the goals of the member as evidenced by his verbalized expressions, the nature of his participation in group activities, and the consistency between his verbalized desires and his patterns of behavior. His own perception of desirable goals as congruent or incongruent with the perception of the worker, the group, and significant others is important. The nature and sources of the resistance forces that operate against the achievement of goals and the use of the group need to be considered.

In making an evaluation of the person, the practitioner is interested in the onset and duration of the problems, previous efforts to cope with the problems, and the person's perception of the severity of the problems. Of great importance is understanding the inner and outer sources of stress that retard effective functioning and the opportunities and resources that enhance functioning. Many factors may be significant: the impact of physical and intellectual assets and disabilities; the adequacy of the ego's functioning; past social and cultural experiences; adequacy of family life as it supports or throttles the members' efforts toward more effective functioning; and the environmental situation. With reference to the environment, factors to be considered are housing, neighborhood conditions, educational and recreational opportunities, and values and norms of other membership and reference groups as these support or conflict with each other and with those of the individual, as well as influences of the structure, composition, and process of the social work group itself on the person's functioning.

Understanding of the group goes hand in hand with diagnostic evaluation of individuals. Similarities and differences among members of the group in relation to their goals, motivations, capacities, and problems need to be assessed. The impact of the individual on the group, members on each other, and the group on individuals is to be considered.

The social worker makes a diagnosis of the current state of the group at a given time. He asks himself whether it is in a state of dynamic equilibrium, or in a fixed and static state so that it is unable to cope with change. He evaluates the nature and severity of the stresses and strains within the group and in its interaction with other systems. He seeks to understand the amount of congruence among the members, and between himself and the members, concerning goals, values, and expectations. He evaluates whether the composition of the group and its organizational structure are faulty or functional to the system. He ascertains the meaning of the pattern of statuses and roles that emerge out of group interaction, both to the individuals and to the development of the group. He ascertains how open are the channels for communication and the nature of the blocks to more effective communication. He evaluates the nature and effectiveness of the decision-making process and both the personal and impersonal controls within the group. He evaluates the relationship of the group to other systems in terms of conformity to, or deviance from, the norms of the community. He assesses the varied facets of group structure and process in order to discover the common ground among the members that can be built on to develop cohesiveness and plan for his participation in the group and its environment.

Clarification of Purpose

The development of preliminary diagnostic evaluations of individuals and the group generally precedes the development of specific goals and plans for helping the group.[4] But the clarification of goals of individuals as related to the general purpose for the group is one essential ingredient of diagnostic evaluation. As understanding of individuals and the group occurs, goals become more specific. The goal-setting process is closely interrelated with other activities of the worker, as part of a dynamic process of interchange within the group.[5]

Explanation and clarification of purpose is not a task to be completed in one or two sessions. It is rather a continuous process of definition and redefinition of both the long-range and immediate purposes as these become more specific and as they undergo gradual change. In first meetings, group members tend to defend themselves from the social worker and each other in myriad ways, and hence it is not usually until the exploration phase that their capacities and problems become known to themselves and the worker, making possible the development of realistic goals. This can be a tremendous relief to the members. The worker's verbal recognition of the com-

---

[4] Main found that treatment goals and plans for individuals tended to be more fully developed when the worker had made a full diagnosis of the individual, an assessment of the individual's own goals, a diagnostic statement of the group's functioning, and used himself appropriately with the group. See: Main, "An Examination of Selected Aspects of the Beginning Phase in Social Work with Groups," p. 85.

[5] For references on the process of determining goals, see: Coyle, *Group Work with American Youth*, pp. 45-90; Konopka, *Social Group Work*, pp. 79-104; Vinter, *Readings in Group Work Practice*, pp. 8-38.

monality of their situations tends to strengthen motivation to use the group. People hear selectively so that, being preoccupied with other concerns in the orientation stage, they take in only part of the explanation and discussion of purpose. Later they are eager to explore and clarify the purpose for the group and its meaning to them. In one group of thirteen- and fourteen-year-old boys, for example, this event did not occur until the fourth meeting. One member commented that he didn't even know how he happened to be in the group. The worker explained that the boys had been referred by the vice-principal of the school. Another boy said he guessed that meant they were the worst boys in the school. Following a spontaneous discussion of the boys' negative feelings toward the vice-principal, the worker explained that all of them were in trouble in school and that, through the group, it was hoped that they could talk about some of these troubles and do things together that would make it possible for them to get along better. He added that he remembered one of them had said that referral to the group meant that they were the worst boys in the school; this was not so and he did not feel this way about them. Other questions then seemed to pour from the boys: Was the worker connected with the police? Would he "squeal on them?" What would he tell the vice-principal and their parents about them? Would he "kick" them out of the group if they "messed up here, too?" Feeling accepted by the worker, the members were ready to listen to the worker's explanation and to discuss the purpose for the group's organization and their reactions to the group.

Motivation for change is related to the extent to which there are shared perceptions by members of the need for change. As the members recognize that the group's purpose is related to shared needs of members, a sense of some pressure toward change develops. An individual's recognition that his own goals can be met within the group, when these are not in conflict with the general purpose of the group, provides strong motivation toward more involvement in and effective use of the group. Not only does the social worker encourage questions and reactions to the purpose for the group, but he also works toward the recognition and elaboration of objectives of individuals, and discussion of how one member's goals are similar to those of others, or how different goals can be accommodated within the group. He recognizes the varied ways by which members make requests for help. A comment by a member, "I'll drop by your office," or "I want to go home last," or a nonverbal request in the form of lingering after other members leave often signify readiness to share concerns and goals with the worker. The worker usually meets these requests, but often clarifies also how the group may be used for help and how the individual's concern, even if unique, can be related to the concerns of others in some way. He takes advantage of opportunities to relate the concern of one to those of others. Development of mutuality of goals is not necessarily achieved through talk alone. Action-oriented experiences may be used to identify problems and hoped-for outcomes. This is illustrated by a group of boys and girls in which the social worker engaged them in playing doctors in order to identify for them some of their feelings and concerns about being in a hospital, and to relate the problems of one child to those of others and to the purposeful use of the group.

When social work service is expected to continue beyond several sessions, it tends to be focused on a constellation of goals, as contrasted with a single purpose typical of brief service. Clarity about goals on the worker's part and the member's part and, more important, congruence between the two perceptions are achieved only over a period of time, usually several sessions. In the course of the early sessions, goals of individuals as perceived by them tend to become partialized and clarified. Thus, one outcome of the first few sessions is that clients come to perceive with greater clarity what they want to achieve for themselves through the use of group experience.[6]

Through research, both Clemenger and Main learned that

[6] The following research tends to confirm the statements made above: Clemenger, "Congruence between Members and Workers on Selected Behaviors of the Role of the Social Group Worker," pp. 63-72; Schmidt, "Purpose in Casework: A Study of Its Use, Communication, and Perception," pp. 87-138; Main, "An Examination of Selected Aspects of the Beginning Phase in Social Work with Groups"; McGuerty, "Individual Group Members' Expectations of Social Work Help as Compared Through Time in a Delinquent Adolescent Group," pp. 15-57.

the social worker's ability to perceive accurately the member's own goals and to formulate treatment goals and plans varied for different members of the group. Clemenger found that a tendency on the part of a worker to stereotype, in a negative way, certain members of a group was related to his lack of skill in assessment of the member's perception of his role and the group's structure and functioning.[7] Main found that workers tended to develop goals and treatment plans, during the first five meetings, for those members who had roles that were regarded as important to the group, and tended to overlook isolates and other less active members of the group.[8]

These findings point up the difficulty, yet necessity, to focus on each individual as well as the developing group system. The overall purpose for the group, being related to individual goals, cannot be furthered fully unless each person's needs are understood.

There has been some assumption in both work with individuals and groups that a client's right to determine his own goals is limited if the worker has professional goals for individuals and the group and shares these with them. There is some evidence, however, that lack of clarity about the worker's goals introduces confusion into the client's perception of what the worker is trying to do. It was found, indeed, that the presence of explicit aims on the part of workers did not deter clients from developing their own objectives. During the course of interviews, the objectives of each partner are communicated to and perceived by the other.[9] In a group, a worker's purpose for individuals and the group is formulated on the basis of his perceptions of the needs, capacities, and goals of individuals and those of the group as a unit. The relationship and focus of the group experience revolves around a purpose recognized and at least partially accepted by all participants in the process.

[7] Clemenger, "Congruence Between Members and Workers on Selected Behaviors of the Role of the Social Group Worker."

[8] Main, "An Examination of Selected Aspects of the Beginning Phase in Social Work with Groups," p. 86.

[9] Schmidt, "Purpose in Casework: A Study of Its Use, Communication, and Perception," pp. 170-72.

Members of groups can perceive with clarity the way in which
the social worker communicates the purpose of the group to
them. Social workers can develop a high degree of skill in
assessing the members' perceptions of the purpose of the group,
as this has evolved through group interaction.[10]

Membership

From an aggregate of individuals who lack clarity about who
does and who does not belong to the group and who may or
may not be admitted to membership, stabilization of membership gradually occurs. In the case of natural groups, the problem is that of inclusion of the worker, and clarity about whether
or not the total group is to be served by the social worker.
Promptness of arrival and regular attendance is important, yet
it may take some time to stabilize these patterns. When there
is irregularity of attendance, the composition of the group is
different each time, and therefore the group itself is different.
It is the worker's task to recognize with the members the difference that these factors make. Their indivdual and group decisions about these matters are important.

A newcomer needs special help from the worker to become
oriented to the group and its prior history, and to find a place
for himself in the group. In some groups, the older members are
still too preoccupied with their own concerns to reach out to
welcome a new member. Members who did not attend earlier
meetings may have special problems about becoming involved
in a group. In a group of mothers in a child guidance clinic,
Mrs. Breen had missed the first two meetings and came late
to the third meeting. This interrupted the group's discussion,
so the worker introduced Mrs. Breen to the others. She reviewed
how the other members had shared with each other their reasons
for coming to the clinic. Mrs. Breen replied quickly, "But, first
I have to know why you are all here. You look so normal,"
with a sigh of relief. The other members took this lightly. One
said, "Oh, we found out that we all have our troubles but that

---

[10] Clemenger, "Congruence Between Members and Workers on Selected
Behaviors of the Roles of the Social Group Worker."

doesn't mean we're not normal." Another member added that Mrs. Breen looked perfectly normal, too. The worker commented that it was true that because parents and their children needed to come to the clinic did not mean that they were abnormal; indeed, to come was a sign of wanting something better for their families and themselves. The feeling of shame and stigma connected with having a child with social and emotional problems runs deep with some parents and they need realistic assurance. Other clients may have similar feelings; often this is true of the mentally ill or physically handicapped, for example.

Stabilization of membership is partly the product of the resolution of problems of ambivalence and resistance on the part of individuals. Partly, it is the result of greater clarity about the purpose and the agency's policies and procedures concerning membership. A distinction needs to be made between a person's initial attraction to the group and his continuation after the first group meeting. During this stage, the worker's ability to involve an individual with other members of the group, as well as with himself, is of crucial importance. Uncertainty about involvement, if not worked through, often leads to withdrawal from the group.

In all forms of psychosocial helping relationships, there is considerable discontinuance, against the judgment of the practitioner. If a group is to benefit a person, he must remain in it long enough to be influenced by it. Some of the reasons for discontinuance are lack of clarity about purpose and means to be used in working toward it, problems of intimacy, deviation from the group in some important characteristic, complications arising from subgroup formation, early provocateurs, inability to share the practitioner, and inadequate orientation to the situation.[11] Thus, it is crucial that the worker take sufficient time to explore the meaning of membership within the group

[11] See: Wolkon and Tanaka, "Outcome of a Social Rehabilitation Service for Released Psychiatric Patients: A Descriptive Study," *Social Work*, XI (2), (1966), 53-61; Yalom, "A Study of Group Therapy Drop-outs," *Archives of General Psychiatry*, XIV (1966), 393-414; Hartford, "The Social Group Worker and Group Formation."

or perhaps, in some instances, through interviews with individuals outside the group itself. Resistance, a trend of forces against membership in the group, occurs frequently during this phase, due to such factors as fear of other members or fear of being changed. Sensitivity to such fears and helping members to deal with them requires tremendous skill on the part of the worker.

The social worker does many small things to stabilize membership in the group. He helps members to know who are members of the group; he follows up on absences; he works separately with some members around their ambivalence toward continuation at times when this does not seem appropriate for group discussion. He discusses openly some of the members' attitudes toward each other and their effect on group belongingness. In natural groups, he engages the members in a problem-solving process concerning the inclusion and exclusion of members, making clear the agency's values and procedures about this. The worker continues to get facts about and evaluate the impact of individuals on each other and on the development of the group. There may be instances in which, in spite of every appropriate effort, the composition of the group is faulty and some decision about changing the membership should be made, whether through the addition of new members or through the withdrawal of existing members. There are groups in which there is a difficult combination of personalities that cannot be helped to fit together, and others in which membership is too heterogeneous for compatibility. In other instances, there are competing subgroups which cannot develop a working relationship and become a part of the group. In other situations, social forces interfere with the group's formation.[12] Decisions to add or drop members to correct faulty composition need to be based on accurate diagnosis and thoughtful planning rather than on the working of the acceptance-rejection process in an unacknowledged way. Usually the group needs to be informed about the decision.

[12] *Ibid.*

Organizational Structure

As a group develops, its members test out the influence of the organizational structure and may make efforts to restructure the group to meet their needs or demands. The practitioner accepts the need for such testing and engages the members in discussion of alternative ways of organizing the group. Aspects of the group to which members acceded in the first meeting may now appear unsatisfactory. There may be realistic obstacles, which were not anticipated earlier, regarding such matters as suitability of time of meeting or payment of fees. Complaints about such matters should be treated as important, and dealt with according to whether they are indeed serious obstacles to attendance, or whether they are symptoms of resistance to other aspects of the group experience. Within the realities of the agency, members' preferences for type of group organization, time, and place of meetings should be considered. Persons need to be highly motivated to overcome some of these obstacles.

Interpersonal Relations

The social worker is an authority figure, but in a particular role that differs in significant ways from the roles of others in positions of authority, such as parents, teachers, policemen, and employers. Each person comes to the group with some attitudes toward and problems with authority. Often he has had little prior experience with social workers and hence has to learn what to expect from his worker. His expectations tend to be colored by experiences with other authority roles. He may become bewildered and confused when the worker does not live up to his expectations concerning the use of his authority. He uses certain devices to learn about the worker's role and the worker's expectations for him. The testing of the worker may be done in subtle or obvious ways.[13] It may last for a brief period. Or it may be prolonged if the worker has difficulty in understanding and accepting the members, if he is inconsistent

[13] See Heldoorn, "Analysis of Testing in Worker-Group Relationships: Testing of the Worker by Group Members."

in his reactions to them, or if he does not clarify the purpose of the group, its operating procedures, and the roles of worker and member. It will be prolonged also in groups that are composed of persons who have had prior unsatisfactory or disturbed relationships with people, particularly with persons in positions of authority. The tension and ambivalence about the members' relationships with the worker have their roots in both reality and in transference reactions.

It is a natural tendency to be uncertain and ambivalent until trust is established. In most groups, the members seek proof that the worker accepts and cares about them. Being absent may be a test of whether or not the worker missed a member. A request for a special favor from the worker or an offer of a gift to the worker may serve the purpose. Learning how the worker reacts to a range of behavioral patterns may be a means of testing acceptance. The members may behave in ways they feel might be disapproved of by the worker in order to test the limits of his acceptance. A group of adolescent girls, for example, asked permission to comb their hair. When told they could do this, the girls tried out very bizarre hair styles to test the worker's reactions to styles that are forbidden by school authorities. They also tested the worker through the use of foul language. When the worker commented that this did not shock her nor make her angry, the behavior stopped. A similar maneuver by members is to confess to feelings of behavior that might bring disapproval. When a worker is able to clarify with the members the fact that he is not interested in placing blame and that his acceptance is not dependent upon conforming behavior, the testing is reduced or stopped. The fact that a social worker can distinguish between acceptance of a person and of his behavior does not mean that a member can perceive this difference. An illustration is that of a nine-year-old girl who was screaming and running around the room. The worker tried to ask her to join in the activity; later the girl was asked to stop the noise. When she stopped, she accused the worker of not liking her. The worker's reply was that she liked the member but not the noise. The member said, "But I am noise." It takes time for such a person to accept the difference between herself as a person and one of her behavioral patterns.

Distrust of a social worker may be tied to prejudice or fear of discrimination. Differences between a worker and a group on any characteristic that tends to create or maintain social distance are bars to mutual acceptance. This distrust is often aggravated when there are efforts to avoid facing, or a denial of, the difference. Some examples are a young worker with a group of aged clients; a Negro worker with a group of Caucasians or vice versa; or a nonhandicapped worker with a group of orthopedically handicapped patients. Open recognition of such differences may not only break down barriers to communication but also lead to enhancement of a positive sense of identity. One example is a group of seven adolescent Negro girls whose members had been adjudicated as delinquents and assigned to a Caucasian social worker for help with the modification of their socially unacceptable behavior. For the fourth meeting of the group, the social worker had invited the members to a neighborhood center for a swim. She knew that the girls loved to swim, but she also knew that the obvious differences in physical characteristics would be accentuated in this situation. As one Negro girl groaned over the problem of straightening her hair, the worker used this opportunity to acknowledge the outward differences between the races and to comment on how this might make it hard for them to trust her and work with her in the group. This led into a discussion of the girls' feelings about their race and their troubles with white people. This activity, designed with a particular purpose, marked the turning point in the group's relationship with the worker. Simple acknowledgment of differences often leads to further exploration of them. The worker may be able to facilitate the exploration of the meaning of differences and the members' expression of feelings about such differences. This contributes to a reduction in distortions of perception of others occasioned by feelings about such differences. The need to accept difference is accompanied by a need to identify and express whatever will tend to further a sense of unity between worker and members.

There are groups in which one or more members are extremely dependent upon the worker. Such members expect the worker to fulfill the role of a parent figure; they show their feelings through making exaggerated efforts to please him, seeking his exclusive attention, being rivalrous with other members for his love and attention, seeking praise or reproof for their actions, or commenting unrealistically, "You never think I do anything right." They may seek a close relationship with the worker but become frightened by the feelings of intimacy. They may fear they will be hurt. They may try to withdraw from the group or provoke rejection. They may make unreasonable demands on the worker and then feel rejected when these cannot be met.

It is a common occurrence for members of groups to test the use the worker will make of his authority to control and limit them. They may provoke him to exert his authority. They may compare him unfavorably with other leaders of groups they have known, to learn whether or not he will become defensive or retaliate. They often test how far the worker will permit them to break rules, behave in unacceptable ways, or hurt themselves before intervening. In such ways, they seek for proof that the worker will protect them against their own and each other's hostile impulses. Such maneuvers also serve as means to discover the boundaries to the right to self-determination of individuals and the group. In natural groups, particularly, some of the behavior of the members may be with the intent of testing out whether or not the worker will usurp the role of the group's elected officials or of its indigenous leadership. As quickly as possible, the worker makes explicit the safeguards that will be provided for the group to take responsibility for itself as soon as possible. The safeguard for self-responsibility is usually the democratic process itself. The right of the group to make its own decision whenever possible is based on the principles that it is important for people in this society to learn to govern their own lives, and that growth can take place only when the change is felt to be self-initiated rather than authoritatively imposed. Therefore, the more active role of the social worker in early group decisions must not continue indefinitely. He must release responsibility to the members as they become able to assume it.

Recognition of the group's tests of the worker is important in establishing and continuing a purposeful, working relationship with the group. To pass these tests, the worker needs to diagnose accurately the meaning of the words or actions of individuals, and the level of the group's development at a given time. He needs to be sensitive to the underlying feelings and concerns. His response needs to be to the feelings behind the content, not the manifest content of the question, comment, or behavior of the members. He needs to be sufficiently secure to be able to accept expressions of indifference or hostility without retaliation. This is not always easy. One worker drove five miles to keep an appointment with a member of his group, only to find no one home. There was a note for the milkman, but not for him. Later, the member explained, "Oh, the milkman has to know—besides the milk will sour."

An awareness and acceptance of his own feelings toward the testing maneuvers is an important prelude to an ability to understand the members' use of the testing process and to respond in appropriate ways. Due to his preoccupation with problems in relationships, a worker might well remember the need for expression and acceptance of positive feelings. Indeed, he welcomes and encourages instances of affection. He assures the members of his interest in them and of his desire to support them in their efforts.

A major task for the worker is to strengthen relationships among the members. He does not just establish his own relationship with individuals and then focus on group relationships, but rather simultaneously works on both. The members not only test the worker; they also test each other, utilizing essentially similar devices as in testing the worker. The worker perceives and helps the group to identify not only positive ties as they develop, but also to recognize difficulties and tensions. Recognition of differences brings them into the arena of the problem-solving processes of the group. Through exploration of differences, the members may come to understand that negative feelings exist side by side with more comfortable ones. The worker needs to reach out and give to members in appropriate ways. He identifies and expresses to the group his awareness of common interests, concerns, and feelings as these develop in the group. He suggests ways in which members can be helpful to each other. What needs to get worked through in this phase is not only ambivalence toward the worker as a person and in his professional role, but also feelings of competitiveness and rivalry among the members. The effective practitioner recognizes that

. . . working on problems of relationships to each other often precedes working on other problems. With each experience in trying to work it out, the members become increasingly able to recognize and handle conflict. It is how the worker helps them to handle these conflicts which determines whether the group bond will become sufficiently strong so that the members can use the group more intensively for help with other problems.[14]

It is during this phase that the structure of interpersonal relationships emerges in the group. Out of the process of ranking, described in Chapter II, leadership emerges in the group. Certain members exert influence upon the purposes and activities of the group. Leadership changes dynamically, either in person or in kind, with the changing needs and conditions of the group system. In this sense, leadership is not necessarily related to the formal leadership positions specified in the organization of the group. To some extent, all persons in a group can be ranked in terms of the degree of influence they exert upon the activities of the group. All things being equal, leadership tends to be situational; that is, it tends to alter according to changing individual and group needs. Leadership is usually a shared phenomenon, rather than a constant role of a par-

[14] Northen, "Social Group Work: A Tool for Changing the Behavior of Disturbed Acting-out Adolescents," in Social Work with Groups, pp. 60-69.

ticular member. Even so, some members will make more important contributions than will others. There is some correlation between individual factors that cause a person to be able to exert influence, and group factors that acknowledge, recognize, or tolerate that influence. Some members may do little but follow others. Certain indigenous leadership roles may become relatively stable in certain members, or they may be performed by different members of the group at different times, as the members expect certain attitudes and behaviors from them.

The reciprocal roles of initiator and follower are especially puzzling in relation to contagion, a particular type of social interaction that is marked by the spontaneous imitation by other members of a feeling or behavior, initiated by one member of the group, that leads to some uniformity of response. The initiator, without conscious intent, starts the ball rolling, or a pattern of action simply seems to "spread like wildfire." The initiator of the action has a status in the group that makes other members susceptible to his influence. In this particular form of influence, the recipients' behavior has changed to become more like that of the initiator, even though the initiator has not communicated overtly his intent to evoke such a change.[15] The dynamics of the process through which contagion occurs are not clear, but following the initiator seems to release otherwise inhibited behavior. Individuals, when infected, often perform in ways they would ordinarily resist quite easily; an unconscious process of identification seems to be operating in the phenomenon of emotional contagion. The followers, who imitate the behavior patterns, have identified with the initiator of those patterns. The basis for identification may be similar etiological needs or a response to latent emotional tensions. It is difficult for an individual to be immune to an emotional infection when the content or cause is antipathetic to the individual's intellectual convictions. In addition to the status of the initiator, other factors seem to influence contagion: the affinity

[15] Polansky, Lippitt, and Redl, "An Investigation of Behavioral Contagion in Groups," *Human Relations*, III (1950), 319-48.

of the behavior to the group code; the commonality of the basic expressional trend; the size, structure, organization, and content of the group; the cohesiveness of the group; and its social climate.

Some patterns of role behaviors of members contribute to the group's movement toward the achievement of its task, whether that task be in the nature of personal problem solving or decision making for corporate action. Each group varies in the particular ways in which these contributions are made. Many of these patterns of behavior, often referred to as group task roles, that are considered to be common to most groups have been identified.[16] There is often an information or opinion seeker who asks for information pertinent to the situation, and for clarification of suggestions and opinions. An opposite role is the information or opinion giver who offers facts, generalizations, experiences, or opinions pertinent to the experience in which the group is engaged. A particular member may be able to express feelings that stimulate others to do likewise or seek out the feelings of others in the group. Another member may typically initiate or suggest a new activity, issue, or means of working on a problem. An elaborator is one who develops further the feelings expressed, or the suggestions of others, in terms of examples, meanings, or consequences of a proposal. A coordinator reconciles the relationships among various points of view or coordinates the activities of subgroups. A critic forms and expresses judgments of other members, things, or the group functioning; or he may question or evaluate the logic or feasibility of a proposal. Other such patterns of behavior may be specified such as the teacher or demonstrator of activities, the spokesman for the group, the procedural technician, and the recorder.

These patterns of behavior may or may not become stabilized into roles in the sense that the particular members are expected to behave in this way regularly. Variability, not consistency, is

---

[16] See Benne and Sheats, "Functional Roles of Group Members," *Journal of Social Issues*, IV (1948), 41-49; Coyle, *Group Work with American Youth*, pp. 91-132; Bonner, *Group Dynamics*, pp. 373-407.

the rule. Remember that individuals have many different inter-
changes with others each day and it is only when a person,
under certain conditions, seems routinely and consistently to
behave in a way toward others, and others toward him, that a
role relationship can be said to exist.[17] Even within institutional
role arrangements, there is usually much room for flexibility
of response in meeting the expectations.

Other role behaviors are oriented toward the social-emotional
needs of the members of the group. There may be an encour-
ager who praises, gives support, reassurance, or acceptance of
the contributions of others. A harmonizer senses the differences
between members, attempts to reconcile disagreements, and
relieves tension in difficult situations. A member may tend to go
along with the movement of the group, passively accepting and
using the ideas of others, and quietly supporting other members
of the group. In a good-humored way, the tension releaser
jokes, laughs, and shows enthusiasm for the group and its activities. The ego-ideal, who embodies the group's values, becomes
an object for identification.

Perhaps more fascinating and more perplexing, however, are
the varied role behaviors that members assume, or those that
they are forced to adopt, which are related to the satisfaction
of the participant's or the group's particular, often unconscious, needs. In some of these situations, the role is created by
the members of the group toward one of its members. In some
situations, the role is assumed by an individual, predominately
as an expression of his own emotional needs. It is necessary to
keep in mind, however, that there is always some interaction
between individual and group needs in the creation and per-
sistence of such role behaviors.

Among the patterns of role behaviors that develop in a group,
the isolate is one that is of special concern to the social worker.
An isolate is one who lacks bonds with his fellow human beings:
isolation is a relative concept, for it is impossible to be com-

[17] Leary, "The Theory and Measurement Methodology of Interpersonal
Communication," in Bennis, Benne, and Chin, eds., The Planning of Change,
p. 315.

pletely separate from other human beings. All isolates are not the same nor in similar positions in a group. Isolation may be temporary or lasting, forced or voluntary. When one is a stranger to a new group, temporary isolation is normal and to be expected, for there is always some ambivalence about joining a new group and some ambivalence toward newcomers by older members. Some people can develop bonds with others in new situations much more easily and rapidly than can others. Another type of isolation is psychological withdrawal from the group. Instead of finding a place in the group, some members withdraw, perhaps due to lack of interest, often due to fear of the group. Some persons are isolates because the group makes them so by rejecting them. There are many reasons for this. One might be that an isolate deviates so far from the values and norms of the group that members cannot understand him. An example would be that of a boy who was a model and an intellectual in a group of nonconformists and nonachievers in school. Another reason might be that an isolate may attempt to break through the usual initial isolation in ways that are inappropriate. With the rejected isolate, a vicious circle is set up. He usually wants affection; because he fails to receive it, he becomes troubled and hostile; he feels guilty because of his hostility; and he feels a great sense of insecurity about his position in the group. The members do not give him the positive responses he hopes for; in the psychological sense, he does not become a member of the group.

Few members of a group are in such desperate situations as is the rejected isolate, and yet others may not truly belong to the group. Some members are fringers or near isolates who feel some minimum acceptance and desire to belong, yet are not quite of the group. They often, however, need the group so badly that they do not seek to withdraw from it.

The role of scapegoat is often one which causes distress to the person and to the social worker who are confronted with such a phenomenon in a group. The members of the group have found a scapegoat among themselves. They turn their aggressions on to one who becomes a symbol of some tendency or characteristic they dislike in themselves and on whom they project their hostility, thus protecting themselves from recognition of their own unacceptable tendencies and freeing themselves from guilty feelings. When a group has a scapegoat, a relatively stable equilibrium is achieved. The scapegoat performs a valuable function in channeling group tensions and in providing a basis for group solidarity.[18] The fact that a scapegoat is not necessarily present continuously suggests that his presence bears a relation to the sense of security of the members. The scapegoat is usually one from whom others do not fear retaliation. Scapegoats are present in family groups as well as in peer groups. There is always interaction between the needs of the individual and the needs of the group. The primary dynamic in such situations, however, often is the group's need to place a person in such a role.

Still other role behaviors seem to be clearly directed toward meeting the emotional needs of a particular member of a group in a way that is not helpful to the group, either in maintaining itself or in accomplishing its purpose. These patterns of behavior are varied, according to the needs and problems of the members of the group. There is often a clown, who seeks for acceptance by offering himself up to be laughed at. The main purpose of clowning seems to be to relieve one's own tensions by breaking the tension of others and getting their amused attention. There is usually, however, an undercurrent of contempt for oneself and for the other members. The monopolizer is another common dysfunctional role in a group situation. The monopolizer feels compelled to hold the center of the stage, becoming anxious when anyone else is the center of attention. The pattern tends to be self-perpetuating since the more the monopolist talks, the more he senses the irritation of others. This makes him talk all the more. He is afraid to stop for fear that other members will attack him. Unconsciously he hopes that by continuing to talk he can appease or divert the group.[19] Members often react through silence. A person in the role of

[18] Powdermaker and Frank, *Group Psychotherapy*, p. 137.
[19] *Ibid.*, pp. 162-63.

aggressor may be present. He may work in many ways to deflate the status of others, or to attack the group or its efforts toward achievement. Varied other roles of this nature are often referred to by such labels as Cinderella, gossip, or bully.

What the social worker does in supporting or influencing change in roles depends upon his diagnostic evaluation of the meaning of the role to the individual and to the group. Generally, he promotes flexibility in role structure so that members may experience varied ways of contributing to the group and testing out their relationship capacities. His supportive comments and actions are directed toward encouraging members to try out new ways of communicating more effectively with others or toward recognizing and modifying inappropriate patterns of behavior. Usually his activities are directed toward both the person in the role and the group. The development of basic trust, through acceptance and empathy, is essential.

With a fearful isolate, great gentleness is required in efforts to involve him with the group. Since behavioral patterns often become stable quite early and other members tend to respond in stereotyped ways, however, efforts need to be made to secure early involvement. Discovering some interest of the isolate, recognizing his feelings, guiding the discussion or action-oriented experience so that success is probable, and avoiding questions that tend to elicit defensiveness are examples of techniques to be tried. Sometimes a period of focus on a simple activity that provides for freedom of expression and that stimulates undemanding relationships with others is useful. Preparation of refreshments, hand arts, and noncompetitive games are other examples.

Involvement of an isolate in role playing may be the key that unlocks spontaneity and brings him into participation with others. An illustration is a group of boys and girls in a child guidance center. For the first two sessions, one eight-year-old boy, Jimmy, did not talk or enter into the activities of the group, in spite of the worker's efforts to help him to do so. During the third session, the children were playing school. Tommy had mentioned that he was in a sight-saving class and the others wondered what that was like. The children were playing school, with Tommy as the teacher. He wanted to have Jimmy play, for Jimmy was the only other child who wore glasses. The worker suggested that Tommy make Jimmy a pupil, even though he stayed across the room. In the role of teacher, Tommy asked Jimmy a question. When Jimmy did not answer, the other children became impatient. One boy said that Jimmy was "dumb." All eyes turned toward Jimmy. The worker took Jimmy by the hand and brought him into the group. All the children watched, quietly. Tommy resumed the class. He soon came around again to Jimmy, who looked down at the floor; Kenny called him "dumb" again. The children looked at Jimmy and in the silence that followed this, Jimmy made the first break in his withdrawal. He began to cry. The worker put his arm around Jimmy, comforted him, and told him that he was coming here to get help with the things that made him cry. The worker asked the other children if they could take time out from playing school to talk with Jimmy. In the following discussion of the things that hurt them, Jimmy was able to stay with the group.[20]

When the developing role behavior is destructive to the group as well as the individual, as in the case of a monopolizer, early efforts of the worker may be directed toward encouraging spread of participation among all of the members through stating this pattern as an expectation, requesting that members take turns, giving nonverbal encouragement to others to enter the discussion or activity, or using comments that summarize so as to encourage others to enter into the conversation. Often the worker needs to set limits on the monopolizer through requests to give others a chance to participate or to wait until others have expressed themselves. If the pattern becomes established, the worker may then use varied means to clarify the nature of the problem, its meaning to the person and the group, what members do to perpetuate the situation, and how they might work it out together. With a scapegoat, the worker uses himself

---

[20] Taken from Ganter, "The Group Worker in the Child Guidance Center," in Trecker, ed., *Group Work in the Psychiatric Setting*, pp. 33-34.

in similar ways, with emphasis on clarification of the conditions that lead to scapegoating, analysis of the stresses in the group that result in this projection of hostilities onto a particular member, and what the scapegoat does to provoke it. Often, the more supportive acts are used first, for the members may not yet be ready to work toward clarification of the meaning of such behavior.

Values and Norms

Following the initial introduction to the policies and rules of the agency, there is a longer phase in which certain values and norms of the group or the agency which differ from an individual's own values and norms are tested. Providing that the worker has maintained the group tension within manageable limits, a set of norms develops that defines the way conflict will be expressed, managed, and resolved. There may be conflict over agency regulations concerning limits on behavior, payment of fees, use of facilities, or ways of solving interpersonal feuds. Some of the conflict in the group during this period is over conformity. There is pressure on each member to behave according to the norms; first, those imposed by the agency and the worker, and then those that develop in the group. Each member deviates to some extent from the norms of the group. These patterns of behavior are determined by the interaction of personality and cultural factors. When a group code develops, it takes over, to some extent, the internalization of standards of behavior. Members test and come to trust that they can express their feelings and bring problems into the group without suffering rejection, punishment, or other severe consequences. In a group of adolescent girls in a maternity home, the members' expression of trust in the worker occurred when they confessed that some of them had violated a rule. The worker listened and then responded in a nonpunitive manner, which led to discussion of the rules and consensus concerning the desirability of this particular rule as necessary for the protection of the girls themselves. The agency rule became a group norm.

Certain acts of the worker are directed toward helping the group itself to recognize norms as these become evident. The worker may do this in a variety of ways: by calling the members' attention to the fact that they are doing things in a certain way, that they now seem to have agreed upon a rule, for example, about confidentiality. He may raise questions that help the members to decide upon norms for the group. Such simple questions as "Do we want to cut off discussions like that?" and "Did you intend to suggest that we do it this way?" help to clarify norms of behavior. Gradual clarification of differences in expectations for this group from other groups to which members belong is helpful. This is often crucial. Adaptation requires that a person be able to distinguish the norms that are suitable in one situation from those of other settings. There may often be confusion concerning conflicting expectations. A common example is that of a norm in a social work group to express angry feelings and the expectation that, in school or at work, these be suppressed. Difficulties are created when the members fail to distinguish between what is appropriate behavior in the group and what is appropriate in other situations.

Development of norms about the distribution of power and control in the group is essential to the group's further development. When desirable, the worker tries to influence the modification of agency rules that affect the group adversely. Hartford found that overly restrictive agency regulations often contributed to the failure of a group to form.[21] The worker permits the testing of rules and policies, recognizing that it is right that the members do this, but also maintaining appropriate limits on behavior. He needs to be nonpunitive in limits and consistent in his actions. He accepts the feelings and the person, but not the behavior that is destructive to the person or to others. He initiates and encourages discussion about the amount and nature of control necessary in the group, when there are indications of misunderstanding about this matter. Through the interaction of members with each other, influenced by certain

[21] Hartford, "The Social Group Worker and Group Formation."

actions on the part of the worker, norms about control develop in the group.

The Content of the Group Experience

Essentially, discussion and action-oriented experiences have as their purpose the facilitation of the exploration of the potential of the group as a context and means for the achievement of individual and group goals.

Discussions among members become less scattered and more focused on particular situations and decisions as the members gain experience in participating together. The topics for discussion vary with each group situation but, as indicated previously, there are some matters that are common to almost all groups such as the clarification of purpose and the selection of specific goals, the structure of the group and its operating procedures, the influence of the agency's structure and policies on the group, and decision making concerning the activities of the group. Opportunities for participation are provided that have potential for testing and strengthening relationships, identifying common interests and concerns, and coping with individual and group problems.

Varied topics for discussion are introduced during the earlier phase, but fuller exploration usually occurs during this stage. As the worker looks underneath the manifest content, he recognizes that certain themes tend to occur and recur in many groups but in specific ways related to needs of individuals and the common characteristics of the group. Some attention is often focused on the attitudes of members as these enhance or detract from effective functioning.

The attitudes toward the self with which the worker deals most frequently are closely interrelated ones of identity and adequacy or self-esteem. Erikson has pointed out that "a common feeling of having a personal identity is based on two simultaneous observations: the immediate perception of one's self sameness and continuity in time; and simultaneous perception of the fact that others recognize one's sameness and continuity." [22] This sense of identity involves knowledge about and acceptance of oneself. As it develops through the life cycle, it incorporates more broadly and fully many aspects that define who a person is, what he can do, and what he will become. So often, members of social work groups feel stigmatized by the nature of their illnesses or handicapping conditions; for example, mental illness, mental retardation, epilepsy, delinquency, or even the "bad mother" or "bad child" label. Feelings that people have about their sociocultural backgrounds often interfere with the development of a positive self-image. This was brought out in work with a group of seven-year-old girls during the course of a game in which the members were parading in front of a mirror and one child said, "Look, how much more black I am than you; guess I'm badder." A sense of adequacy is closely related to, indeed may be a part of, identity. To feel adequate, persons need to master the demands placed on them in their varied roles at home, school, work, church, and play. Certain events threaten the sense of adequacy of even the healthy ego. Report cards, civil service examinations, work evaluations, or comparisons of development between children arouse fears of failure and worries about adequacy. These events force the person to find out how his performance stands in relation to his own expectations and in relation to others. Sexual adequacy is a recurrent theme in groups of adolescents, related to the underlying theme of sexual identity. For the aged person, forced retirement and loss of relatives and friends through death are threats to his identity and sense of adequacy. Conflicts in identity also often come to the fore with clarity as members come to feel some success in their achievements. One typical example is the delinquent adolescent's struggle as he realizes that in order to achieve certain goals he needs to give up his identification with his gang. Whether members approach an experience with competence and hope or a devastating sense

[22] Erikson, "Identity and the Life Cycle: Selected Papers," *Psychological Issues*. For a paper on identity specifically related to social work practice, see Solomon, "Conceptualization of Identity in Social Work Practice," *Social Service Review*, XLI (1967), 1-9.

of inadequacy with its accompanying hopelessness, is of deep concern to the social worker.

Attitudes toward others—members of the group, other peers, family members, the social worker, and other persons in positions of authority—are brought into the group situation. These are closely intertwined with a sense of identity and self-esteem. Prejudice, fears, hostilities, and acceptance or rejection of others are expressed directly or indirectly and focused on in the group. During this phase, there is a great deal of expression of feelings about other people, often in the form of complaints about them or deep feelings of being misunderstood or rejected by others.

Some experiences provide a means for the free communication of feelings, desires, and ideas; some involve nonverbal communication, a primary means of communication as contrasted with the more abstract medium of language. In groups of children, play tends to predominate. In play, for example, the child expresses feelings and perceptions about his world which he cannot verbalize. Through exploration with many materials, the young child begins to learn cognitive skills in understanding colors, shapes, textures, sounds, and spatial relations, and to identify many common actions. Later, he learns to label what he has experienced. The child draws upon his prior experiences and repeats those that have made an impression upon him. As he relives experiences in play, he expresses anger, hate, love, joy, and other emotions. Not only does the unpleasant character of the experience not prevent the child from using it as a game, but he often chooses to play out the unpleasant experience. By so doing, he attempts to master the problematic situation. The content of a child's play indicates with what basic problems he is coming to terms and it gives clues as to what disturbs him. But, at least as important, are the patterns that occur in play. Some of these, for example, are rigidity or functional adaptation, evidence of body image and identity, stereotyping or creativity, accommodation to cultural norms, balance of emotional attachment to things or to people, activity or passivity, and realistic use of objects as contrasted with objects used in a highly affectively charged way. Older children and adults express their feelings and needs through food, more structured games, and cultural interests such as music, painting, and dramatics.

In groups of older children and adults, numerous simple devices may be used with the group to open up or extend verbalization. The display of a thing that is a symbol of unexpressed interest or concern may open up discussion. Examples are books or magazine articles on the discipline of children for use in a parent education group; or on boy-girl relations or sex for use with adolescents; a family of dolls or a dollhouse for use with children; and a movie, a painting, or a drawing that portrays people in situations somewhat similar to those of the members. Some people find it much easier to talk into a microphone, a toy telephone, or through puppets, for example, than directly to the worker and other members of the group. The "I'm only pretending" quality to such devices makes them useful when members are not yet ready to face directly their feelings, thoughts, and situations. Such experimentation with props often leads to direct verbal expression. The quality of pretending is also present in role playing, an activity in which a group observes some of its members enact roles in a skit for the purposes of analyzing some real-life situation in which the group is interested. The quality of spontaneity in role playing makes it possible for members to communicate more freely their feelings and thoughts to others. It provides an opportunity to practice what a person might do when faced with realistic, stressful situations outside the group.

The development of a group into a cohesive unit is fostered when members develop meaningful relationships with each other, through sharing experiences. Each experience provides a somewhat different kind of opportunity and challenge in relating to other members of the group. By providing fresh experiences common to the members but differentiating this group from other groups, identification with the group is enhanced. Some people share more fully of themselves when they engage in activity that is more varied than "just talk"; hence their identification with each other is apt to be enhanced. The value of opportunities to do as contrasted with talking only is illustrated by experiences with patients:

Our experience suggests that the severely demoralized, defensive and resentfully dependent chronic patients tend to use free-interaction group therapy to bolster their pathological defenses. A structured, activity-oriented group setting is less threatening, offers the patients more support and provides an atmosphere which evokes more healthy trends in functioning.[23]

With certain other groups, too, properly selected experiences facilitate the development of relatedness, and are an aid in sustaining and deepening them. Experiences, in which each member participates, tend to equalize participation. They make for group-centeredness by stimulating interaction around a current shared experience. Activity rituals, no matter how simple, tend to differentiate the culture of the group from that of other associations.

Some social workers avoid the use of activities, because of faulty notions that their use requires that they have special skills in a host of cultural, recreational, and social activities. It can be assumed that any social worker has had varied experiences in group living and in social and cultural activities. It is out of these life experiences, with special efforts perhaps to recall the many things one has done in the past, that ideas for activities come. The worker can capitalize on his own interests and skills, providing that through the use of these he can meet the needs of the group. In some groups, members can help with activities or outside resources can be used. The most simple everyday tasks, too, may be the most valuable for the group and these are readily learned by workers.

In using an activity, a worker makes an assessment of the usefulness of a particular activity in furthering the group's purpose.[24] It seems essential that the following questions be considered:

[23] Wheat, Slaughter, and Frank, "Rehabilitation of Chronically Ill Psychiatric Patients," unpublished paper, undated.
[24] For a somewhat different outline for the analysis of activities, see Vinter, Readings in Group Work Practice.

1. Relationship and participation demands. Can the activity be done alone, in subgroups, by the entire group? What intensity of relationships is required by the activity? Does the activity suggest cooperation or competition, sharing, blocking, asserting, demanding, or attacking behaviors? How much closeness and intimacy are required? Does the activity foster withdrawal from relationships or movement toward others at an appropriate pace?

2. Performance skills that are required. What does the experience require in terms of physical movement, coordination, cognitive ability, verbalization, and obedience to rules?

3. Impact on behavioral expression. Does the nature of the activity itself tend to free, inhibit, or control impulses? Does it free or bind? What are the extent and forms of control exercised over the participants—those that are personalized as contrasted with those that are depersonalized in nature coming from rules or the nature of the material that is being worked with? What are the freedoms and limits in the activity? What are the implicit and explicit rewards for participating successfully in the activity? How abundant or scarce are they? How are they distributed?

4. Decision making. How much opportunity for personal choice and group decision making is inherent in the activity? Who makes the choices and how widespread are opportunities for individual choice and participation in decision making?

5. Cultural attitude. What cultural attitudes and values are perceived as being connected to the activity? What are the anticipated feeling responses, related to cultural backgrounds, to participation in a given activity? How is the activity adaptive to the ethnic, racial, or social class backgrounds of members and the surrounding culture?

The social worker takes responsibility for working with the group to select and use experiences. His contribution may be one of introducing, supporting, modifying, or enriching the experience that a group is engaged in at a given time. The worker uses all he knows about the members and their situations in his use of social experiences. Action-oriented experiences are purposeful. They are means by which the group moves toward its specific goals for individuals and the group as a unit within the context of the agency and the wider socio-cultural milieu. Thus, clarity of goals for the use of a particular experience is essential. The worker needs to clarify the nature of the hoped for outcome and what from this experience might be carried over to other experiences both within and outside of the group. Any given activity may be modified so that it can be used in relation to the needs and capacities of the members and the readiness of the group at a given time. Many different experiences may be used to achieve the same objective. Among the appropriate ones, members' interests, the worker's preference and competence, and the availability of materials and facilities may guide the selection and particular use of experience. During this stage of the group's life, activities need to be selected that lead to successful accomplishment, promote interaction, require little self-control, allow for individual differences, permit the worker to be free to give recognition and acceptance to members, and provide for expression of feelings in ways that do not jeopardize the members' sense of security.

The social worker needs to learn to understand the meaning of play, gestures, and other actions just as he needs to understand the verbal language of the persons he serves. Words and actions are seldom separated. Many activities make use of words, but within a framework of playing, rehearsing, or learning something new, one step removed from the demands and consequences of performance in the world outside the group. It must be remembered that the development of facility with language remains an important area of ego adequacy. It is easy for a social worker and a group to come to rely on activities as a means of avoiding verbal sharing of feelings, problems, and plans, in which cases activities serve as a defense against intimacy of relationships. Clarity of understanding by the worker is equally important, whether the medium of communication is verbal, nonverbal, or a combination of both. The two tools of conversation and action-oriented experiences are closely interrelated. The essential question for the worker is when and under what conditions can discussion or an action experience contribute to the achievement of the goals of the individuals who comprise the group or to the development of the group as a whole.

In finding a focus for discussion or other activity, the social worker's intent is to involve the members in a process that utilizes both emotion and cognition, considers differences and similarities in feelings and thoughts among the members, and relates means to ends.

In many situations, the practitioner needs to work toward improved communication with individuals and among the members of the group. All events which hinder communication lead to disturbance in the system. When efforts to communicate become too frustrating, a person protects himself through such means as withdrawal, silence, forgetting, and verbosity. Discomfort in the situation may make it difficult for a member to tell others what he feels, thinks, or desires. Physical handicaps such as defects in speech, sight, and hearing make communication difficult. There may be differences in language, particularly the choice and nuances of words or differences in the degrees of verbal facility among members. The channels of communication may develop in such a way that some members seem to be excluded from participation or so that some members seem to dominate the discussions. Differences in norms governing the nature and spread of communication may create problems. A person relates to others according to the implied assumption that the others share his views of reality. Lack of sufficient commonage of experience among the members may interfere with the achievement of common meaning and mutual understanding. To the extent that norms are not shared and there is little common experience, meaningful communication is difficult. The worker's activity is focused on identifying blocks to communication and implementing ways to overcome them, to the extent possible in the light of members' problems and capacities.

In work with disturbed children, discussion is difficult for them because they lack the requisite skills, and are well defended against looking at their own involvement in situations.[25] They tend to react to any discussion of their part in situations as an attack on them. They use denial, conscious lying, distortion, and projection when they attempt to discuss what happened. The members gradually take a natural step, substituting angry verbal outbursts for physical action. It is only later that talking becomes a tool for problem solving.

The social worker has available to him many procedures for improving communication among the members. The provision of information necessary to the group's progress in discussion, or of interesting social experiences which expand the area of common knowledge and experience, is very useful. Often, in a conflict situation, the worker is helpful if he notes the power of words to help or to hurt. He may need to request that the members develop willingness and ability to listen to and hear each other accurately. He may comment upon garbled expressions of feelings and opinions, using understandable language. He may work with members toward the development of a commonly understood vocabulary and gestures. He may review with the group its troubles and successes in communication. He needs to encourage decision making, clarify relevant issues, and indicate realistic obstacles.

The social worker supports the ventilation of feelings and concerns unless this action seems to be counterindicated. Communication of feelings is often indirect in this stage. An example is of a natural group in which members talked to the worker through each other. In complaining about each other, the real target of the communication was the worker. The members of this group also asked questions such as: "Why does teacher always meddle with us?" referring to their feelings toward the worker. The worker can often assess the real target of the communication through the tone of voice used, the direction of eye movements, or the accompanying gestures. Likewise, members may talk with each other indirectly. As mentioned earlier, the content of discussion often takes the form of complaints about

[25] Churchill, "Part-time Group Work Practice in Nontreatment Institutions," in Maier, ed., *Group Work as Part of Residential Treatment*, p. 106.

things or other people, often a projection away from the self. Complaining is often a way that persons test out how freely they can talk about the things that concern them deeply. This point may be illustrated by new patients in a mental hospital who complained about the physical arrangements and facilities as a mask for their deep feelings of not being welcomed and cared for by the staff. The worker was supportive of the expression of complaints, but then moved the patients toward acknowledgment of their feelings. To continue to talk about physical inconveniences about which nothing could be done but not the feelings that mattered to them was a pattern of behavior of these women. The worker, by communicating his perceptions of the feelings, could test the readiness of the members to face their feelings more directly. The worker's attitude that it was desirable to explore feelings that are troublesome gave the members sanction to talk about themselves as an early step toward clarification of the meanings attached to these feelings.

As the members test out each other's feelings, they become aware of the similarities among them. People often express publicly attitudes that are not their own because they feel that their private attitudes are unique and different.[26] It was noted earlier in Chapter II that there is a tendency to act in ways that are consistent with the norms of the group. Through their focus on communication of honest feeling, the members' public attitudes become more consistent with their private ones. They realize that they are not alone, that certain attitudes are shared which makes it possible for them to work toward evaluating them and either confirming or modifying them.

Essentially, discussion and action-oriented experiences have as their purpose the facilitation of the exploration of the group. Within the members' abilities to tolerate it, the worker works toward more expression of conflicted feelings and toward differences in points of view and attitudes toward things and people. The worker is active in eliciting from members their

[26] Blum, "The A-ha Response as a Therapeutic Goal," in Maier, ed., *ibid.*, pp. 47-56.

proposals for alternative ways of dealing with issues and for resolving conflicts. Early detection of uncertainty and stress makes it possible for the worker to help the members to deal with differences among them before conflict occurs. The worker's comments and questions may be directed toward the partialization of an issue, so that the immediate conflict that requires a solution is manageable. Rather than taking sides, the worker supports all factions by giving concrete assistance in finding means to explore and resolve the differences. If he can perceive some rationale for the various views expressed, he is more likely to be able to help each side to communicate with each other with a view toward mutual understanding. This often leads from accusatory comments such as "But you did say that" to "What was it you meant to say?" The worker needs to step in to regulate conflict when it is too threatening to one or more members of the group, or when it threatens the very continuance of the group itself. He may do this through placing a direct limit on a member or the group. He may point out the self-defeating aspects of behavior. Without being punitive, he may confront the members involved with the unacceptability of the behavior and the need to stop it. Attention to supporting the group in its efforts to deal with conflict and to accrediting each bit of progress in working through the testing of relationships and use of the group is essential. Continuous evaluation of the members' capacity to handle conflict and acting on the basis of this evaluation are not easy, but there really are no easy answers.

While recognizing with the members some of their inner conflicts and interpersonal conflict, the worker guides discussion and other activity toward some strong common interests or concerns. He emphasizes similarities and positives as well as differences and negatives. He has a responsibility to provide new opportunities for participating in content that has the potential for testing and strengthening relationships, identifying common interests, concerns, and capacities; or affirming preferences and making decisions. The use of action-oriented experiences, as well as discussion, will have much merit with some groups. For members to explore capacities and relationships, test out authority of worker and agency, and identify common and divergent norms, there must be a real situation in which the persons can be truly ego-involved and act out the meaning of these objectives. The action is upon a stage where the chips are not down, where a mistake can be retrieved, where amends can be made.

Exploration of the external situation and the feelings and concerns of the members usually result in enhanced readiness to reconsider goals with greater specificity and to make decisions concerning the content of the group experience. Differences among members in needs to defend themselves from facing their problems, or in uncertainty about the means through which the group can be helpful, may lead to conflict in the group. Some members will be ready to move into the use of the group for focused problem solving earlier than will others. This is illustrated in the third meeting of a group of adult men in a hospital in which, for the first time, there was expression of deep feeling by Mr. Brantner and Mr. Partens concerning their inability to return to full-time employment due to physical handicaps. Mr. Boysen and Mr. Santz, with more optimistic prognoses for work, empathized with them. Another severely handicapped patient, Mr. Miner, became restless and then wise-cracked, "Who wants to work anyway—only fools, not me." "Yeah, a life of Riley's what I want," quipped Mr. Derry. The four men who had been discussing seriously what it means to a man to be unable to work, looked taken aback. Mr. Brantner, who had emerged as a leader in this group, told Mr. Miner and Mr. Derry to: "Cut out the wisecracks. You know this is no joke," but the two men continued their behavior. The worker commented that perhaps it was hard to talk about what their lives might be like when they leave the hospital, most members seemed ready to do this: could the others give them a chance? The facetious remarks stopped, but it took some time before Mr. Miner and Mr. Derry were able to verbalize some of their fears and problems about illness and return to families and communities. The group was then able to make a decision about a few problems that seemed most pressing to all of them and to use the group for working on these concerns. This meeting marked a transition for this group into the next stage.

Many times in the course of a group session, the social worker appears to be doing nothing, but this inactivity is a means of communicating something, often support of the ongoing activity of the group. The worker maintains the inactive behavior consciously and for a purpose. Maintaining silence is often one means through which the worker can enhance self-direction and the progress of the group's discussion or other activity. Silence may convey disinterest or it may convey support of and confidence in the group's progress. Silences may indicate that there is a shared feeling or, simply, that the members are reflecting on their feelings and thoughts before verbalizing them. If prolonged, silences may be symptoms of resistance that require the worker's verbal participation. Certainly, the worker controls his own need to speak and remains silent except when he has a purposeful contribution to make to the group, based upon his evaluation of the situation. Knowing when to act and when to remain silent is one of the important skills of the social worker in a group situation.

The purposeful use of silence requires deep understanding of individual behavior, group development, and the range of alternatives available to the worker. "The art of creative listening lies in the ability to remain receptively silent," according to Slavson.[27] Even when silent, the practitioner must be able to convey, through nonverbal messages, that he is interested in and supportive of the group's activities. Phillips refers to this quality as containment, a conscious deliberateness, allowing the members to interact without his manifest participation. It is not to be equated with passivity, but rather it is a purposeful use of restraint that supports the members' own efforts. It reflects faith in the capacity of the members to give to each other. Skill is possessed by a worker when he "is able with sureness to

[27] Slavson, *A Textbook in Analytic Group Psychotherapy,* p. 420.

select when he will be active and when, in silence, he will let the group carry the process." [28]

In whatever discussion or action-oriented experience the group is engaged, the worker's intent is to develop working relationships and productive participation. A number of professional activities are particularly important. One is the provision of support to individuals, subgroups, or group as a whole, combined with limitations on behavior that is harmful to self or the group. A major responsibility is a focus on the clarification of the agency's purpose, policies, and operating procedures; the social worker's role with the group; and the nature of the means through which objectives hopefully will be achieved. There is some identification of problems in intragroup communication as well as consistent efforts to seek fuller and deeper understanding of individuals and the group. Some of the worker's efforts are directed toward the identification, elaboration, and initial working with feelings, behavior, and situations that are troublesome to the members. The worker initiates or he supports discussion or action-oriented experiences initiated by the members themselves that help the group to test out and master certain situations, primarily those related to the development of the group itself. He works with the members to identify and resolve conflict about their involvement in the group, in relationships with himself and with each other, and in regard to the norms that govern individual behavior and group development.

Conferences between the worker and individual members are an integral part of the social worker's practice with groups. The worker's use of himself in interaction with the group is, in one sense, the essence of social work practice with groups. Yet the worker is extremely limited if he views this as the only means of treatment. He often works directly, on a one-to-one basis, with some members of the group.

There are brief interviews between the worker and a member within the life space of the group, often referred to as life space

[28] Phillips, *Essentials of Social Group Work Skill*, p. 148.

or marginal interviews.[29] Such interviews are held immediately prior to, following, or even during a group session. The member may seek out the worker for a particular reason. The conference may be initiated by the worker, usually when his particular concern about a member is not apt to be brought into the orbit of the group session itself. There are times when conflict between a member and other members of the group becomes so intense and the group is so unready to handle it that individual conferences may be necessary. In one group in a community center, for example, Janice was critical of the staff in the game room; she perceived them as "picking on her," disliking her, and blaming her for things that were not her fault. One of the members, Kathy, criticized Janice for not being able to say anything good about anybody, and other members agreed with Kathy. Janice angrily turned her chair to the wall, sat there for awhile, and then left the room, slamming the door behind her. The worker acknowledged with the remaining members some of their feelings. She suggested then that the group continue with its planning while she went to see if Janice was still in the building so she could talk with her and help her to return to the group. In a brief conference, the worker commented to Janice that she knew she was troubled about a number of things which seemed to make it hard for her to get along in the group. After some discussion, Janice responded to the worker's suggestion that she return to the group and the worker would support her in trying to work things out there. This was done.

The important skill is to use such brief interviews to meet the immediate needs of the individual, yet not detract from the group itself as the primary means of service. A great deal of diagnostic acumen is necessary to decide wisely whether to deal with the concern privately with the member or to encourage the person to bring his concern into the group. The skilled worker can often find ways to relate what seems like a unique problem

[29] Redl, "Strategy and Technique of the Life Space Interview," *American Journal of Orthopsychiatry*, XXIX (1959), 1-18.

to the concerns of the group, through his search for likeness in seemingly unlike situations.

Interviews with individual members of the group, or other persons in their behalf, often take place in privacy, usually by appointment. There are several purposes for which such interviews are used. One purpose is to orient and prepare new members for making a satisfactory initial entry into the group. Another purpose is to help a member to cope more effectively with a pressing problem that seems unsuitable for discussion within the group at a particular time, due either to the situation in the group or to the fact that, at the time, the person cannot bear to express feelings and thoughts or to present a problem to the group. A conference may enable the person to bring it into the group or indicate that individual treatment is necessary. In groups in which certain responsibilities have been assigned to officers or chairmen of committees, a conference may be used to aid such persons to fulfill their responsibilities as effectively as possible. Relatives or other relevant persons in the community may be interviewed to secure or enhance their support of the member's use of the group. Another common purpose of the interview is to refer a member to another service in the community for forms of assistance that cannot be provided through the group, or to provide special support to a member as he gets connected with a special service.

The worker constantly needs to remind himself that a group does not exist in a vacuum; that it is part of a larger social system which encompasses the agency, the families of the members, and the community. The means for achieving improved psychosocial functioning are indeed partly with the individuals and the group interaction, whenever a determination has been made to use the group for purposes of treatment. But, working with the environment is crucial also, as the environment supports or impedes the group's efforts. This is especially important in this phase of the group's development. Concrete needs of members as seen by them must often be met if the group experience is to be helpful. Often, it is desirable that relatives be involved in appropriate ways. A family centered approach is preferable, wherever possible in terms of agency function. Conferences with other personnel, such as teachers or nurses, are usually focused on members who are having difficulty. The content may be an exchange of information, joint planning for integrated service to the person, attempts to modify the behavior of others toward the client, or reports on the client's progress with the hope that this will start a chain reaction in the client's favor. A social worker serves as a bridge between a member, his family, and the community. He may refer members to other resources; then he may participate with other institutions that are serving the family to insure that all efforts in behalf of the family are meshed for its benefit. He may make use of his observations of unmet needs in calling these to the attention of appropriate social planning and action bodies.

A Group Forms

If all has gone well, a social worker has a group with the characteristics that make it a potent force in the lives of its members. The members have delineated goals for themselves that are in harmony with the group purposes. They have come to accept each other sufficiently to want to continue together. They have given up some of their earlier self-centered attitudes and behavior, or overdependency on the worker, and moved into a relationship of interdependency. They have developed some understanding and acceptance of the worker's role in relation to their roles in the group. They have accepted a norm of experimentation and flexibility and of responsibility for both supporting each other and stimulating each other toward the achievement of individual and group goals. They have come to some acceptance of a set of norms through which necessary control is effectuated within a general climate of acceptance of difference.

Essentially, a major outcome of the process of exploration and testing out is that there is achieved considerable congruence between each member's perception of the group and the worker's perception of it. Members of groups usually have come to perceive quite clearly the activities of the worker in contributing to the members and the group as a whole. The diagnostic skill of the worker has become translated into accurate judgments about the perceptions that members have of the nature of the functioning of the group and the worker's role in it. With this common understanding of both purpose and means toward its achievement, the members use the group for more intensive work on their problems in psychosocial functioning.

CHAPTER VII

The Group As a Problem-Solving Medium

THERE IS general recognition of two major emphases in this stage of group development; the emergence of a cohesive group in which members are interdependent on each other, and the use of the group as a vehicle for work or working through of problems. The phrases used by various authors to depict the essence of the group are varied and reflect particular interests. The theme of interdependence has been expressed in such phrases as mutual interaction, interdependence among members, a therapeutic attitude of mutuality, mutual identification, and engagement in cooperative activity. The notion of an integrated cohesive group is conveyed by such expressions as: a cohesive, integrated, identified group; a total group orientation to replace the earlier polarized individual and subgroup operation; increased awareness and acceptance of the group; consciousness of group dynamics and group process problems; the group as an effective, integrative, and creative social instrument; cohesiveness; development of a strong sense of group feeling; a group-directed phase; ingroup consciousness; and consolidation. There is emphasis on work, and exchange of methods of dealing with emotions and problems. There is some emphasis, too, on the tendency of a group to relate to other groups and the broader community in a more natural and comfortable manner.

A group, in which members accept and are interdependent on others, has emerged. This stage is characterized by the interdependence of the members in sustained work on problems in personal and social functioning which are related to the goals of the members. The patterns within the group, always dynamically changing, have achieved some stability. As most members find an accepted place in the group, they experience feelings of security and freedom. The group is a cohesive one. It has become a means for both supporting and stimulating its members toward the achievement of individual and group goals. A major characteristic of the group is acceptance and utilization of differences for collaborative work on problem-solving activities. The focus of the social worker is on maintaining the group as a viable modality so that increasingly the members are able to help each other. The worker's activities are directed toward supplementing what the members themselves are able to accomplish. Actually, no group moves along in an orderly sequence, but progress is made unevenly with steps forward and backward and then ahead to a new level of consolidation of gains. Most groups are in transition somewhere between identifiable stages of development.

Characteristics of the Group

In this stage, there is sufficient congruence about goals that the members can work together toward their achievement. The group is important to the members, who use it as a source of help in working through their problems and concerns. The social worker, based on his diagnostic evaluations, continuously helps the members to modify individual and group goals. He emphasizes individual and group problem solving, using the group itself as the major medium. One of his intermediary goals is to help members to help each other. He helps members to extend and make more specific the more proximate goals through which further progress in psychosocial functioning will occur. There is continued clarification of the goals that individuals seek for themselves as these are similar to or different from those of others in the group.

Usually, members have achieved considerable involvement in the group; they feel that belonging is important to them and they know who belongs. The worker has a responsibility to maintain members in the group when the group can be beneficial to them: this is done through follow-up of absences, and provision of encouragement and support when resistance or ambivalence recurs. Members usually are able to accept a newcomer to the group without being threatened, unless the new-comer upsets the norms that govern the group's operations. Addition of new members to an ongoing group dilutes and interferes with the progressive deepening of feelings among the members until the newcomer is accepted by the group.

The newcomer to a cohesive group is in a difficult position. He has the feelings typical of entry into any new group situation, but in addition he needs to become socialized into the member role in a group that has developed its patterns of goals, relationships, communication, and norms.[1] In many cases, the new member is left with the responsibility of finding his place in the group rather than the old members sharing this responsibility with him. Assimilation into the group is dependent upon learning to take roles, to perceive oneself in relation to others and to acquire the commonly shared frames of reference. The nucleus group already has a common frame of reference, although the values have become so much a part of the members that they cannot readily be verbalized. The new person needs to discover these and test them out before he finds a place in the group. In the case of disturbed persons, the process may be prolonged and fraught with hesitating and belabored efforts to find acceptance.

Preparation of the group for the arrival or departure of a member helps the group to maintain its cohesiveness even while absorbing a new member or feeling threatened by the loss of a member. Through discussion of changes in membership, some members may recall their own feelings around entering and separating from groups and generalize about what makes it easy or difficult to find one's place in a group. Assimilation of new members seems to be easier in open groups than in closed ones, but it should be remembered that the developmental process in open groups tends to be slower. The timing of the entry of a newcomer is important. He may at one time bring in a desirable new stimulation. At other times, he may seriously disrupt the stability of the group. These changes in membership pro-

---

[1] Phillips, Shenker, and Revitz, "The Assimilation of the New Child into the Group," *Psychiatry*, XIV (1951).

vide opportunities for solving problems of acculturating new members, breaking affectional ties with departing members, and realigning roles and friendship patterns. It is the social worker's responsibility to prepare the group for the entry of new members or a new practitioner as well as to prepare the newcomer for the group.

Discontinuance of members from closed groups is not frequent during this stage. Some members, however, cannot accept the increasing demands of the group for give and take, or they cannot tolerate the demands that participation in the content of the group makes of them. They become anxious and resistant. Feelings about exposure of self in the group may reoccur as its content touches upon more areas of the life experiences of its members. It is crucial that the person "have confidence that his real self can be understood and accepted by others in the group." [2] Until the point is reached in which there is openness and acceptance of self and others, some members may consider withdrawal from the group. The worker's task is to support such a person in staying, through making very clear that the worker wants him to remain in the group. Hopefully, the members themselves can reassure him that he has a place in the group and can put gentle pressure on him to continue. Departure of a member stirs up myriad reactions: a sense of loss, fear that the group will disintegrate, ambivalence about wanting the person in the group, with accompanying guilt reactions. When a member terminates from the group, the worker helps both him and the remaining members to accept the termination.

The predominant qualities of relationships in this phase are trust, acceptance, and interdependence. There is a noticeable decrease in the ambivalence of members toward the worker and each other. Members more often feel accepted and understood. More frequently, they are able to empathize with each other.

The relationship with the worker is predominantly positive. There is less dependence on him and more reliance on each other, combined with a realistic dependence upon the worker

[2] Powdermaker and Frank, *Group Psychotherapy,* p. 433.

at times when this is still necessary. Within the general atmosphere of acceptance and support, negative feelings toward the worker should be recognized and accepted. The worker recognizes whether the feeling about him is limited to one or two members or is widely shared and, if the latter, the extent to which contagion has occurred. Some hostile feelings toward the worker are very natural reactions to certain realistic situations, in which instances the members concerned have every right to be angry with the worker as, for example, when the worker does not follow through on a promise. In other instances, hostility toward the worker may be an effort to avoid involvement, or feelings may be displaced or projected onto the worker from other life experiences. Some negative feelings may stem from resistances in the relationship that have not been understood or explained to individuals or the group. Facing things in himself that he finds difficult to tolerate may anger a member and cause him to project the reason for his discomfort onto the worker. Hostility may be expressed against the worker who represents to him a parent or other persons whom he feels are against him. Even though such hostility stems from feelings that were realistic in the past, the irrational elements should not be continued in the present if the member is to cope with such experiences constructively. Resistance that results in negative feelings may take many forms. Some common ones are forgetting appointments, tardiness, silence, lack of response to efforts in his behalf, belittling the contributions of the worker to the group, denial of progress, or overt expressions of hostility.

Members often develop strong positive feelings toward the worker that are expressed in a desire to have him to oneself, difficulty in sharing, strong overidentification with him, or dependence on him. In a group of mentally ill young women being prepared for leaving a hospital, for example, the worker took the members on a shopping trip. As she took them to a coffee shop and helped them to make decisions about their orders, the members were necessarily dependent upon the worker for guidance and concrete help. Later, as the worker helped the members to select and buy small articles in a nearby store, one of the members said, "Come on, Mommy, we want to show you what we want to buy." More often, perhaps, this type of transference occurs in groups of young children. Usually, the relationship of worker to members is based on a realistic perception of his qualities and his role as a helping person.

Although generally positive feelings among members predominate, the demands of the group result in some conflict among the members that is acompanied by hostility, rejection, or withdrawal. Some members may project their feelings or problems onto other members. In a group of women, Mrs. James glowered at Mrs. Perkins when the worker asked Mrs. James to wait until Mrs. Perkins had a chance to speak. Mrs. Perkins noted Mrs. James's behavior and asked why she was angry with her. Mrs. James looked startled and then said, "Well, I've a right to be—I was cut off." Mrs. Blaine said, "But the rest of us have a right to talk, too." Mrs. Perkins said she couldn't understand why Mrs. James reacted so strongly against her; Mrs. James did not reply. There was a silence which Mrs. James interrupted to say that she did react too strongly; Mrs. Perkins had done nothing. The worker commented that it was he who had suggested that Mrs. Perkins be given a turn. Mrs. Blaine wondered if Mrs. James might be jealous of Mrs. Perkins because the worker turned his attention away from Mrs. James and toward Mrs. Perkins. Mrs. Wender affirmed this opinion, commenting that it was natural to be jealous of the attention that another member receives from the worker, "Just like children who want the mother's attention all to themselves." The members all laughed at this. Mrs. Wender, in a light way, said that the group sometimes acted like a family of kids who get jealous of each other. Mrs. James thought it was natural for children to feel this way, but not for adults. The members continued to express their feelings and to reassure Mrs. James that other adults often reacted as she had done. This example is but one of the many ways in which member-to-member transference may be expressed in the group.

During the preceding phases, the members found a place

within the group. Some members may have been stereotyped into roles that prevent their use of the group in a flexible manner, according to their particular needs. The worker can attempt to alter the expectations that a particular member has for himself and that others have for that member, which in turn can modify self-expectations and behavior of others toward the person.[3] A member's pattern of behavior may be changed or extended as the worker and other members come to expect different things of him. The worker may need to confront the members directly with some of their tendencies to stereotype others, just as he comments on any other behavior that is destructive to an individual or the group. He may observe, "What makes you use Jack as a scapegoat?" or "I notice you just won't listen to Mrs. Price." The relationships among members are a valid part of the content of the group experience. A norm of flexibility and experimentation is crucial in making possible the changing of maladaptive role behavior.

Subgroups have emerged by this time which can generally be accommodated by the group and which can contribute to the group as a whole. This does not mean that there will be no subgroups that are inimical to the welfare of individuals and the group. Indeed, there may be unhealthy pair relations that develop, or are continued from the earlier stages, which are indicative of problems in interpersonal relationships, and their modification becomes an important goal for those members. It is natural that transitory negative relationships will develop within the group, as the members try to solve the many problems of an individual and group nature.

The practitioner's responsibility is to diagnose the shifting and changing relationships of the members with him and with each other, plan for means of building on the strengths of the members and the group, work with members to set goals for improvement in relationships, and contribute his own knowl-

[3] For fuller discussion of maintenance of negative roles, see Lippitt, "Unplanned Maintenance and Planned Change in the Group Work Process," in Social Work Practice, pp. 75-95; Glasser, "Social Role, Personality, and Group Work Practice," ibid., pp. 60-74.

edge and skills to the group's efforts to cope with interpersonal problems as these arise.

A group code has developed, consisting of norms that are recognized, understood, and generally accepted by the members. The social worker's efforts have been directed toward influencing the nature of the code. If this has been successful, differences are now perceived as being potentially useful, although they may create discomfort. Individual differences and talents are acknowledged and used. Prestige is now attached to a person's efforts to express himself and to work on problems. The members recognize that conflict can be used constructively toward the achievement of purposes.

The social worker continues to help members to recognize and clarify the developing norms in the group and some of the underlying values. He supports the members' efforts to establish desirable rules and to take mutual responsibility for their enforcement. He accredits and supports the norms that are positive to the achievement of goals; he questions openly those that are negative in influence. He encourages the examination of existing norms and the consideration of alternative ones. He continues to help the group to find an appropriate balance between control and freedom in feeling and behaving. It is a temptation for a practitioner to overstress group loyalty and group standards, regardless of their influence on individuals. Group loyalty and group standards do strengthen the impact of the group on its members; the crucial consideration is that the code of standards approve and support flexibility and experimentation.

Behavior that deviates from the norms of the group poses a threat to the stability of the group. The other members tend to respond with efforts to control the deviator. The deviator's failure to conform to the group's expectations makes life difficult for all concerned. The other members cannot count on him, so they tend to respond by penalizing him in order to influence him toward conformity to the expectations of the group. This is essential to the group's ability to continue its activities.[4] The worker's task is to assess the bases for the deviancy and the members' behavior toward the deviator, and to work toward mutuality of understanding.

Patterns of communication that are appropriate to the purpose of the group have been established. There is greater ease in communication about feelings, problems, and opinions. There is a greater spread in verbal communications by members. Conflict, however, continues to be present and serves as a dynamic for change. Although many interpersonal and intergroup conflicts were expressed and worked out during earlier phases, resolution of major conflicts usually cannot occur until the group has developed a basic consensus that provides strength to face and weather serious differences. In this phase, when the social climate of the group is apt to be marked by mutual acceptance and support, members are more willing to risk exposure of themselves and their ideas than in earlier phases when they are uncertain of their acceptance and the consequences of self-expression. They recognize that expression of difference need not mark the end of the relationship. In the words of George Simmel:

It is by no means the sign of the most genuine and deep affection never to yield to occasions for conflict. . . . On the contrary, this behavior often characterizes attitudes which lack the ultimate unconditional devotion. . . . The felt insecurity concerning the basis of such relations often moves us . . . to the avoidance of every possible conflict. Where, on the other hand, we are certain of the irrevocability and unreservedness of our feeling, such peace at any price is not necessary. We know that no crisis can penetrate to the foundation of the relationship.[5]

Generally, the group has developed means for the resolution and management of conflict that are appropriate to the members' capacities. More often, conflict is resolved through means of compromise or integration, rather than elimination of some members or subjugation of some by others.

[4] Merton, "Social Problems and Sociological Theory," in Merton and Nisbet, eds., *Contemporary Social Problems*, p. 805.
[5] Simmel, *Conflict*, p. 46.

Cohesiveness is generally present to a great extent in that the members are mutually attracted to the group. The degree of cohesiveness is, however, relative. It is dependent upon the members' common interests and goals and their abilities to enter into intimate relations with others. It is unlikely that very sick mental patients will develop into as cohesive a group as might persons with greater competence in interpersonal relations. But the group has come to have meaning to the members. As the members become more secure in their own relationships, and in the identity of their group, they become more able to relate to other groups in an effective manner. The worker continues to pay attention to the development of the dimensions of group structure and process in order to maintain the group as a viable modality for the achievement of the goals of its members.

Content

During this phase, the predominant focus is on the problematic situations of members of the group, as these are connected with those of others and with the general purpose of the group. The focus is also on major group problems, those that are concerned with the functioning of the group as a unit. This focus does not mean that the earlier phases were devoid of problem-solving activities. By the time an integrated group emerges, members have made modifications in their attitudes, relationships, and competencies. The early changes tend to be in their abilities to adapt to a new situation, relate more effectively with a professional person, and identify and explore individual and group problems. Then there is, in this stage, a greater focus on working through the identified problems, with members being more effective in helping each other. The particular problems that become the focus of the group's discussions and action-oriented experiences are those that are primary concerns of individuals and the group at a given time.

The work on problems of identity, adequacy, and attitudes toward other people that was begun in the preceding stage continues. There now tends to be more direct expression of feelings and ideas and more realistic readiness to face problematic situations. In a group of male adolescents who were in foster families, there was discussion of the boys' views of the feelings that foster parents have toward natural parents; then more direct expression of their own feelings toward natural parents; and then the reasons why their parents were unable to care for them. Deep insecurity concerning living with families with whom they have no biological ties and uncertainty concerning the attitudes of foster parents toward them were evident in the ensuing discussions. Still later, discussion focused on some of the members' behavioral patterns that made it difficult for them to live in their foster homes. There was within this general sequence of activity, however, considerable moving back to earlier topics and then moving ahead to a new one. This is one illustration of the way in which progression toward working through of problems in attitudes and behavior occurs.

Some working through of problems of behavior that interfere with the successful performance of social roles is, in a sense, the major content of this phase. The varied aspects of failure to perform to the extent of the members' potentialities in one or more of their roles is brought directly into the group experience. Knowledge about the tasks typical of stages of development in the life cycle, as described by such writers as Erikson,[6] is useful to the worker in locating common interests and concerns, providing that the worker assesses individual differences and group deviations from such norms. Unresolved problems from earlier stages may be brought into the group. Differences in life styles concerning such matters as orientation to time, patterns of child rearing, age and sex role typing, group associational patterns, and educational and vocational aspirations need to be included in the worker's assessment of the adequacy of the members' performance of roles. The fact that most members have achieved a sense of satisfaction in their roles as members of the group enhances their readiness to examine their per-

[6] Erikson, *Childhood and Society.*

formance in other roles in which they have difficulty or the variables that seem to account for greater success in one role than in others.

Movement toward more focused discussion of the members' own functioning in their roles may take different routes. In earlier stages, for example, there may have been concern with concrete problems that impede effective performance of roles, such as environmental stresses, or lack of opportunities for education, job training, child care, and so forth. This frequently happens in groups of public assistance clients. When such stresses are relieved, or opportunities provided, there often is consideration of attitudes and behavior that limit effectiveness of functioning and efforts to cope more effectively. In other groups, the progression may be from concern about the behavior of others to concern about one's own behavior. To illustrate, one group was organized to help husbands of wives who were in outpatient psychiatric treatment to cope more effectively with their fears of mental illness and their roles in relation to their wives.[7] The principal expressed concern of the men was to be helpful to their wives. During the orientation and exploration stages, the members shared their concerns about their wives' symptoms and problems, slowly developing the feeling that they were all in the same boat. Through this focus, the men developed a substantial degree of positive identification with each other on a conscious and realistic level. The feeling of mutual support enabled them to begin to look at themselves. The members became ready to stimulate and challenge each other to look at their own attitudes and behavior in relation to their wives' illnesses, or in relation to job or family functioning. They began to modify modes of communication at home and to try out different ways of behaving in varied situations, reporting the results back to the group. This group experience was designed to reinforce ego strengths so as to enable each member to use his capacities in improving his current characteristic patterns of functioning.

[7] Taken from "Ego Psychology and Its Application to Group Counseling," in Vigilante, ed., *Ego Psychology*, pp. 46-64.

In other groups, discussion occurs in relation to making decisions concerning action-oriented experiences and around the experiences themselves. Movement may occur much more slowly than in the preceding example. A group, composed of chronically ill and quite regressed schizophrenic men who had been placed in family care homes after many years in a mental hospital, was organized for the purpose of improving the men's social relationships and functioning in the local community.[8]

The stage of orientation was prolonged. Activities were designed to interest individuals, but at the same time, to make possible the development of interpersonal relations. Verbal communication was minimal. The men were helped by the worker to participate in such simple activities as serving coffee and baking cookies, simple crafts such as mosaics and painting, and quiet games of checkers or pool. By the end of six months, the patients had developed some semblance of a group. They referred to each other by name, developed some sense of trust in the social worker, and participated together in some activities. Activities were graduated in complexity so as to make increased demands on the patients, in accordance with their responses to earlier demands. It took two or three more months for the members to test the worker and themselves in the group through participating in cooperative activities, making decisions, and testing out the safeness of expressing feelings and ideas.

In the next stage, there was more group cohesion. Projects were designed to involve all of the members. As the demands on them increased, there were some altercations and disappointments, despite which the men maintained relationships with each other. The movement had been from a group of silent, isolated men to a group in which absentees were missed and discussion was often sustained. Two patients who had been mute for years were now talking in sentences. Activities were of a more masculine nature: building toys, constructing outdoor play equipment, and repairing bicycles with the accompanying planning, shopping for supplies, and evaluating the results. As

[8] Lane, "Psychiatric Patients Learn a New Way of Life," in *New Perspectives on Services to Groups,* pp. 114-23.

new men joined the group at intervals, the more able old-
timers helped them to become oriented to the group and the
community. A later development was the use of the group
for some focused discussion of the men's reactions to the varied
situations they faced, and ways in which they could behave
more effectively in the group and community. Discussion of
opportunities in the community and visits to the mobile library,
adult education school, a recreation center, and a community
council resulted in each man's use of at least one of these
facilities, and the use of the group for discussion of problems
and progress in their new roles as students, members of organizations, volunteers in community service, and part-time
employees.

In children's groups, play is developed into a semblance of
cooperative activity, focused on the problems of the members.
A picture of group integration has emerged around themes
through which children work out their troubling situations.
These themes have to do with "goodness" and "badness," being
born and growing up, parent-child or sibling relationships,
feelings of deprivation, conflict over ownership of materials
and property, or adaptation to the demands of school.

In one group of economically disadvantaged Negro children
in the second grade, the children often pretended to be what
they feared—lightning, thunder, abandonment, and death.
They played house, exposing their feelings about being pun-
ished, not loved, and discriminated against by their parents.
They played school, exposing their feelings of failure and
being disliked by teachers and other pupils. They played
games in which white children always won out over black
children. In a more directive type of play, the worker set up
situations with which the members needed help. The play
period was often followed by a short period of group conversation in which the children reviewed the play, and the worker
gave information or clarified misperceptions that the children
seemed to have. Through such means, the children engaged
in problem-solving processes.

These illustrations have been presented to emphasize the

varieties of discussion themes and action experiences that may
be utilized to contribute to the enhancement of members'
competence to meet their own and other's expectations, and
the progression that occurs in the content of the group. Discussion of attitudes toward and skills necessary to improved performance in selected roles may comprise a considerable amount
of the content of the group. Communication skills, rehearsals
of behavior, preparation of budgets, conflict over selection of
alternative new roles, doubts about ability to meet expectations,
differences between aspirations and the realistic demands of
situations are but a few examples of specific content in this
area. Reports of progress or successes in meeting expectations
of roles outside of the group become more frequent as the
group progresses. The social worker's focus is not limited to
the content of specific roles, but is also on the development of
affective and cognitive styles or processes of acquiring mastery
over oneself and environment.

Crises are bound to occur in any group. Crises faced by
members outside of the group may be brought into the content
of the group. The group, with its potential for support and
stimulation, may be an effective aid in helping the person to
resolve the problem. Some crises, such as death or attempted
suicide, may make desirable the use of an individual service to
help the person to cope with the situation, or the group itself
may be the most useful unit of service.

Members of some groups are faced with crises over and over
again: lack of water and heat due to nonpayment of bills,
suspensions from school, arrests, interpersonal conflicts, and
illness. This is particularly true of low income, multiple-prob-
lem families, and of persons with character disorders. The
worker's initial focus is on resolution of the immediate problem.
As such members become able to tolerate it, the worker uses
procedures that help them to clarify those situations and behavioral patterns that contribute to the development of crises,
and to make realistic plans for preventing new crises.

Crises may occur also within the internal system of the group.
The absence of the worker, the transfer of the group to another

worker, the loss of a member, or any other change in the group may be perceived as a crisis by the members. Such situations may stir up suppressed feelings about prior separations, so that the event itself is magnified beyond the reality of the situation. Within the climate of acceptance that tends to pervade the group during this stage, conflict between members or subgroups may be severe enough to constitute a crisis for the group.

Whenever stress is present, whether only moderate in nature or severe as in a crisis, the principal activities of the social worker are to provide support and control, to open and maintain communication about the situation, and to provide opportunities for clarifying and coping with the situation. In an intragroup crisis, the worker often needs to limit destructive argument, identify with the members some of the feelings and issues involved, and pick up on some area of agreement, thereby tacitly demonstrating that an underlying consensus exists and can be utilized to weather the conflict. He expresses confidence that, if this crisis can be resolved, there is hope for the future of the group.

Along with the need to find new ways of coping with the crisis, the intensification of stress enhances motivation to find new ways of resolving problems. A person or a group may be especially open to influence during a period of crisis. Usually, the anxieties, interest, and concern of all members heightens. To work constructively with the group taxes the social worker's understanding, stamina, and skill. But if he is able to do this, progress toward further goal achievement is likely to be hastened. By way of illustration, a group of mentally retarded, adolescent girls, on a trip to the community nearest to the hospital, was stopped by a policeman, who said that some of the girls had stolen merchandise from a store. All of the members seemed upset by this encounter. When learning that the group was from the hospital, the officer was willing to forget the charges. But the worker suggested that it was important for the girls to face and learn from the crisis. During the discussion with the officer, there were both denials of the charges and accusations of each other. When the officer assured the group that he was not going to put the girls in jail, one girl confessed, another did so only after the officer found a pair of earrings and no receipt for them in her shopping bag. After lecturing the group, he shook hands with the two girls who had stolen the merchandise. The girls were concerned that the worker was angry with them and intended to punish them. She reassured them, suggested that the trip be continued, and that the incident could be discussed later. During the ride back to the hospital, the members talked about their feelings about the incident and the difficulties they had in controlling their behavior. Later in the day, the group brought the worker a card addressed to: "A very nice lady we like who helps us to learn many things." The incident marked the members' willingness to examine their behavior and the consequences of it.

Participation in planning and decision-making processes is often a means through which members of groups gain in social competence. How difficult this is for some people is often underemphasized. During the sixth month of service to a group of very disturbed boys, ages twelve to fourteen, in a residential treatment center, the boys requested a trip to an amusement park. The worker, assessing that the boys were ready for it, engaged them in detailed planning for the trip. One of the first steps was to consider the nature of the decisions to made: where to go, how to get there, how much money was needed, what to bring, and so forth. The tension became almost unbearable as the group decided that Billy should make a telephone call to get information about the amusement park. All of the boys tried to instruct Billy on how to use the telephone and what questions to ask. None really knew how to do this. What a great sense of accomplishment the boys had when Billy was able to get at least some of the information desired.

Members of a group are usually very invested in goal-directed activity during this stage, but the group does not neglect the socioemotional needs of its members. Some areas of content are in the nature of shared experiences that strengthen relationships and group morale and that provide the necessary relaxation following periods of effort. Spontaneity and seemingly trivial events, as mentioned earlier, are important in the life of a group. All groups alternate their attention between working on tasks and on the relationships among members. This alternation occurs because efforts in behalf of the task which confronts the group bring about strains in the socio-emotional area. A group can tolerate the accompanying tension and conflict only so long. The group then needs to turn its attention to the socio-emotional area in order to reduce the strain. There are times also when progress in a group reaches a temporary plateau. At such times, the members are using their energies to integrate the gains they have achieved. Such a plateau may last for one session or several, and is usually followed by a spurt of forward progress.

Activities of the Social Worker

SUPPORT. The social worker, as in earlier phases, supports the members and the group as needed. He tends, however, to be less active in this regard than he was earlier. The group has developed some sustaining and nurturing power of its own. Generally, also, the members are more confident in their ability to face and cope with problems. The worker identifies, recognizes, and approves the attempts of one member to support the constructive efforts of another.

There are times when, as members move into facing, clarifying, and working toward new or modified modes of functioning, anxiety is aroused that goes beyond what is useful for the enhancement of motivation. Such anxiety may take the form of questions about, or verbal attacks on, the usefulness of the group or the worker. Argumentative behavior, rationalization, denial, and other maneuvers are used to defend the members concerned. Sensitivity to such signs of anxiety and keeping it within manageable bounds are necessary.

Support may be offered through such means as nonverbal gestures that convey the worker's feelings of empathy with the members; recognition of the naturalness of having feelings about an experience or reassurance that it is all right to move on to another focus at this time. The use of limits may be necessary. Limits are supportive if they reduce anxiety and, simultaneously, motivate the members to continue to work on the task at hand. Granting permission may also relieve anxiety. It is knowing when to limit and when to permit that taxes the diagnostic skills of the social worker. At times, the worker supplements the support that the members give each other through such means as physically supporting a member who is very fearful of talking or of trying out an activity; expressing confidence that a member can succeed, providing this expression of confidence is realistic to the member's capacities; and accrediting efforts and achievements as this seems to be needed by the members. As the group takes on a more supportive quality, the practitioner encourages and accredits this progress.

SKILL IN COMMUNICATION. During earlier meetings, in order for the group to have formed, some satisfactory channels for communication were developed, and communication among members became adequate to the achievement of the tasks typical of those phases. Most problems in communication now tend to be directed toward relevant people in the members' environments. The members use the group for help in working through problems in communication with such persons as their parents, children, siblings, employers, teachers, or colleagues. When Chata, aged fifteen, announced that she had been "kicked out of school," the worker suggested this was a good place to talk about it. Chata replied, "Oh, no, I never could." But when she felt the worker's acceptance of her feelings, she told the group about the situation. When another member asked if the suspension were final, it developed that Chata could be reinstated only if her mother would go to school, and her mother had refused to do this when her brother had been in similar trouble. Chata brought out much anger toward school and a feeling of hopelessness about her mother's cooperation. The worker suggested that the group act out the situation to try out ways that Chata might talk with her mother. The worker knew that the members were ready and able to help with the problem and that, as they did so, they would also learn more effective ways of communicating with their own parents.

Members of groups often continue to need help to communicate effectively about more difficult subjects within the group itself. When members of a group find it difficult to talk about their feelings and problems, comments from the worker that mention the universality of certain feelings and concerns, if appropriate to the situations of the members, often release inhibitions. Examples would be the recognition by the worker that it is perfectly normal for teen-agers to feel rebellious against their parents at times, or to have frightening feelings about sex. Those things that people are often ashamed of, or are embarrassed about, are also of deep concern to them, for example, sexual attitudes and experiences, racial differences, and failures.

In a group of fifteen- and sixteen-year-old girls, when Ernestine was absent, the worker asked about her. Her older sister, Vernelda, obviously embarrassed, said that she'd be back in a few months. The other girls looked knowingly at each other. The worker said that she thought she understood. Vernelda, after a long pause, said, "Yeah, I think you do. She got herself in trouble—she's pregnant," and then hurriedly walked away from the worker. The worker said that it was all right for the girls to talk about this, and that Ernestine was still welcome in the group. The girls could hardly believe this, and required reassurance from the worker that she really meant it. This opened up discussion of feelings about pregnancy, unmarried motherhood, and means of dealing with sexual feelings. In such ways, permission is given by the worker to open up topics that have been taboo previously. Naming the taboo subject makes of it a normal concern, and tends to enhance readiness to deal with it. The skill is in being able to stay with the members' feelings and thinking, rather than veering away from such subjects. With permission to explore and work on such topics is the explicit or implied understanding that such discussions rest on mutual trust and confidentiality.

CLARIFICATION OF REALITY. During earlier phases, there was clarification and some acceptance of the group's purpose and the means toward its achievement. There was work on understanding the members' varied feelings and situations. Some beginning was made in identifying and elaborating behavior that was unsatisfying to self or unsatisfactory to others. As the members become ready, the worker's focus is on continuation of the progress made earlier and on further clarification of the feelings, behavior, situations, and progress of the members.

Sharing of feelings is more open, and often produces mitigation of fear, guilt, hopelessness, or other strong emotions. Members often talk about situations in which they have been unable to express their feelings either because they didn't have the words to symbolize the feelings, were afraid of offending other persons, felt guilty about the feelings, or were fearful of the consequences of acknowledging the feelings.

It was not until the fourth month that a group of seriously disturbed young women in a mental hospital were able to share deep feelings and respond to each other's expressions in a helpful manner. The topic for discussion was reaction to experiences in the hospital. One member, Martha, said that she'd spent a lot of time in the back ward. "It's just awful when you're back there." Sara said, "I know, I've been there." Three other members said they'd been there, too. Martha continued to repeat several times that it was the most awful feeling she'd ever had. When she repeated it directly to the worker, the latter commented, "I'm sure it must feel awful, Martha." Martha's response was, "But you can't really know." The worker acknowledged this was so, but she'd like to try to understand, and perhaps the members could share this experience more fully. Martha went on to talk about: "Feeling so lonely; you're all alone in a little room, very afraid, and strapped to that bed so you can hardly move." Other members shared their feelings, too. Then Sara commented that what they said was so true, yet sometimes she felt she ought to be there, because she was afraid of what she might do. To break the silence that followed, the worker asked, "Afraid of what you might do to yourself and others?" This comment led to further feelings about the "awfulness" of the back ward, interspersed with comments that it was sometimes necessary to be there for one's own protection. When Martha later reiterated her deep feelings of loneliness, she added, "But, you know, you can be lonely sitting out on that ward with eighty-five people, too." The worker nodded to indicate this could be true. Jane said this was part of being mentally sick. Recognizing, naming, facing, and integrating some of these feelings were important steps for this group toward efforts to reach out to other people or to respond to efforts of others to relate to them.

According to his understanding of the needs of the members and their motivation and capacity to deal with problems, the worker helps the group to focus on clarification of patterns of behavior that are helpful or destructive to them. To repeat what has been noted before, there seems to be a natural progression from recognition of the behavior in the situation to elaboration of the situation more fully in its many facets—the feelings about it, the behavior patterns and the situations in which they occur, and the consequences of the behavior. In some situations, such understanding is sufficient; in others, further work is desirable in order to clarify the meaning of the situation or the behavior.

The social worker's major efforts build on and support the use of the members' positive motivations and capacities and encourage members to support or to question the comments and behavior of each other. For example, in a group of adolescent boys, one member asked Pete directly about school. Pete, aged seventeen, replied that he had quit. One member said it was stupid to have done that. The other members agreed. One member commented, "We'd better stop jumping Pete and find out what happened." Here, the worker supported, through purposeful silence, the group's work in understanding one of its members and then helping him to face his behavior more realistically.

There are times when inability to perceive reality is an obstacle to the group's progress. The worker then needs to confront such members with the irrationality of their thinking, the destructive use of defenses, the unacceptability of their behavior, or their lack of progress. Under such circumstances, "a force is needed within the learning group system that will challenge the obstacles as they appear by calling attention to their existence and asking the group to come to grips with them." [9] The practitioner may use confronting questions or comments with the intent of encouraging the members to face and work on such problems. To confront people enables them to face and work on such problems, honestly and openly. To confront people enables them to face the reality of a feeling, act, or situation. In order to use confrontation effectively, the worker's diagnosis of the situation must be a sound one. The confrontation must be accompanied by empathy. There is some empirical support for the view that when it is accompanied by a high degree of empathy, confrontation is an effective therapeutic ingredient. When employed by practitioners with little empathy, it is not.[10]

The worker's attitude and choice of words make a vast difference in the extent to which the members will feel attacked, and retreat from facing reality, or will be enabled to move into coping with it. For example, "I know you're lying," sounds far different from, "Sometimes it's hard to say what really happened; let's try to look at that." When they are not able to do so themselves, the members need a worker who can face them with some of the feelings, ways of thinking, and behavior that is destructive, thus freeing them to move forward constructively. The worker may share directly his feelings about a member's behavior in order to face him with it and then help him with it. One example would be a worker's sharing with a father who covered up for his son's stealing, "I feel angry with you because you're contributing to Bob's delinquency instead of helping him to get along better."

Supportive techniques often accompany confronting ones.

[9] Schwartz, "The Social Worker in the Group," in *The Social Welfare Forum*, p. 148.
[10] Hallowitz et al., "The Assertive Counseling Component of Therapy," *Social Casework*, XLVIII (1967), 546.

An example is that of a worker's use of herself with a group of Negro high-school girls, all with problems in school and from deprived economic backgrounds, under the auspices of a YWCA. A frequent topic of discussion in this group was feelings of being discriminated against and feelings of prejudice toward others. The sensitivity of these girls created frequent outbreaks of emotion in the group.

At first, the worker supported the expression of feelings about the girls' race and toward others, then gradually worked toward clarification of what part was the reality and what was displacement and projection of feelings onto others. When a teacher, also Negro, asked the girls to be less noisy, one member screamed, "Oh, I hate her; she is just prejudiced. She doesn't stick up for her own race." Others joined in the ventilation of feelings against teachers and white students who were perceived as being discriminatory. Gross distortions were evident, one complaint being that no Negro had ever been an officer of the student organization.

When the worker expressed understanding of the members' feelings but confronted them with the reality of the situation, including the fact that the president of student organization was a Negro, the girls stopped to ponder this. One grudgingly admitted, "That's true, but I just hate white kids." Later, the worker commented that the members seemed to feel at one about this. All agreed. The worker asked, "And there are no exceptions?" Two teachers were mentioned as being all right, but the expressions of hatred continued. To the two girls who expressed most of these feelings, the worker commented, "You seem to be full of hate today." The response was, "Well, yes, we've a right to." The worker acknowledged that sometimes there were reasons to feel hatred. Gradually, the members themselves began to confront each other with the facts. One girl said, "After all, Mrs. Grant [the worker] is white too." The most vociferous of the members looked startled, and said, "Oh, no," and broke into tears, then added, "But, but, I like you." From that point, the girls began to individualize people, with more realistic evaluations of people and situations.

When members confront each other, the worker needs to understand the motivations of the confronter as to whether his intent was to hurt or to help, the influence of the confrontation on the member or members toward whom it was directed, and on the other members, and the needs and readiness of the group to use it. Based on such diagnostic considerations, he supports the efforts of the confronter; directs attention of the group to another matter; encourages the group to continue with the train of thought; or sets a limit. Gradually, the members become more able to empathize with each other and thereby become more helpful than hurtful in the intent and nature of their confronting comments.

Within the protection of the social work group, the worker may create an awareness among the members of the discrepancy between their private attitudes and behavior and their public statements. He may do this by encouraging a member with high status in the group to tell the group about his feelings and behavior that deviate from his earlier public expressions. One example is of a group in which a high-status boy revealed that his earlier exaggerations concerning his sexual conquests and his sexual security were not true; that he really felt very uncomfortable with girls. Following their expressions of surprise at this admission, the other members openly expressed their anxieties and fears. The façade of sexual adequacy gave way to efforts to achieve more adequate masculine identification. Thus, instead of continuing to support each other's denials, the members could move toward support of efforts to modify attitudes and behavior. When possible, the selection of a member with high status is deliberate; if such revelation emanates from a member with low status, there is danger that he will become a scapegoat. Such a member also is less likely to be able to influence the behavior of other members.[11]

To carry understanding further, when the worker judges this to be desirable, clarification in the form of explanation of the underlying meaning of behavior or its roots in the past may be

[11] Blum, "The A-ha Response as a Therapeutic Goal," in Maier, ed., *Group Work as Part of Residential Treatment*, pp. 47-56.

used. The diagnosis of each member deals with the nature of the obstacles and the capacity of the ego to use such explanations. The worker considers the readiness of the members to participate, in relation to the nature of the common and unique needs in the group, mutuality of empathy, and potential effect on each member. It is futile and may be hurtful to present information about the meaning of behavior before it can be comprehended or related to the current situation. Working toward such understanding should be a natural process, with members participating and the worker supplementing or affirming what the members are able to do. In a group of patients in a mental hospital, one member, Mrs. Jennings, said she was hiding under her blanket and keeping her eyes shut. The worker commented that the members might like to discuss the idea of using physical hiding to shut out reality. Another member suggested that this was so Mrs. Jennings would not need to admit that she was daydreaming. Mrs. Jennings said that she wanted to shut out her problem from the view of others. The worker wondered if she might want to shut out problems from her own view, too. Mrs. Jennings did not respond verbally, but others acknowledged that this could be so, and two members gave examples from their experiences. At the next meeting, Mrs. Jennings freely brought out deep feelings of hurt and said she no longer needed to hide behind her blanket.

Seeking for the meaning of behavior or underlying emotions may help persons to make connections between various aspects of problems, as they appear in current functioning, or to make connections between the past and the present. The focus is on bringing to conscious awareness such feelings and experiences as are not readily verbalized and acknowledged, but which can be recalled, verbalized, and acknowledged with some assistance from others. The worker may ask the group to consider connections between feelings, behavior, or events. He may point up the consequences of behavior. When members or the worker suggest explanations, these are related to the particular situation, not generalized to the total personality. It is generally accepted in social work that the practitioner refrains from "interpretation of unconscious mechanisms to individuals in the group, although he may help group members to deal with conscious or preconscious material." [12] It is generally recognized, too, that probes for connections and interpretations of meanings are apt to be more effective with middle-class clientele with fairly good ego integration than with clients who are of lower socioeconomic status or are more emotionally disturbed.[13]

An example of the use of interpretation of the meaning of behavior is taken from a group of mothers of preschool children in a child guidance clinic. During this stage, the group was a cohesive one. The members had considerable ability to support and stimulate each other. All of the members, including Mrs. Johnson, had made progress in understanding and modifying their feelings and behavior toward their children who were being served by the clinic.

In spite of progress in many areas, when the worker asked the members what things were still hardest for them to cope with, Mrs. Johnson said with much feeling, "Toilet training." She expressed despair that her four-year-old boy would ever become trained and her feelings of disgust with his behavior. The other members expressed empathy and understanding of her feelings. The worker said she could agree that some of Tommie's behavior would be very hard to accept. Following ventilation of feelings, the women talked about alternative ways of dealing with the problem. At the suggestion of one member, Mrs. Johnson acknowledged that she indeed was over-anxious about the problem, but could not help it. Two weeks later, Mrs. Johnson, upon entering the room, immediately expressed discouragement and growing impatience with her son, threatening severe punishment. Another member noted that Mrs. Johnson was really mad at her son and she replied explosively, "Yes, I am mad at him." One member said that shame and punishment did not work. Mrs. Johnson said she

[12] Coyle, "Social Group Work: An Aspect of Social Work Practice," *Journal of Social Issues,* VIII (1952), 29.
[13] Reid, "Client and Practitioner Variables Affecting Treatment," *Social Casework,* XLV (1964), 586-92.

knew this, but what on earth could she do—she'd tried everything? The members reflected on alternative ways of dealing
with such a situation.

The worker suggested that perhaps it might help to focus
more on the feelings of the parents toward behavior that dis-
gusted them, pointing up certain similarities in the feelings
that had been expressed in spite of differences in the children's
overt behavior. At one point, Mrs. Adams suggested that maybe
Mrs. Johnson's feelings about Tommie's toilet training might
go back to something else. Mrs. Johnson responded with a
burst of feeling, "It's just especially hard for me; it's the only
thing I can't stand." Mrs. Adams said she could remember some
unpleasant things about her own toilet training. After giving
an incident in which she had felt shamed and humiliated, she
asked if Mrs. Johnson had had similar experiences. Mrs. Johnson said that she had not; then she turned to the worker and
asked if something in the past could possibly have anything to
do with her feeling of difficulty with Tommie now. The worker
said that sometimes past experiences have a great deal of meaning because the feelings that were experienced then can carry
over into our present lives. Mrs. Johnson said that perhaps the
worker had a point. She began to recall some of her own feelings
about her mother's reactions to accidents she had before toilet
training was fully achieved.

Every member participated in the ensuing discussion about
how understanding some of one's feelings and behavior might
result in changes in those feelings and behavior. Mrs. Johnson
said that she felt some sense of relief and hope that she could
deal with Tommie's behavior with less sense of panic. This was
a turning point in the nature of Mrs. Johnson's efforts to be
helpful to Tommie. But it is important that, as in this instance,
one member's problem can be dealt with in such a way that
other members benefit.

In some groups, the members gradually come to fuller recognition of patterns of attitudes or behavior. They become aware
that these patterns have developed over a period of time. They
have learned to distinguish which patterns of behavior are

gratifying and adequate to their situations and which are harmful to self or to others. They may come to understand the meaning of the patterns of feelings or behavior. Questions, exploratory comments, or explanations that are intended to enhance understanding of the meaning of feelings and behavior are helpful to the members only under certain conditions. The interpretations must, of course, be accurate. The worker or member who makes comments about the meaning of behavior needs to seek feedback or reactions to the interpretation and to work toward evaluation of the comments. Again, interpretations are not helpful unless the intent is to understand and help, and unless the atmosphere of the group is one of mutuality of support. The most effective comments are made at the time the individuals who are targets of the communication are nearly ready to discover the meaning for themselves and to relate it to their particular situations. The understanding that has developed needs to be repeated in different forms over a period of time if it is to result in more adaptive behavior. The principle holds true: the selection of a given technique is based on sound diagnosis of both individual and group.

A special characteristic of the use of interpretation in groups is that, in order to be useful to an individual, it need not be directed specifically to him.[14] During a period in which a particular problematic situation is developing, various members may present their experiences, express their feelings, and make relevant comments. To the extent that the underlying theme of the content is relevant to a particular person's concerns, he may derive understanding of himself and his experiences. This is what Konopka refers to as the anonymity of insight.[15] Often when feelings or explanations are universalized, they touch closely on some member's particular concerns.

ACHIEVEMENT OF COMPETENCE. In this stage of development, there are many opportunities to help the members to learn adaptive behavior. The competencies acquired in the group are

[14] Whitaker and Lieberman, *Psychotherapy through the Group Process,* p. 170.
[15] Konopka, *Social Group Work,* p. 128.

then tested out in the community which, after all, is the real proof of changes in adaptive capacity.

As the group progresses through time, its decisions extend from those that influence the group's purpose, structure, and process and the patterns of behavior of its members to the life of members outside the group. The social worker helps the group to work toward decisions applicable to the life situations of the members. It is not realistic to hope that, if members learn how to make decisions about their group life, this ability can be transferred automatically to other situations. The members need to perceive the carryover to other areas of social functioning. Thus, the focus on problems in the interaction between individuals and the social environment needs to be maintained. It is important that the participant experience the relevance between what he does in the group and what he does or can do in his environment.[16]

Arriving at a decision is in and of itself not necessarily helpful. It is crucial that alternative solutions be considered, and the consequences of each alternative explored thoroughly. To look at alternative modes of behavior and act on the basis of such examinations tends to enhance social competence. In a group of delinquent boys on probation, John exploded that his father was angry and had had enough of him. Tom asked about the trouble. John said he had been forbidden to use the car one night, but some of his friends insisted so he gave in. Later that evening he was arrested for speeding. The worker commented that John seemed caught between two pulls: his father and his friends. He suggested that the group go back to the time when John made the decision to take his father's car, and think about other ways that John might have dealt with the problem. He was thus helping the boys to understand conflicting desires and pressures, weigh circumstances, and make decisions based on what solutions bring satisfaction and have

[16] In a demonstration research project, it was found that decision-making abilities learned in the group are not carried over into situations outside the group unless the decisions made in the group are clearly related to those outside the group. See McLarnan and Fryer, "Improving Decision-making among Young Low-income Couples," pp. 74-80.

utility. Once implemented, decisions need to be reviewed, evaluated, and often modified on the basis of experience. Thus, there is a recurrent cycle of problem identification, decision making, and action on the part of an individual or of the group as a unit. Such problem-solving activities can enhance the members' general competence to make decisions that are based on understanding of one's own motives and the demands of the situation.

Rehearsal is useful in work with certain persons, regardless of their age, to clarify situations and plan how to face difficult situations. How to tell the teacher that one needs help, apply for a job, communicate effectively with parents or spouse, talk with a probation officer or employer, or behave when challenged to fight are common situations that can be discussed and rehearsed in the group. Follow-up of what happened when efforts were made to apply learning from the group to situations outside the group provides oportunity for evaluation and, when necessary, further efforts to solve the problem.

Another way that members can be helped with problems in their functioning in particular roles is through encouragement of members to report incidents of problematic situations, exploration of the nature of the situation and consideration of alternative means for dealing with the situation more effectively. Other members who have observed or been involved in similar situations can be effective in modifying each other's false perceptions of the situation, or their own behavior, and in proposing alternative coping methods. When decisions have been made about the modes of behavior and means for achieving desired objectives, the worker suggests ways they can be put into practice between meetings. Through such means, persons can learn that new efforts are worthwhile, and progress is often more rapid. Role playing may be used to recreate the stressful encounters and to test out alternative solutions.[17] Participation in

---

[17] For examples of the use of such procedures with groups, see Vinter and Sarri, "Malperformance in the Public School: A Group Work Approach," *Social Work*, X (1), (1965), 3-13; Glasser, Resnick, and Sarri, "Social Group Work in the Psychiatric Setting: A Report on Two Instructional Programs"; Klein, *Role Playing*.

new behaviors, accompanied by emotional involvement, is sometimes necessary if antisocial roles are to be modified. As new roles are explored, the person gains experience with different attitudes and a clearer perception of both the dynamics behind the action and how others perceive him. Such activities may be effective as practice for reality.[18]

Concern with dependency-interdependency conflicts and the concomitant need to both give and take is prevalent with many members of groups. With people in hospitals and other residential settings, particularly, there is necessary dependence on many staff. It is a sign of maturity in relationships to be able to give as well as receive. The group itself fosters interdependency among its members, but there is often a need also to give to others outside the group within the institution or the wider community. The ego-enhancing opportunities to give to others, either in terms of contributions of time, ideas, or material things, should not be underestimated.

A group of mothers of hospitalized children, toward the end of their experience in a group, used the last session to plan and carry out special holiday programs for all the children and staff in the hospital. A group of crippled children were enthralled when, instead of only being entertained and given to at a community party, the members could contribute cookies and take responsibility for registering guests. A group composed of mentally ill patients sent representatives to a meeting that was held to plan a community action program on mental health. A group of Negro adolescent girls, following discussion of their own feelings about experiences with discrimination, initiated and participated responsibly in a social action project directed toward making a recreational activity available to people of all races. A parent education group, in cooperation with a church, developed a playground for young children and volunteered to supervise it. Low income parents, previously fearful of ap-

---

[18] Antisocial women prisoners who participated in group sessions that included psychodrama showed a significantly stronger sense of personal identity than did those in a control group. See Maas, "The Use of Actional Procedures in Group Psychotherapy with Sociopathic Women," *International Journal of Group Psychotherapy*, XVI (1966), 190-97.

proaching school personnel, became active in a Parent-Teachers Association, and thereby helped to achieve a school lunch program.[19] Interdependence, then, is important not only within the group, but between the group and the community.

The social worker progressively extends the experience of the members to other areas of community life. Expectations for members are raised gradually as they show the capacity to modify behavior, and as they indicate readiness for more complex tasks. Through broadening the experience of members and evaluating with them their responses to new situations, members become able to handle a greater variety of experiences in an adequate manner. Soon they will become ready to leave the group.

[19] See Del Valle and Alexander, "Effects of the Project on Family Service Agencies and Urban Leagues," *Social Casework,* XLVIII (1967), pp. 633-38.

CHAPTER VIII

The Termination Stage

SOCIAL WORK intervention is time-centered. "The goal of treatment," said Gordon Hamilton, "is always to help the person return as soon as possible to natural channels of activity with strengthened relationships." [1] At its best, social work service has been directed toward the realization of goals that are specific enough so that progress can be measured in relation to them. The final phase is one during which the efforts of the social worker are directed mainly toward helping the members to stabilize the gains they have made and to prepare them for termination. Termination is a dynamic and vital process in social work. It is a process through which a social service is discontinued to an individual or a group. This does not necessarily mean that the group itself cannot continue to exist. In most instances, however, the group itself is approaching its end.

The purposeful nature of social work implies that from time to time it is necessary to assess the desirability of continuing service to the members. The judgment may be that there has been progress toward the achievement of goals and there is potential for further improvement, in which case the service should be continued. Another decision may be that little, if any, progress has been made; if this is combined with little potential for changing the situation, the service should be discontinued. Still another evaluation may be that progress toward the achievement of goals has been sufficient, and the service should be terminated. The social worker undoubtedly has anticipated termination from the beginning of his work with the group and has clarified with the members its possible duration, so that the goals and the means toward their achievement

[1] Hamilton, *Theory and Practice of Social Case Work*, p. 236.

have been related to the plans for both individuals and the group. Nevertheless, there comes a time when the worker and the members must face the fact of separation from each other and often, also, the end of the group itself.

Planned and Unplanned Termination

Termination occurs for a number of reasons, some of them planned as an integral part of treatment, and some of them unplanned or unanticipated. Ideally, termination occurs when a person or a group no longer needs the professional service. The social worker is required to make a judgment that there has been sufficient progress to enable the person to continue to consolidate the gains he has made without the help of the social worker, and often also without the group. All people have problems, but usually they can cope with them with the support and help of families, friends, and nonprofessional community resources. It is unrealistic to continue service until the members have achieved their full potential: the question rather is one of whether or not there has been sufficient progress to assume that the members can continue to improve outside of the group.

Too often, termination occurs that is not the natural outcome of a plan for individuals and the group. Changes in the interests and situations of members often result in premature termination from a group; for example, a move away from the locale in which the group is meeting, a change in the work or school schedule of a member, an illness, the removal of a child from a group by a parent, lack of continued eligibility for public assistance, or other situations over which the social worker has no control. An administrator may transfer workers from one assignment to another or financial exigencies may force the termination of groups before the members are really ready to give up the service. There are times, too, when progress is not made, due to a variety of facets of an individual or group nature, resulting in the dissolution of the group. A natural decline in a group sometimes occurs, leading to its dissolution, when the social work purposes have not been achieved. Some groups may become less cohesive and lose their sense of identity as groups. The interdependence among members may be clearly gone and not recoverable. The social worker's responsibility is to use the reality of these changes in the group to help the members to face the changes and to make other appropriate plans for service to individuals or subgroups.

Evaluation of Progress

INDIVIDUAL PROGRESS. Evaluation, the appraisal of the quality of the service and of the members' use of it, is an ongoing process. For the social worker, it involves a capacity to make sound judgments in relation to purpose. The ultimate test of the effectiveness of social work practice is the extent to which the persons who were served have made positive changes toward the goals set with them, associated with the group experience. The progress or regression of a member is appropriately made in relation to his particular characteristics, background, problems, and needs, rather than in relation to fixed or uniform standards. In some instances, notably work with families or other groups that will continue to exist when social work service is terminated, the concern is with changes in the structure and interacting processes of the group, as well as in the individuals who comprise it. If goals for each member and the group have been developed, evaluated, and modified periodically, they naturally become the criteria for evaluating progress.

Evaluation of the progress of members is made more precise and easier for the worker if some plan is developed for tracing changes in attitudes, relationships, and behavior periodically during the course of the group experience. Perhaps, minimally, summary reports should be made at the end of the first meeting, toward the end of the exploration phase, and when termination is being considered. The first report would include pertinent data about the individual: his characteristics, problems, capacities, and motivations; goals as seen by the member, relevant others who may have referred him, and the worker; and an initial description and evaluation of the member's beginning in the group. As changes occur, these can be noted from week to week or periodically. These changes are usually those in attitudes toward self and others, changes in the quality and range of social relationships, and changes in problematic behavior. Necessary data are then available for the practitioner to assist him to understand and evaluate the nature and extent of progress and regression. The movement of each individual is evaluated in relation to the trend of changes in the group, and the impact of environmental influences on it. According to Chin:

. . . it is important to emphasize that evaluation studies of goal achievement or outcome are of limited importance unless the evaluation study also tries to pinpoint the components which "cause" the degree of attainment or hindrance of goals.[2]

Whenever termination is being considered, a thorough review and evaluation of what has or has not been accomplished, and the determinants thereof, is imperative. So, too, is a set of realistic goals for the periods of time that remain before the final termination.

GROUP DEVELOPMENT. As the group moves toward readiness for termination, there are clues to guide the practitioner in his activities with the group. The goals that members have for themselves and for each other have been partially achieved, at least, although movement in the group may have been faster for some than for others. Members come to talk about some of the changes that have taken place in them and in the group. Attendance may become irregular unless the worker makes special efforts to motivate members to continue until the final meeting. Some members may feel ready to terminate before the time set for the group; others may want to drop out due to insecurity, having been left behind by members who have made more rapid progress. The structure tends to become more flexible; for example, by giving up official roles within the membership or by changes in time, place, and frequency of meetings. Although acceptance of each other is mutual, there is

[2] Chin, "Evaluating Group Movement and Individual Change," in *Use of Groups in the Psychiatric Setting,* p. 42.

a movement toward the breaking of interpersonal ties as members find satisfaction in relationships outside the group. Exceptions are in work with family units or peer groups which will continue to meet together after the termination of social work service. The norms of members have become more nearly in harmony with those of appropriate socially desirable segments of the community where the members live or of which they are a part. The members' norms evidence confidence in the future. Communication is free and easy. There is a lessening of group controls and a greater increase in inner controls on the part of the members. Cohesiveness weakens as the members begin to find satisfactions and new relationships outside the group.

Termination of Individuals

In group situations, members may be ready to terminate at different times. In open-ended groups, a member leaves a group that is going to continue without him. Even in closed membership groups, some members may need to leave the group due to changes in their situations, or they may be ready for termination before the other members. Such situations pose both special problems and opportunities for the worker and the members. Time needs to be taken to prepare an individual for termination, and to help the remaining members with their reactions to the person who is leaving and to the change in the composition and dynamics of the group occasioned thereby. In some instances, the fact that a member is ready for termination provides both hope and stimulation toward change for other members. In other instances, it points up the slower progress of the others and is reacted to with a sense of failure or discouragement. It may arouse feelings of rivalry and competition among the members. It requires some time for a readjustment of members' roles to occur, and this upsets the equilibrium of the group. The practitioner needs to deal with the feelings of the person who is leaving the group and the feelings of those who remain. He works toward using this change for the benefit of all.

Termination of the Group

Once the worker has made a thorough evaluation of where each individual and the group is, related to goals and to agency policies concerning length of service and criteria for termination, he anticipates and plans for making maximum use of the remaining sessions. The purpose is to stabilize gains that have been made, and to help the members to leave the relationship with the worker and with each other as members of this particular group with this particular focus. In many instances, this also means leaving the agency. The worker needs to anticipate the responses of the members to termination, and to make plans concerning timing and specific content to be dealt with. He needs to make plans for supplementing the group service, and for follow-up services to members; when indicated by his evaluations.

Some groups are established for a particular period of time, and the members have known this fact since the time of intake. Ideally, planning for the length of service was related to the agency's purpose for offering the group service. Knowledge about the duration of the group has been an important factor in the determination of specific purposes by the members and of the content and focus of the activity in the group.

Many groups of predetermined duration are short-term ones, consisting of from one to ten sessions. They are used for such purposes as orientation, preparation for a new experience, coping with crises, or the resolution of specific situational problems. The short duration of the group does not mean that it has been less meaningful to its members than has a group of longer duration. The greater specificity of the shared problems or the crises situations may indeed have influenced the development of intensive relationships among the members and with the social worker and a deep sense of accomplishment. A short-term group moves through all of the stages of development, but in a condensed manner. Knowledge of the duration of the group has, to some extent, eased the trauma of leaving a meaningful experience. But the members of such a group still have many ambivalent reactions to the reality of the group's termination similar to those of members of continued service groups.

There comes a time when the worker must inform the group about the reality of the termination. The initial clues that one or more members of the group are ready to terminate often come from the members themselves. The content of the group tends to include more reports from members about their successful efforts to try new things, or to modify their patterns of behavior outside of the group. The social worker is alert to such a development in the group. He responds to these cues, if his own evaluation of progress confirms the members' views, by introducing the possibility of termination of a member, or the group, in the near future. The responses of the members indicate to him whether or not he should pursue the subject further or await developments. But, the practitioner cannot wait for the group to introduce the matter of termination and to make the decision about it. When it does not come from the group, it is his responsibility to introduce the reality of termination, and to shift his focus toward preparing the members for it.

The need for termination should be discussed well in advance of the termination date, to allow sufficient time to make of it a positive experience for the members. But, if termination is discussed too early, anxiety and hostility may be aroused which detract from motivation to use the group fully toward goal achievement. The time span between the initial information about termination and the final meeting of the group will vary with many factors, including the group's purpose, the length of time the group has been together, the problems and progress of the members, their anticipated reactions to termination, and the press of the environment on them. If a tentative date for termination is set, work can proceed with that time in mind, yet allow for some flexibility.

REACTIONS OF MEMBERS TO TERMINATION. A group experience may feel so good and be so gratifying to the members that they want to continue, even though they have made many positive gains and could probably maintain these in the community. The conflict between the acknowledgment of improvement and movement away from social work help, and the fear of the loss of the worker's special attention and the support of the group, leads to varied reactions to termination on the part of members.[3]

Termination is viewed with ambivalence by almost all members of groups and by the social worker, for that matter. The harboring of conflicting emotions and desires constitutes a drain on the ego. In a group of adult women, as an example, the social worker commented that people usually have mixed feelings about ending with a group, and asked if some of them could express feelings about termination. Mrs. Blaine spoke up, saying that she knows she still needs to come—she is not ready to leave. The worker wondered if she was feeling pushed out, to which Mrs. Blaine replied, "That's exactly what I feel," and elaborated on this. Two other members said that they also felt this way. Mrs. Jones said that she would miss the group, but she would feel good to be able to manage without professional help.

Expression of ambivalent feelings about termination makes it more possible for the members to evaluate the experience realistically, rather than have it clouded or blackened by unrecognized feelings. If ambivalences are worked through, the members' energies are released for other purposes. Doubt, hesitancy, and unresolved tugs between positive and negative feelings are characteristic in this stage of development. Members recognize the progress they have made and want to move on to new relationships and new activities, yet they also want to continue the gratifications provided by the worker and the sense of belonging to the group. A variety of defenses are mobilized to deal with the ambivalence. The strength of the

[3] See Garland, Jones, and Kolodny, "A Model for Stages of Development in Social Work Groups," in Bernstein, ed., *Explorations in Group Work,* pp. 12-53; Green, "Terminating the Relationship in Social Casework: A Working Paper"; Flesch, *Treatment Considerations in the Reassignment of Clients;* Morton, "The Role of the Social Worker in the Termination of Service to Groups"; Valle, "The Role of the Social Group Worker within the Process of Planned Termination."

dependency needs, the nature of his relationships in the group, and the amount of improvement he has made will influence how a particular member will respond. The diversity of reactions set off by the confrontation that the group will definitely terminate is reminiscent of the range of maneuvers displayed during the earlier phases when the group was forming. Anxiety similar to that experienced over coming together is felt now in relation to moving apart and breaking the bonds that have been formed. Some members do not know their own feelings, and are bewildered by them. Many maneuvers are employed by the members both to avoid and forestall termination and to face and accomplish it.[4]

In one study, the major separation anxiety was expressed in regard to the threatened loss of the group as an entity, rather than to the loss of the therapist.[5] As one member of a prerelease group in a mental hospital expressed it, "I came to say good-bye to you [the worker] again. It's hard to do this, and hard to leave the hospital after so many years here. But leaving our group is the hardest of all." Then, following the social worker's comment, "Yes, I know," the patient continued, "But it's easier knowing others are facing the same thing, trying to make a go of life outside." The group which is being dissolved is probably a meaningful reference group and a vehicle for social gratifications for the members, which fact creates additional anxieties and resistances concerning termination.

One typical reaction is that of denial that the group is terminating. The members refuse to accept the notion of termination, behave as though it were not going to happen, and forget the prior explanations by the worker of the plan for termination. Another frequent response to the need to terminate is to return to earlier patterns of behavior. This action may be in the form of inability to cope with situations and tasks that had

[4] Garland, Jones, and Kolodny, "A Model for Stages of Development in Social Work Groups," in Bernstein, ed., *Explorations in Group Work*, pp. 41-49.

[5] Scheidlinger and Holden, "Group Therapy of Women with Severe Character Disorders: The Middle and Final Phases," *International Journal of Group Psychotherapy*, XVI (2), (1966), 174-89.

apparently been mastered earlier, or in the reactivation of conflicts among members. Sometimes the members behave in ways
that are dramatically reminiscent of earlier developmental
phases, reflecting a desire to begin all over again.

It is not unusual for a group to face the fact of termination
in an explosion of behavior which says, in effect, "You thought
we were better or more able, but you were wrong, we really
are not; we still need you and the group." Negative symptoms
may recur. It is important that the worker not take this for actual
retrogression, nor agree with the group that it is back to the
beginning. Rather, it is necessary to understand the acts as the
members' way of reassuring themselves that the worker continues to accept them and be interested in them. The negative
behavior expresses anxiety that the worker will put the members
out before they are ready to leave. The flare-up is an indication
of difficulty in leaving relationships and experiences which have
been important. Such members need the practitioner's reassurance that he will not leave until the members are ready.

Another problem is that of the group member who is so
fearful of being left that he is impelled to break off the relationship precipitously, as if to say, "I'll leave you before you
leave me." This is one pattern of behavior in leaving meaningful relationships. People who have never experienced much
trust in parents and others in positions of authority are particularly fearful of the intimacy of the social work relationship.
Through the many hurts of their life experiences, they are
easily triggered to withdraw if they have a glimmer that they
might be hurt again. The impulse to flee from the warm group
climate may be great. With such a problem in the termination
phase, the worker's activity needs to be geared to helping the
members to stay in the relationship until its official ending.

Reactions to termination frequently are based on a perception
of being rejected by the social worker. As aptly put by Schiff,
"The therapist has been a big liar. What good parent would
throw his child out?" [6] Some members may react through a

[6] Schiff, "Termination of Therapy," *Archives of General Psychiatry*, VI
(1962), 80.

denial of the positive meaning of the experience for them, to prove that the worker never really did care for them. Some may feel that the group is terminating as a punishment for their unacceptable behavior. To this end, the members exhibit a variety of rejecting and rejection-provoking behavior. They may be absent, leave the group, or express verbally their feelings of being rejected by the worker or of rejecting him.

Not all reactions to the group's termination are related to inability to accept it. Another set is concerned with accepting and making constructive moves toward separating from the worker and often from other members, too. Activities used for such ends include review of the experiences the members have had in the group, and reminiscences about the satisfactions they have achieved and the conflicts they have weathered. There is spontaneous evaluation of what is different about individuals and the group now and the ways in which the members have made progress. The members make constructive moves to find new activities and relationships outside the group.

A combination of varied reactions tends to occur, with modifications in tendency and duration, in most groups which have continued with sustained attendance over a significant period of time. There is a tendency for reactions to occur in flashes and in clusters, even within the space of a single session. Over a period of time, there seems to be a certain progression in rationality among the reactions, for example, from denial or reactivation of symptoms to review and evaluation. Nevertheless, the actual emergence is not always in sequence. It is not uncommon for members to evaluate their experience together in a reflective manner and later explode into mutual recrimination over responsibility for unacceptable behavior that occurred some time ago.[7]

[7] Garland, Jones, and Kolodny, "A Model for Stages of Development in Social Work Groups," in Bernstein, ed., *Explorations in Group Work*, pp. 44-45.

The Activities of the Social Worker

In the terminal stage, the social worker's contribution becomes centered on helping the members to cope with the stressful situation of ending. He faces a complexity of feelings: the separate reactions of each individual which may be like or different from those of the other members. But, through mutual influence, a group feeling or mood emerges to which he needs to address his attention. He works with the members to help them to express their ambivalent feelings toward termination. If a reaction is one of feeling abandoned or rejected, additional support is needed. At times, the worker needs to help the members to identify and clarify their feelings. He may need to point out how the present reactions are similar to modes of dealing with other problematic situations in order to help members to understand and modify them. He recognizes that, unless the group is to continue as a unit, the feelings tend to revolve around the loss of the group as well as of the worker.

The social worker is not immune from feelings about terminating with members of the group. Facing termination stirs up feelings about both the members and his role in the group. It is natural that a worker will feel pleased about the progress of the group and his part in it. It is natural, too, that he will feel a sense of loss, for it is not easy to separate from persons with whom one has developed a meaningful relationship. Termination also stirs up feelings about the quality of the worker's performance, for example, certain guilt feelings for not having had the time or the skill to have been more helpful to more members. The worker may have doubts about the nature and permanence of the gains made by the members, leading to a desire to hang onto the group. If he is to use his feelings in a helpful, rather than hurtful way, the worker needs to acknowledge them and to renew his faith in the members' capacities to continue to grow after his relationship with them is terminated.

Four weeks before the planned termination day, the social worker reminded a group of high-school girls that there were only three more meetings before school was out and the group would end. The members protested that they did not know time would go so fast—they wanted to continue. After the meeting closed, the girls insisted upon staying. Later, they went to the worker's office and gave her a letter in which they expressed their feelings about leaving her and the group. The worker read it and said that she was very touched by it. One girl said it made her want to cry, and the others agreed. The worker commented that it would be hard for her to leave them also. In the next meeting, in response to the comments of the girls, the worker said she guessed it felt to them as if she were deserting them. One girl replied, "Yeah—that's it." Others said it made them feel angry. The girls spent considerable time talking about how much help they still needed. At the last meeting, the girls had a surprise party for the worker. The worker took pictures of the group with her Polaroid camera and gave each girl one. Later, the worker shared with each member her impressions of the gains each had made in the group, which pleased them very much. She took each of the girls home and said good-bye to their families.

The social worker engages the members in discussions and action-oriented experiences to help them stabilize the changes they have made. These activities are a natural progression from those in the preceding phase of development. They tend to be oriented to the community, such as visits to schools or employment offices, or participation in sophisticated social experiences that test the members' capacities for adaptive behavior. Sometimes, there is a desire by members to repeat earlier experiences, either those that were gratifying or those in which they failed in some way. Through such repetition, the members confirm their judgment that they are more able to deal with problematic situations now than previously. Opportunities and resources in the community are discussed or used in order to foster mobility into the community.

One common focus during the last meetings is a review of the group's purpose and individual purposes and an evaluation of the extent to which the members have moved toward the achievement of these goals. The social worker accepts differences in progress made. He may need to work with the group to help bring about acceptance of differences or give special help to a particular member of the group who feels disappointed that he has not made as much progress as he had hoped for. He has a responsibility to share his observations of progress and his confidence in the growing ability of the members to get along without him and usually also without the group. As the group evaluates its experience together, the worker needs to be secure enough to accept and elicit evaluations of things that could have been done differently by him, as well as of those things that he did that were most useful and satisfying to the members.

The social worker supports the members' efforts to move away from the group, to develop new relationships outside the group, and to find their place in the usual activities of the community. The worker's activity is pinpointed on helping the members to develop a sense of their own identity apart from the group, a natural extension of earlier work on problems of identity. For the members need now to be able to get along without the group, to have further help in integrating the gains, and to make decisions about their own futures. The worker supports the efforts of the members to move away from the group, to make new friends and to develop new interests outside of the group, and to find their place in the normal activities in the community. He accredits the members' developing interests in other things, and is pleased when other interests come to take precedence over group meetings:

The painful aspects of terminating a helpful relationship are diminished by the clients' own growing sense of strength, by a comforting feeling of improvement because of the channelizing of his activities into ego building and enlarged social activities and interests with the realization of the worker's continuing good will and the fact that he can return to the agency if necessary.[8]

The worker needs to indicate and clarify the nature of any continuing relationship he may have with individuals, their families, or with the group. He makes plans to be available for

[8] Hamilton, *Theory and Practice of Social Case Work*, p. 81.

help on an individual basis if problems are encountered, to follow up with interviews for the purpose of evaluating how members are getting along later, or to have reunions with the group.

In many situations, it is not sufficient that the social worker notify and prepare the members of the group for termination. In work with children, parents need to participate in the review and evaluation of the child's progress in the group and in the decisions concerning any follow-up services to be provided by the worker or referrals to another agency. In serving groups within an institutional setting, other staff members who have responsibilities to the members need to be either notified about or to participate in the actual decision to terminate the group service, depending upon circumstances. When group work is one part of a constellation of services to a member, the other personnel within the agency or in the community need to be involved in the plans for the member after he has left the group. For no group is an island unto itself: its members are parts of other social systems which may be affected by the discontinuance of the group.

Groups often have a final ceremonial to symbolize the ending. In one group of former mental patients, ready to apply for official discharge from the mental hospital, the members brought their letters requesting discharge to the meeting, read them to each other, and made suggested improvements in the letters. There was an exchange of statements of hope that each would be able to get along well, and a statement by one member, in behalf of the group, of the meaning the experience had to them and of their appreciation to the worker for his help. A group of parents brought elaborate refreshments and a note of appreciation to the worker to symbolize the ending of that group. In such instances, the worker accepts graciously the members' appreciation for help given.

In the actual final disengagement, the social worker makes clear that the door is open, when this is within agency policy, that the worker will be available for interviews with members if they feel it necessary to have them. He assures the members of his continued interest in them, even though the old relationship will not be available. The worker's concern for the members does not stop on the last day and the members need to know this. Hope is held out that the new strengths and outlooks gained through the group experience will provide a basis for each member's continued coping in his own way with the problems of daily living.

Bibliography

Alexander, Franz, and Helen Ross, eds. *Dynamic Psychiatry*. Chicago, University of Chicago Press, 1952.

Allport, Floyd. *Theories of Perception and the Concept of Structure*. New York, John Wiley, 1955.

Arieti, Silvano, ed. *American Handbook of Psychiatry*. 2 vols. New York, Basic Books, 1959.

Aronson, H., and B. Overall. "Treatment Expectations of Patients in Two Social Classes," *Social Work*, XI (1), (1966), 35-41.

Austin, David M. "Goals for Gang Workers," *Social Work*, II (4), (1957), 43-50.

——— "What about Reaching-out—An Account of the Boston Youth Project," *The Round Table*, National Federation of Settlements, XIX (1955), 1-5.

Bales, Robert F. *Interaction Process Analysis: A Method for the Study of Small Groups*. Cambridge, Mass., Addison-Wesley, 1950.

Bales, Robert F., et al. "Structure and Dynamics of Small Groups: A Review of Four Variables," in Joseph Gittler, ed., *Review of Sociology: Analysis of a Decade*. New York, John Wiley, 1957.

Bales, Robert F., and Edgar Borgatta. "Size of Group as a Factor in the Interaction Profile," in A. Paul Hare et al., eds., *Small Groups; Studies in Social Interaction*. New York, A. A. Knopf, 1955.

Bartlett, Harriet. "Toward Clarification and Improvement of Social Work Practice," *Social Work*, III (2), (1958), 3-9.

Bell, Norman W., and Ezra F. Vogel, eds. *Modern Introduction to the Family*. Glencoe, Illinois, Free Press, 1960.

Benne, Kenneth D., and Paul Sheats. "Functional Roles of Group Members," *Journal of Social Issues*, IV (1948), 41-49.

Bennis, Warren G., Kenneth D. Benne, and Robert Chin, eds. *The Planning of Change; Readings in the Applied Behavioral Sciences*. New York, Holt, Rinehart and Winston, 1961.

Berelson, Bernard, and Gary A. Steiner. *Human Behavior: An*

Inventory of Scientific Findings. New York, Harcourt, Brace and World, 1964.

Bernstein, B. "Language and Social Class," *British Journal of Sociology.* XL (1960), 23-30.

Bernstein, Saul, ed. *Explorations in Group Work.* Boston, School of Social Work of Boston University, 1965.

―――― "Self Determination: King or Citizen in the Realm of Values," *Social Work,* V (1), (1960), 3-8.

Bettleheim, Bruno, and Emmy Sylvester. "Therapeutic Influence of the Group on the Individual," *American Journal of Orthopsychiatry,* XVII (1947), 684-92.

Biestek, Felix P. *The Casework Relationship.* Chicago, Loyola University Press, 1957.

Bion, W. R. *Experiences in Groups and Other Papers.* London, Tavistock Publications, 1961.

Blum, Arthur. "The A-ha Response as a Therapeutic Goal," in Henry Maier, ed., *Group Work as Part of Residential Treatment.* New York, National Association of Social Workers, 1965.

―――― "Values and Aspirations as a Focus for Treatment," in *Social Work Practice, 1963.* Selected Papers, 92nd Annual Forum, National Conference on Social Welfare. New York, Columbia University Press, 1963.

Boehm, Werner W. "The Nature of Social Work," *Social Work,* III (2), (1958) 10-18.

Bonner, Hubert. *Group Dynamics: Principles and Applications.* New York, Ronald Press, 1959.

Brager, George. "Organizing the Unaffiliated in a Low-income Area," Social Work, VIII (2), (1963), 34-40.

Brenner, Charles. *An Elementary Textbook of Psychoanalysis.* New York, International Universities Press, 1957.

Briar, Scott M. "Use of Theory in Studying Effects of Client Social Class on Students' Judgments," *Social Work,* VI (3), (1961), 91-97.

Buhler, Charlotte. *Values in Psychotherapy.* New York, Free Press of Glencoe, 1962.

Building Social Work Knowledge. New York, National Association of Social Workers, 1964.

Burns, Mary E., and Paul H. Glasser. "Similarities and Differences in Casework and Group Work Practice," *Social Service Review,* XXXVII (1963), 416-28.

Cartwright, Dorwin, and Alvin Zander. *Group Dynamics: Research and Theory.* 2nd ed. Evanston, Illinois, Row Peterson, 1960.

Cattell, Raymond B. "New Concepts for Measuring Leadership in Terms of Group Syntality," *Human Relations,* IV (1951), 161-84.

Chin, Robert. "Evaluating Group Movement and Individual Change," in *Use of Groups in the Psychiatric Setting.* New York, National Association of Social Workers, 1960.

Churchill, Sallie R. "Part-time Group Work Practice in Non-treatment Institutions," in Henry Maier, ed., *Group Work as Part of Residential Treatment,* New York, National Association of Social Workers, 1965.

Clemenger, Florence. "Congruence between Members and Workers on Selected Behaviors of the Role of the Social Group Worker," Unpublished D.S.W. Dissertation, School of Social Work, University of Southern California, 1965.

Cloward, Richard A. "Agency Structure as a Variable in Services to Groups," in *Group Work and Community Organization, 1956.* Selected Papers, 83rd Annual Forum, National Conference on Social Welfare. New York, Columbia University Press, 1956.

Cohen, Jerome. "Social Work and the Culture of Poverty." *Social Work,* IX (1), (1964), 3-11.

Cohen, Mabel B., ed. *Advances in Psychiatry; Recent Developments in Interpersonal Relations.* New York, W. W. Norton, 1959.

Confidentiality in Social Services to Individuals. New York, National Social Welfare Assembly, 1958.

Cooley, Charles. *Social Process.* New York, Scribner's Sons, 1918.

Coser, Lewis A. *The Functions of Social Conflict.* Glencoe, Illinois. Free Press, 1956.

Cottrell, Leonard S., and Rosaland Dymond, "The Empathic Responses, A Neglected Field for Research," *Psychiatry,* XXI (1949), 355-59.

Council on Social Work Education, *A Conceptual Framework for the Teaching of the Social Group Work Method in the Classroom.* New York, Council on Social Work Education, 1964.

Coyle, Grace L. "Concepts Relevant to Helping the Family as a Group," *Social Casework,* XLIII (1962), 347-54.

——— *Group Experience and Democratic Values.* New York, Woman's Press, 1947.

———— *Group Work with American Youth.* New York, Harper and
Bros., 1948.

———— *Social Process in Organized Groups.* New York, Richard
R. Smith, 1930.

———— "Some Basic Assumptions about Social Group Work," in
Marjorie Murphy, *The Social Group Work Method in Social
Work Education.* New York, Council on Social Work Education,
1959.

———— "Social Group Work: An Aspect of Social Work Practice,"
Journal of Social Issues, VIII (1952), 23-34.

———— ed. *Studies in Group Behavior.* New York and London,
Harper and Bros., 1937.

Coyle, Grace L., and Margaret E. Hartford. *Social Process in the
Community and the Group.* New York, Council on Social Work
Education, 1958.

Cumming, John, and Elaine Cumming. *Ego and Milieu; Theory
and Practice of Environmental Therapy.* New York, Atherton
Press, 1962.

Cunningham, Ruth, and Associates. *Understanding Group Behavior of Boys and Girls.* New York, Teachers College Press,
Columbia University, 1951.

Curriculum Policy Statement for the Master's Degree Program in
Graduate Professional Schools of Social Work. New York, Council on Social Work Education, 1962.

Del Valle, Alline, and Felton Alexander. "Effects of the Project
on Family Service Agencies and Urban Leagues," *Social Casework,* XLVIII (1967), 633-38.

Deutsch, Martin. "The Role of Social Class in Language Development and Cognition," *American Journal of Orthopsychiatry,*
XXXV (1965), 78-88.

Deutsch, Martin et al. *The Disadvantaged Child: Studies in the
Social Environment and the Learning Process.* New York, Basic
Books, 1967.

Durkin, Helen E. *The Group in Depth.* New York, International
Universities Press, 1964.

Elliott, Harrison. *The Process of Group Thinking.* New York,
Association Press, 1928.

Erikson, Erik H. *Childhood and Society.* 2nd ed., New York, W.
W. Norton, 1963.

———— "Growth and Crisis in the Healthy Personality," in Kluckhohn, Clyde, and Henry A. Murray, eds., *Personality in Nature, Society, and Culture,* 2nd ed., New York, A. A. Knopf, 1953.

——— "Identity and the Life Cycle: Selected Papers," in *Psychological Issues.* New York, International Universities Press, 1959.

——— "The Problem of Ego Identity," *Journal of the American Psychoanalytic Association,* IV (1956), 56-121.

Eubank, Earle E. *The Concepts of Sociology.* Boston, D. D. Heath, 1932.

Falck, Hans S. "The Use of Groups in the Practice of Social Work," *Social Casework,* XLIV (1963), 63-67.

Falsberg, Martin. "Setting Limits with the Juvenile Delinquent," *Social Casework,* XXXVIII (1957), 138-42.

Fantl, Berta. "Integrating Psychological, Social, and Cultural Factors in Assertive Casework," *Social Work,* IV (4), (1958), 30-37.

Feldman, Francis Lomas, and Francis H. Scherz. *Family Social Welfare: Helping Troubled Families.* New York, Atherton Press, 1967.

Fenton, Norman, and Kermit T. Wiltse, eds. *Group Methods in the Public Welfare Program.* Palo Alto, California, Pacific Books, 1963.

Fisher, Raymond. "Use of Groups in Social Treatment by Caseworkers and Group Workers," in *Use of Groups in the Psychiatric Setting.* New York, National Association of Social Workers, 1960.

Flesch, Regina. *Treatment Considerations in the Reassignment of Clients.* New York, Family Service Association of America, 1947.

Follett, Mary Parker. *Dynamic Administration,* the collected papers of Mary Parker Follett. Edited by Henry C. Metcalf and L. Urwick, New York and London, Harper and Bros., 1942.

——— *The New State.* New York, Longmans-Green, 1920.

Foote, Nelson N., and Leonard S. Cottrell, Jr. *Identity and Interpersonal Competence.* Chicago, University of Chicago Press, 1955.

Frank, Jerome. *Persuasion and Healing: A Comparative Study of Psychotherapy.* Baltimore, Johns Hopkins Press, 1961.

Frank, Lawrence K. "Change through Group Experience," in *The Social Welfare Forum,* 1957. Official Proceedings, 84th Annual Forum, National Conference on Social Welfare, New York, Columbia University Press, 1957.

Freud, Anna. *The Ego and the Mechanisms of Defence.* New York, International Universities Press, 1946.

Freud, Sigmund. *Group Psychology and the Analysis of the Ego.* London, Hogarth Press, 1948.

Frey, Louise. "Support and the Group: Generic Treatment Form," *Social Work,* VII (4), (1962), 35-42.

———— ed. *Use of Groups in the Health Field.* New York, National Association of Social Workers, 1966.

Frey, Louise, and Ralph Kolodny. "Illusions and Realities in Current Social Work with Groups," *Social Work,* IX (2), (1964), 80-90.

Friedlander, Walter A., ed. *Concepts and Methods in Social Work.* Englewood Cliffs, New Jersey, Prentice-Hall, 1958.

Gans, Herbert J. *The Urban Villagers, Group and Class in the Life of Italian-Americans.* New York, Free Press of Glencoe, 1962.

Ganter, Grace. "The Group Worker in the Child Guidance Center," in Harleigh B. Trecker, ed., *Group Work in the Psychiatric Setting.* New York, Whiteside and W. Morrow, 1956.

Ganter, Grace, and Norman Polansky. "Predicting a Child's Verbal Accessibility to Individual Treatment from Diagnostic Groups," *Social Work,* IX (3), (1964), 56-63.

Garland, James A., Hubert E. Jones, and Ralph Kolodny. "A Model for Stages of Development in Social Work Groups," in Saul Bernstein, ed., *Explorations in Group Work.* Boston, Boston University School of Social Work, 1965.

Garrett, Annette. *Interviewing, Its Principles and Methods.* New York, Family Welfare Association of America, 1942.

"Girls in Crisis." Proceedings of a Conference sponsored jointly by the Welfare Federation of Cleveland, Ohio, and the School of Applied Social Sciences, Western Reserve University, 1962.

Gittler, Joseph B., ed. *Review of Sociology: Analysis of a Decade.* New York, John Wiley, 1957.

Glasser, Paul H. "Group Methods in Child Welfare: Review and Preview," *Child Welfare,* XLII (1963), 213-19.

———— "Social Role, Personality, and Group Work Practice," in *Social Work Practice, 1962:* Selected Papers, 89th Annual Forum, National Conference on Social Welfare. New York, Columbia University Press, 1962.

Glasser, Paul, Herman Resnick, and Rosemary Sarri. "Social Group

Work in the Psychiatric Setting: A Report on Two Instructional Programs," School of Social Work, University of Michigan, 1963.

Goffman, Erving. *Behavior in Public Places; Notes on the Social Organization of Gatherings,* New York, Free Press, 1963.

Gold, Bertram M. "Some Guiding Principles in the Work with Individuals Outside the Group," in *Toward Professional Standards.* New York, Association Press, 1947.

Goodrich, D. Wells, and Donald S. Boomer. "Some Concepts about Therapeutic Intervention with Hyperaggressive Children: Part I," *Social Casework,* XXXIX (1958), 207-13; "Part II," *ibid.,* 286-92.

Gore, Ellen. "Analysis of Members' Expressions of Feelings in First Meetings of Groups," Unpublished M.S.W. Thesis, School of Social Work, University of Southern California, 1960.

Gordon, William E. "A Critique of the Working Definition," *Social Work,* VII (4), (1962), 3-13.

Gouldner, Alvin W. "Red Tape as a Social Problem," in Robert Merton et al., eds., *Reader in Bureaucracy.* Glencoe, Illinois, Free Press, 1952.

Green, Rose. "Terminating the Relationship in Social Casework: A Working Paper." Paper read before the Annual Institute on Corrections, University of Southern California, April, 1962.

Gross, Neal, Warren S. Mason, A. W. McEachern. *Explorations in Role Analysis; Studies of the School Superintendency Role.* New York, John Wiley, 1958.

Group Methods and Services in Child Welfare. New York, Child Welfare League of America, 1963.

Hacker, Frederick J., and Elisabeth Gelered. "Freedom and Authority in Adolescence," *American Journal of Orthopsychiatry,* XV (1945), 621-30.

Hallowitz, David, et al. "The Assertive Counseling Component of Therapy," *Social Casework,* XLVIII (1967), 543-49.

Hamilton, Gordon. "Helping People—The Growth of a Profession," in *Social Work as Human Relations.* New York, Columbia University Press, 1949.

——— *Theory and Practice of Social Case Work.* 2nd ed., revised. New York, Columbia University Press, 1951.

Hare, A. Paul. *Handbook of Small Group Research.* New York, Free Press of Glencoe, 1962.

Hare, Paul A., Edgar F. Borgatta, and Robert F. Bales, eds. *Small*

Groups: Studies in Social Interaction. New York, A. A. Knopf, 1955.

Hartford, Margaret E., ed. "Working Papers toward a Frame of Reference for Social Group Work." New York, National Association of Social Workers, 1964.

—— "The Social Group Worker and Group Formation," Unpublished Ph.D. Dissertation, School of Social Service Administration, University of Chicago, 1962.

Hartman, Heinz. *Ego Psychology and the Problems of Adaptation*. New York, International Universities Press, 1958.

Hayakawa, Samuel, ed. *Language, Meaning, and Maturity*. New York, Harper and Bros., 1954.

Hearn, Gordon. "Group Change and Development," Unpublished Paper, 1962.

—— *Theory Building in Social Work*. Toronto, University of Toronto Press, 1958.

Heldoorn, Jean. "Analysis of Testing in Worker-Group Relationships," Unpublished M.S.W. Thesis, School of Social Work, University of Southern California, 1955.

Herrick, James C. "The Perception of Crisis in a Modified Therapeutic Community," Unpublished D.S.W. Dissertation, School of Social Work, University of Southern California, 1966.

Hersko, Marvin. "Group Psychotherapy with Delinquent Adolescent Girls," *American Journal of Orthopsychiatry*, XXXII (1962), 169-75.

Herzog, Elizabeth. "Some Assumptions about the Poor," *Social Service Review*, XXXVII (1964), 389-401.

Hoffman, Martin L., and Lois Wladis Hoffman, eds. *Review of Child Development Research*. Vol. I. New York, Russell Sage Foundation, 1964.

Hollingshead, August B., and Frederick C. Redlich. *Social Class and Mental Illness, A Community Study*. New York, John Wiley, 1958.

Hollis, Florence. *Casework: A Psychosocial Therapy*. New York, Random House, 1964.

Homans, George. *Social Behavior: Its Elementary Forms*. New York, Harcourt, Brace and World, 1961.

—— *The Human Group*. New York, Harcourt-Brace, 1950.

Inkeles, Alex. "Social Structure and the Socialization of Competence," *Harvard Educational Review*, XXXVI (1966).

Jennings, Helen Hall. *Leadership and Isolation: A Study of Personality in Interpersonal Relations.* New York, Longmans Green, 1950.

Johnson, Arlien. *School Social Work: Its Contribution to Professional Education.* New York, National Association of Social Workers, 1962.

Kaiser, Clara A. "The Social Group Work Process," *Social Work,* III (2), (1958), 67-75.

—— "Characteristics of Social Group Work," in *The Social Welfare Forum, 1957.* Official Proceedings, 84th Annual Forum, National Conference on Social Welfare. New York, Columbia University Press, 1957.

Kahn, Alfred J., ed. *Issues in American Social Work.* New York, Columbia University Press, 1959.

Katz, Daniel, and Robert L. Kahn. *The Social Psychology of Organizations.* New York, John Wiley, 1966.

Katz, Robert L. *Empathy, Its Nature and Uses.* New York, Free Press of Glencoe, 1963.

Kelley, Harold H., and John Thibaut. "Experimental Studies of Group Problem Solving and Process," in Gardner Lindzey, ed. *Handbook of Social Psychology.* Cambridge, Addison-Wesley, 1954.

Kendall, Katherine. "New Dimensions in Casework and Group Work Practice, Implications for Professional Education," *Social Work,* IV (4), (1959), 49-56.

Klein, Alan F. "Exploring Family Group Counseling," *Social Work,* VIII (1), (1963), 23-29.

—— *Role Playing in Leadership Training and Group Problem Solving.* New York, Association Press, 1956.

—— *Society, Democracy, and the Group.* New York, Woman's Press and William Morrow, 1953.

Klein, Joyce Gale. "Social Group Work Treatment: Some Selected Dynamics," in *New Perspectives on Services to Groups.* New York, National Association of Social Workers, 1961.

Kluckhohn, Florence. "Cultural Factors in Social Work Practice and Education," *Social Service Review,* XXV (1951), 38-47.

—— "Variations in the Basic Values of Family Systems," *Social Casework,* XXXIX (1958), 63-72.

Kogan, Leonard S. "The Short Term Case in a Family Agency,"

Social Casework, XXXVIII (1957), Part I, 231-38; Part II, 296-302; Part III, 366-74.

Konopka, Gisela. *Group Work in the Institution—A Modern Challenge.* New York, Whiteside, Morrow, 1954.

——— "Resistance and Hostility in Group Members," *The Group,* XVI (1953), 3-10.

——— *Social Group Work: A Helping Process.* Englewood Cliffs, New Jersey, Prentice-Hall, 1963.

——— *The Adolescent Girl in Conflict.* Englewood Cliffs, New Jersey, Prentice-Hall, 1966.

——— *Therapeutic Group Work with Children.* Minneapolis, University of Minnesota Press, 1949.

Kraft, Ivor, and Catherine S. Chilman. *Helping Low-Income Families through Parent Education, Survey of Research.* Welfare Administration, U.S. Department of Health, Education, and Welfare, Washington, D.C., 1966.

Lane, Dorthea. "Psychiatric Patients Learn a New Way of Life," in *New Perspectives on Services to Groups.* New York, National Association of Social Workers, 1961.

Landes, Ruth. "Minority Groups and School Social Work," *Social Work,* IV (3), (1959), 91-97.

Leader, Arthur. "The Role of Intervention in Family Group Treatment," *Social Casework,* XLV (1964), 327-32.

Leary, Timothy. "The Theory and Measurement Methodology of Interpersonal Communication," in Warren G. Bennis, Kenneth D. Benne, and Robert Chin, eds. *The Planning of Change.* New York, Holt, Rinehart and Winston, 1961.

Leichter, Elsa. "The Interrelationship of Content and Process in Therapy Groups," *Social Casework,* XLVII (1966), 302-06.

Lennard, Henry L., and Arnold Bernstein. *The Anatomy of Psychotherapy; Systems of Communication and Expectation.* New York, Columbia University Press, 1960.

Lerner, Raymond C. "The Therapeutic Social Club: Social Rehabilitation for Mental Patients," *International Journal of Social Psychiatry,* VI (1960).

Levine, Baruch. *Fundamentals of Group Treatment.* Chicago, Whitehall Company, 1967.

——— "Principles for Developing an Ego-supportive Group Treatment Service," *Social Service Review,* XXXIX (1965), 422-32.

Levinger, George. "Continuance in Casework and Other Helping Relationships: A Review of Current Research," *Social Work,* V (3), (1960), 40-51.

Lewin, Kurt. *Field Theory in Social Science, Selected Theoretical Papers.* Edited by Dorwin Cartwright. New York, Harper and Bros., 1951.

Lifton, Norman and E. M. Smolen. "Group Psychotherapy with Schizophrenic Children," *International Journal of Group Psychotherapy,* XVI (1966), 23-41.

Lindenberg, Ruth Ellen. "Hard to Reach: Client or Casework Agency?" *Social Work,* III (4), (1958), 23-29.

Lindzey, Gardner, ed. *Handbook of Social Psychology.* 2 vols., Cambridge, Mass., Addison-Wesley, 1954.

Lippitt, Ronald. "Unplanned Maintenance and Planned Change in the Group Work Process," in *Social Work Practice, 1962.* Selected Papers, 89th Annual Forum, National Conference on Social Welfare. New York, Columbia University Press, 1962.

Lippitt, Ronald, Jeanne Watson, and Bruce Westley. *The Dynamics of Planned Change.* New York, Harcourt-Brace, 1958.

Loeb, Martin. "Social Class and the American Social System," *Social Work,* VI (2), (1961), 12-17.

Lowry, Fern. "The Caseworker in Short Contact Services," *Social Work,* II (1), (1957), 52-56.

Lucas, Leon. "Content of the Group Experience," in *Use of Groups in the Psychiatric Setting.* New York, National Association of Social Workers, 1960.

Maas, Henry, ed. *Five Fields of Social Service; Reviews of Research,* New York, National Association of Social Workers, 1966.

———— "Group Influences on Client-Worker Interaction," *Social Work,* IX (2), (1964), 70-79.

———— et al. "Socio-cultural Factors in Psychiatric Clinic Services for Children," *Smith College Studies in Social Work,* XXV (1955), 1-90.

———— "The Role of Member in Lower-class and Middle-class Adolescents," *Child Development,* XXV (1954), 241-42.

Maas, Jeannette. "The Use of Actional Procedures in Group Psychotherapy with Sociopathic Women," *International Journal of Group Psychotherapy.* XVI (1966), 190-97.

McGuerty, Patricia. "Individual Group Members' Expectations of

Social Work Help as Compared Through Time in a Delinquent
Adolescent Group," Unpublished M.S.W. Thesis, School of
Social Work, University of Southern California, 1963.

McLarnan, Georgiana, and Gideon W. Fryer. "Improving Decision-
making among Young Low-income Couples," School of Social
Work, University of Tennessee, 1966.

Maier, Henry W. "Adolescenthood," *Social Casework,* XLVI (1965),
3-9.

——— ed. *Group Work as Part of Residential Treatment.* New
York, National Association of Social Workers, 1965.

Maier, Norman R. F. *Problem-Solving Discussion and Conferences,
Leadership Methods and Skills.* New York, McGraw-Hill, 1963.

Main, Marjorie. "An Examination of Selected Aspects of the Beginning Phase in Social Work with Groups," Unpublished Ph.D.
Dissertation, School of Social Service Administration, University of Chicago, 1965.

Maloney, Sara E., and Margaret H. Mudgett. "Group Work—
Group Casework: Are They the Same?" *Social Work,* IV (2),
(1959,) 29-36.

Maloney, Sara E. "The Interview in Group Work and Casework:
A Comparison," in *Social Work with Groups, 1958.* New York,
National Association of Social Workers, 1958.

Masser, Alfred A. "Ethnocultural Identity and Mental Health,"
in *Social Work Practice, 1963.* Selected Papers, 90th Annual
Forum, National Conference on Social Welfare. New York,
Columbia University Press, 1963.

Mayer, John E., and Aaron Rosenblatt, "The Client's Social Context: Its Effect on Continuance in Treatment," *Social Casework,*
XLV (1964), 511-18.

Mehr, Anita. "Ego Psychology and Its Application to Group
Counseling," in Joseph L. Vigilante, ed., *Ego Psychology: Its
Application to Social Work with Groups in the Mental Hospital.*
New York, Adelphi University School of Social Work, 1963.

Meier, Elizabeth G. "An Inquiry into the Concepts of Ego Identity
and Identity Diffusion," *Social Casework,* XLV (1964), 63-70.

——— "Culturally Deprived Children: Implications for Child Welfare," *Child Welfare,* XLV (1966), 65-73.

Mencher, Samuel. "The Concept of Authority and Social Casework," in *Casework Papers, 1960.* New York, Family Service
Association of America, 1960.

Menninger, Karl. *Theory of Psychoanalytic Technique*. New York, Basic Books, 1958.

Merton, Robert K. "Social Problems and Sociological Theory," in Robert K. Merton and Robert A. Nisbet, eds., *Contemporary Social Problems*. New York, Harcourt, Brace and World, 1966.

———— *Social Theory and Social Structure*. Glencoe, Illinois, Free Press, 1949.

Merton, Robert K., et al., eds. *Reader in Bureaucracy*. Glencoe, Illinois, Free Press, 1952.

Meyer, Marguerite, and Edward Power. "The Family Caseworker's Contribution to Parent Education Through the Medium of the Discussion Group," *American Journal of Orthopsychiatry*. XXIII (1953), 621-28.

Middleman, Ruth R. *The Nonverbal Method in Working with Groups*. New York, Association Press, 1968.

Miller, Walter B. "Implications of Urban Lower-Class Culture for Social Work," *Social Service Review*, XXXIII (1959), 219-36.

Milner, John G. "Freedom and Authority in Social Work," *Social Work Papers*, University of Southern California, VIII (1961), 9-15.

Montagu, Ashley. *The Cultured Man*. Cleveland, World Publishing Co., 1958.

Moreno, Jacob L. *Who Shall Survive? A New Approach to the Problem of Human Interaction*. Washington, D.C., Nervous and Mental Disease Publishing Co., 1934.

Morgan, Ralph W. "Is it Scientific to be Optimistic?" *Social Work*, VI (4), (1961), 12-21.

Morton, Donald. "The Role of the Social Worker in the Termination of Service to Groups," Unpublished M.S.W. Thesis, School of Social Work, University of Southern California, 1964.

Mudgett, Margaret H. "Social Group Work, A Method not a Program," *Social Work Papers*, University of Southern California, V (1957), 14-21.

Murphy, Marjorie. *The Social Group Work Method in Social Work Education*. A Project Report of the Curriculum Study, XI, New York, Council on Social Work Education, 1959.

Myers, Jerome K., and Bertram H. Roberts. *Family and Class Dynamics in Mental Illness*. New York, John Wiley, 1959.

National Federation of Settlements and Neighborhood Centers.

Serving the Teenage Girl. New York, National Federation of Settlements and Neighborhood Centers, 1964.

Neighborhood Youth Association. *Changing the Behavior of Hostile Delinquency Prone Adolescents, I,* Los Angeles, Neighborhood Youth Association, 1960; *Follow-up Study,* II, 1962.

Neiman, Lionel J., and James W. Hughes. "Problem of the Concept of Role—A Re-survey of the Literature," *Social Forces,* XXX (1951), 141-49.

Newcomb, Theodore M. "Role Behaviors in the Study of Individual Personality and of Groups," *Journal of Personality,* XVIII (1950), 273-89.

Newstetter, Wilber I., Marc J. Feldstein, and Theodore Newcomb. *Group Adjustment: A Study in Experimental Sociology.* Cleveland, School of Applied Social Sciences, Western Reserve University, 1938.

Northen, Helen. "An Analysis of Stages of Group Development." Unpublished Paper, 1966.

———— "Evaluating Movement of Individuals in Social Group Work," in *Group Work Papers, 1957.* New York, National Association of Social Workers, 1958.

———— "Interrelated Functions of the Social Group Worker," *Social Work,* II (2), (1957), 63-69.

———— "Social Group Work: a Tool for Changing the Behavior of Disturbed Acting-out Adolescents," in *Social Work with Groups, 1958.* New York, National Association of Social Workers, 1958.

———— "Social Group Work and Work with Groups," *Social Work Papers,* School of Social Work, University of Southern California, V (1957), 1-13.

Olds, Victoria. "Role Theory and Casework: A Review of the Literature," *Social Casework,* XLIII (1962), 3-8.

Olmsted, Michael S. *The Small Group.* New York, Random House, 1959.

Osborn, Hazel. "Some Factors of Resistance which Affect Group Participation," in Dorothea Sullivan, ed., *Readings in Group Work,* New York, Association Press, 1952.

Overton, Alice. "Serving Families Who Don't Want Help," *Social Casework,* XXXIV (1953), 304-09.

———— "Establishing the Relationship." Paper read before the Annual Institute on Corrections, University of Southern California, April, 1962.

Overton, Alice, and Katherine Tinker. *Casework Notebook*. St. Paul, Minnesota, Greater St. Paul Community Council, 1957.

Oxley, Genevieve B. "The Caseworker's Expectations and Client Motivation," *Social Casework*, XLVII (1966), 432-38.

Panter, Ethel J. "Ego-Building Procedures in Social Functioning," *Social Casework*, XLVII (1966), 139-45.

Papell, Catherine, and Beulah Rothman. "Social Group Work Models: Possession and Heritage," *Journal of Education for Social Work*, II (1966).

Parad, Howard, ed. *Crisis Intervention: Selected Readings*. New York, Family Service Association of America, 1965.

Parad, Howard J., and Roger R. Miller, eds. *Ego-Oriented Casework: Problems and Perspectives*. New York, Family Service Association of America, 1963.

Parnicky, Joseph J., et al. "A Study of the Effectiveness of Referrals," *Social Casework*, LXII (1961), 494-501.

Parsons, Talcott, and R. F. Bales. *Family: Socialization, and Interaction Process*. Glencoe, Illinois. Free Press, 1955.

Peck, Harris B., and Virginia Bellsmith. *Treatment of the Delinquent Adolescent: Group and Individual Therapy with Parent and Child*. New York, Family Service Association of America, 1954.

Peirce, Francis J. "A Study of the Methodological Components of Social Work with Groups," Unpublished D.S.W. Dissertation, School of Social Work, University of Southern California, 1966.

Perlman, Helen H. *Social Casework, A Problem-Solving Process*. Chicago, University of Chicago Press, 1957.

——— "Social Work Method: A Review of the Past Decade," *Social Work*, X (4), (1965), 166-78.

Pernell, Ruby B. "Identifying and Teaching the Skill Components of Social Group Work," in *Educational Developments in Social Group Work*. New York, Council on Social Work Education, 1962.

Phillips, E. Lakin, Shirley Shenker, and Paula Revitz. "The Assimilation of the New Child into the Group," *Psychiatry*, XIV (1951), 319-25.

Phillips, Helen U. *Essentials of Social Group Work Skill*. New York, Association Press, 1957.

Pigors, Paul. *Leadership or Domination*. Boston and New York, Houghton-Mifflin, 1935.

Polansky, Norman, Ronald Lippitt, and Fritz Redl. "An Investigation of Behavioral Contagion in Groups," *Human Relations,* III (1950), 319-48.

Polansky, Norman, and Jacob Kounin. "Clients' Reactions to Initial Interviews: a Field Study," *Human Relations,* IX (1956), 237-64.

Polsky, Howard. *Cottage Six—The Social System of Delinquent Boys in Residential Treatment.* New York, Russell Sage Foundation, 1962.

Powdermaker, Florence B., and Jerome D. Frank. *Group Psychotherapy, Studies in Methodology of Research and Therapy.* Cambridge, Mass., Harvard University Press, 1953.

Powell, John W. "The Dynamics of Group Formation," *Psychiatry,* II (1948), 117-24.

"Project Enable." Five articles based on a project sponsored jointly by the Child Study Association of America, the Family Service Association of America, and the National Urban League. *Social Casework,* XLVIII, 1967.

Pumphrey, Muriel W. *The Teaching of Values and Ethics in Social Work Education.* A Project Report of the Curriculum Study, XIII, New York, Council on Social Work Education, 1959.

Rae-Grant, Quentin A., Thomas Gladwin, Eli M. Bower. "Mental Health, Social Competence, and the War on Poverty." Unpublished Paper, National Institute of Mental Health, 1965.

Redl, Fritz. "Diagnostic Group Work," *American Journal of Orthopsychiatry,* XIV (1944), 53-67.

——— "Resistance in Therapy Groups," *Human Relations,* I (1948), 307-20.

——— "Strategy and Technique of the Life Space Interview," *American Journal of Orthopsychiatry,* XXIX (1959) 1-18.

——— "The Art of Group Composition," in Suzanne Schulze, ed., *Creative Group Living in a Children's Institution.* New York, Association Press, 1953.

Redl, Fritz, and David Wineman. *Controls from Within; Techniques for the Treatment of the Aggressive Child.* Glencoe, Illinois, Free Press, 1952.

Reid, William. "Client and Practitioner Variables Affecting Treatment," *Social Casework,* XLV (1964), 586-92.

Reynolds, Bertha C. *Learning and Teaching in the Practice of Social Work*. New York, Farrar and Rinehart, 1942.
────── *Social Work and Social Living*. New York, Citadel Press, 1951.
Richmond, Mary. 'Some Next Steps in Social Treatment," in *The Long View*. New York, Russell Sage Foundation, 1930.
────── *Social Diagnosis*. New York, Russell Sage Foundation, 1917.
Riessman, Frank. *The Culturally Deprived Child*. New York, Harper and Bros., 1962.
Riessman, Frank, Jerome Cohen, and Arthur Pearl, eds. *Mental Health of the Poor; New Treatment Approaches for Low Income People*. New York, Free Press of Glencoe, 1964.
Ripple, Lilian. "Factors Associated with Continuance in Casework Service," *Social Work*, II (2), (1957), 87-94.
────── *Motivation, Capacity, and Opportunity; Studies in Casework Theory and Practice*. Chicago, School of Social Service Administration, University of Chicago, 1964.
Rosenbaum, Max, and Milton Berger, eds. *Group Psychotherapy and Group Function*. New York, Basic Books, 1963.
Rosenfield, Jona M. "Strangeness Between Helper and Client: A Possible Explanation of Non-Use of Available Professional Help," *Social Service Review*, XXXVIII (1964), 17-25.
Rosenblatt, Aaron. "The Application of Role Concepts to the Intake Process," *Social Casework*, XLIII (1962), 8-14.
Ruesch, Jurgen, and Gregory Bateson. *Communication: The Social Matrix of Psychiatry*. New York, W. W. Norton, 1951.
Ruesch, Jurgen, and Weldon Kees. *Nonverbal Communication; Notes on the Visual Perception of Human Relations*. Berkeley, University of California Press, 1956.
Ryland, Gladys. "Use of the Small Group as an Association Pattern within which Professional Intervention Can Take Place," in *New Developments in the Theory and Practice of Social Group Work*. New York, Council on Social Work Education, 1959.
────── "Social Group Work in Medical Settings," in *Group Work and Community Organization, 1956*. Selected Papers, 83rd Annual Forum, National Conference on Social Welfare. New York, Columbia University Press, 1956.
Saloshin, Henrietta. "Development of an Instrument for the An-

alysis of the Social Group Work Method in Therapeutic Settings," Unpublished Ph.D. Dissertation, School of Social Work, University of Minnesota, 1954.

Sampson, Timothy. "An Inquiry into Knowledge about Stages and Phases of Group Development," Unpublished M.S.W. Thesis, School of Social Work, University of Southern California, 1962.

Sanford, Nevitt. *Self and Society; Social Change and Individual Development.* New York, Atherton Press, 1966.

Sarri, Rosemary C., and Maeda J. Galinsky. "A Conceptual Framework for Teaching Group Development in Social Group Work," in *A Conceptual Framework for the Teaching of the Social Group Work Method in the Classroom.* New York, Council on Social Work Education, 1964.

Satir, Virginia. *Conjoint Family Therapy.* Palo Alto, California, Science and Behavior Books, 1964.

Schatzman, Leonard, and Anselm Straus. "Social Class and Modes of Communication," *American Journal of Sociology*, LX (1955), 329-38.

Scheidlinger, Saul. "Experiential Group Treatment of Severely Deprived Latency-Age Children," in Frank Riessman, Jerome Cohen, and Arthur Pearl, eds. *Mental Health of the Poor.* New York, The Free Press of Glencoe, 1964.

―――― *Psychoanalysis and Group Behavior.* New York, W. W. Norton, 1952.

―――― "The Concept of Empathy in Group Psychotherapy," *International Journal of Group Psychotherapy*, XVI (1966), 413-24.

Scheidlinger, Saul, and M. A. Holden. "Group Therapy of Women with Severe Character Disorders: The Middle and Final Phases," *International Journal of Group Psychotherapy*, XVI (2) (1966), 174-89.

Scherz, Frances H. "Family Treatment Concepts," *Social Casework*, XLVII (1966), 234-40.

Schiff, Sheldon K. "Termination of Therapy," *Archives of General Psychiatry*, VI (1962), 77-82.

Schmidl, Fritz. "A Study of Techniques Used in Supportive Treatment," *Social Casework*, XXXII (1951), 413-19.

Schmidt, Julianna. "Purpose in Casework: A Study of Its Use, Communication, and Perception," Unpublished D.S.W. Dissertation, School of Social Work, University of Southern California, 1966.

Schulze, Suzanne, ed. *Creative Group Living in a Children's Institution.* New York, Association Press, 1951.

Schwartz, Betty. "Knowledge and Skills Used in Social Group Work Practice," in *Social Work with Groups, 1959.* New York, National Association of Social Workers, 1959.

Schwartz, William. "The Social Worker in the Group," in *The Social Welfare Forum, 1961.* Official Proceedings, 88th Annual Forum, National Conference on Social Welfare. New York, Columbia University Press, 1961.

Selby, Lola. "Social Work and Crisis Theory," *Social Work Papers,* School of Social Work, University of Southern California, X (1963), 1-9.

—— "Supportive Treatment: The Development of a Concept and a Helping Method," *Social Service Review,* XXX (1956), 400-14.

Shatton, S. P., et al. "Group Treatment of Conditionally Discharged Patients in a Mental Health Clinic," *American Journal of Psychiatry.* CXXII (1966), 798-805.

Shepherd, Clovis R. *Small Groups: Some Sociological Perspectives.* San Francisco, Chandler Publishing Co., 1964.

Sherif, Muzafer. *The Psychology of Social Norms.* New York, Harper and Bros., 1936.

—— "Group Influences upon the Formation of Norms and Attitudes," in Guy E. Swanson, ed. *Readings in Social Psychology.* Rev. ed. New York, Holt, 1952.

Sherif, Muzafer, and Carolyn W. Sherif. *An Outline of Social Psychology.* Revised ed., New York, Harper and Bros., 1956.

Sherif, Muzafer, and M. O. Wilson, eds. *Group Relations at the Crossroads.* New York, Harper and Bros., 1953.

Sherman, Sanford. "Family Treatment: An Approach to Children's Problems," *Social Casework,* XLVII (1966), 368-72.

Shoemaker, Louise P. "Social Group Work in the ADC Program," *Social Work,* VIII (1), (1963), 30-36.

—— "Use of Group Work Skills with Short-Term Groups," in *Social Work with Groups, 1960.* New York, National Association of Social Workers, 1960.

Shulman, Lawrence. "Scapegoats, Group Workers, and Pre-emptive Intervention," *Social Work,* XII (2), (1967), 37-43.

Shyne, Ann W. "What Research Tells us About Short-term Cases in Family Agencies," *Social Casework,* XXXVIII (1957), 223-31.

Siller, J. "Socioeconomic Status and Conceptual Thinking," *Journal of Abnormal and Social Psychology*, LV (1957), 365-67.

Simmel, George. *Conflict*. Translated by Kurt H. Wolff. Glencoe, Illinois, Free Press, 1955.

———— *The Sociology of George Simmel*. Edited and translated by Kurt H. Wolff. Glencoe, Illinois, Free Press, 1950.

Slavson, S. R. *A Textbook in Analytic Group Psychotherapy*. New York, International Universities Press, 1964.

Sloan, Marion B. "Factors in Forming Treatment Groups," in *Use of Groups in the Psychiatric Setting*. New York, National Association of Social Workers, 1960.

Smalley, Ruth Elizabeth. *Theory for Social Work Practice*. New York and London, Columbia University Press, 1967.

Social Work as Human Relations; Anniversary Papers of the New York School of Social Work and the Community Service Society of New York. New York, Columbia University Press, 1949.

Solomon, Barbara. "Conceptualization of Identity in Social Work Practice," *Social Service Review*, XLI (1967), 1-9.

Somers, Mary Louise. "Four Small Group Theories: An Analysis and Frame of Reference for Use in Social Group Work." Unpublished D.S.W. Dissertation, School of Applied Social Sciences, Western Reserve University, 1957.

———— "The Small Group in Learning and Teaching," in "Learning and Teaching in Public Welfare," Report of the Cooperative Project on Public Welfare Staff Training, I. Bureau of Family Services, Welfare Administration, U.S. Department of Health, Education, and Welfare, 1963.

Sommers, Vita S. "Identity Conflict and Acculturation Problems in Oriental Americans," *American Journal of Orthopsychiatry*, XXX (1960), 637-44.

Spellmann, Dorothea. "Nucleus and Boundaries in Social Group Work: Seven Propositions," *Social Work*, VI (4), (1961), 90-95.

Spergel, Irving. *Street Gang Work, Theory and Practice*. Reading, Mass., Addison-Wesley, 1966.

Spiegel, John. "Resolution of Role Conflict within the Family," *Psychiatry*, XX (1957), 1-6.

———— "The Social Roles of Doctor and Patient in Psychoanalysis and Psychotherapy," *Psychiatry*, XVII (1954), 369-76.

Stamm, Isabel L. "Ego Psychology in the Emerging Theoretical

Base of Casework," in Alfred J. Kahn, ed., *Issues in American Social Work*. New York, Columbia University Press, 1959.

Stark, Frances B. "Barriers to Client-Worker Communication at Intake," *Social Casework*, XL (1959), 177-83.

Stein, Herman D., and Richard A. Cloward, eds. *Social Perspectives on Behavior; A Reader in Social Science for Social Work and Related Professions*. Glencoe, Illionis, Free Press, 1958.

Stranahan, Marian, Cecile Schwartzman, and Edith Atkin. "Group Treatment for Emotionally Disturbed and Potentially Delinquent Boys and Girls," *American Journal of Orthopsychiatry*, XXVII (1957), 518-52.

Strean, Herbert S. "Role Theory, Role Models and Casework: Review of the Literature and Practice Applications," *Social Work*, XII (2), (1967), 77-88.

Studt, Elliot. "Correctional Services," in Harry L. Lurie, ed. *Encyclopedia of Social Work*. New York, National Association of Social Workers, 1965.

―――― "Worker-Client Authority Relationships in Social Work," *Social Work*, IV (1), (1959), 18-28.

―――― "The Nature of Hard-to-reach Groups," *Children*, IV (1957), 219-24.

Sullivan, Dorothea, ed. *Readings in Group Work*. New York, Association Press, 1952.

Swanson, Guy E. ed. *Readings in Social Psychology*. Rev. ed. New York, Holt, 1952.

Theodorson, George A. "The Function of Hostility in Small Groups," *Journal of Social Psychology*, LVI (1962), 57-66.

Thibaut, John W., and Harold H. Kelley. *The Social Psychology of Groups*. New York, John Wiley, 1959.

Thomas, Edwin, and Clinton Fink. "Effects of Group Size," in A. Paul Hare et al., eds., *Small Groups; Studies in Social Interaction*. New York, A. A. Knopf, 1955.

Towle, Charlotte. *Common Human Needs*. 2nd ed. New York, National Association of Social Workers, 1952.

Trecker, Harleigh B. *Social Group Work—Principles and Practices*. Revised ed. New York, Whiteside, 1955.

―――― ed. *Group Work: Foundations and Frontiers*. New York, Whiteside, 1955.

―――― ed. *Group Work in the Psychiatric Setting*. New York, Whiteside and Wm. Morrow, 1956.

Tropp, Emanuel. "Group Intent and Group Structure; Essential Criteria for Group Work Practice," *Journal of Jewish Communal Service,* XLI (1965), 229-50.

Truax, Charles B. "A Scale for Measurement of Accurate Empathy," *Psychiatric Institute Bulletin.* University of Wisconsin (1961), 1-23.

Tyler, Ralph W. "Implications of Research in the Behavioral Sciences for Group Life and Group Services," in *The Social Welfare Forum, 1960.* Official Proceedings, 87th Annual Forum, National Conference on Social Welfare. New York, Columbia University Press, 1960.

Use of Groups in the Psychiatric Setting. New York, National Association of Social Workers, 1960.

Valle, Juan Ramon. "The Role of the Social Group Worker within the Process of Planned Termination," Unpublished M.S.W. Thesis, School of Social Work, University of Southern California, 1964.

Vigilante, Joseph L., ed. *Ego Psychology; Its Application to Social Work with Groups in the Mental Hospital.* New York, Adelphi University, 1963.

Vinter, Robert D., ed. *Readings in Group Work Practice.* Ann Arbor, Michigan, Campus Publishers, 1967.

——— "Social Group Work," in Harry L. Lurie, ed. *Encyclopedia of Social Work.* New York, National Association of Social Workers, 1965.

Vinter, Robert D., and Rosemary Sarri. "Malperformance in the Public School: A Group Work Approach," *Social Work,* X (1), (1965), 3-13.

Visotsky, Harold M. "Approaches to the Treatment of the Socially Deprived and Culturally Different," in *Social Work Practice,* 1963. New York, Columbia University Press, 1963.

Warner, W. Lloyd. *Life in America: Dream and Reality.* New York, Harper and Bros., 1952.

Wax, John H. "Criteria for Grouping Hospitalized Mental Patients," in *Use of Groups in the Psychiatric Setting.* New York, National Association of Social Workers, 1960.

Webster's New World Dictionary of the American Language, College Edition. New York, The World Publishing Co., 1962.

Weiner, Hyman J. "Social Change and Social Group Work Practice," *Social Work,* IX (3), (1964), 106-112.

Weisman, Celia B. "Social Structure as a Determinant of the Group Worker's Role," *Social Work*, VIII (3), (1963), 87-94.

Wheat, William D., Regina Slaughter, and Jerome D. Frank. "Rehabilitation of Chronically Ill Psychiatric Patients," Maryland State Department of Education, Division of Vocational Rehabilitation, mimeographed, no date.

Whitaker, Dorothy Stock, and Morton A. Lieberman. *Psychotherapy through the Group Process*. New York, Atherton Press, 1964.

White, Robert W., "Motivation Reconsidered: The Concept of Competence," *Psychological Review*, LXVI (1959), 297-333.

Williams, Robin M. *American Society: A Sociological Interpretation*. New York, A. A. Knopf, 1965.

Wilson, Gertrude. *Group Work and Case Work, Their Relationship and Practice*. New York, Family Welfare Association of America, 1941.

——— "Measurement and Evaluation of Social Group Work Practice," in *The Social Welfare Forum*. New York, Columbia University Press, 1952.

——— "Social Group Work—Trends and Developments," *Social Work*, I (4), (1956), 66-75.

——— "Social Group Work Theory and Practice." in *The Social Welfare Forum, 1956*. Official Proceedings, 83rd Annual Forum, National Conference on Social Welfare. New York, Columbia University Press, 1956.

——— "The Social Worker's Role in Group Situations," in Marjorie Murphy, *The Social Group Work Method in Social Work Education*. New York, Council on Social Work Education, 1959.

Wilson, Gertrude and Gladys Ryland. "The Family as a Unit of Service," *Social Work Practice, 1964*. Selected Papers, 91st Annual Forum, National Conference on Social Welfare, New York, Columbia University Press, 1964.

——— "Social Classes: Implications for Social Group Work," in *The Social Welfare Forum, 1954*. Official Proceedings, 81st Annual Forum, National Conference on Social Welfare. New York, Columbia University Press, 1954.

——— *Social Group Work Practice: The Creative Use of the Social Process*. Boston, Houghton-Mifflin, 1949.

Wiltse, Kermit T. "Orthopsychiatric Programs for Socially Deprived Groups," *American Journal of Orthopsychiatry*, XXXIII (1963), 803-13.

———— "The Hopeless Family," *Social Work*, III (4), (1958), 12-22.

Wittenburg, Rudolph M. *The Art of Group Discipline; A Mental Hygiene Approach to Leadership*. New York, Association Press, 1951.

Wittenburg, Rudolph, and Janice Berg. "The Stranger in the Group," *American Journal of Orthopsychiatry*, XXII (1949), 89-97.

Wolkon, G. H., and Henry Tanaka. "Outcome of a Social Rehabilitation Service for Released Psychiatric Patients: A Descriptive Study," *Social Work*, XI (2), (1966), 53-61.

Worby, Marsha. "The Adolescents' Expectations of How a Potentially Helpful Person Will Act," *Smith College Studies in Social Work*, XXVI (1955), 19-59.

Yalom, I. D. "A Study of Group Therapy Drop-outs," *Archives of General Psychiatry*, XIV (1966), 393-414.

Index